Telling Lies

PAUL EKMAN

Telling Lies

Clues to Deceit in the
Marketplace, Politics, and Marriage

W · W · NORTON & COMPANY · *New York* · *London*

Printed in the United States of America.

First published as a Norton paperback 1991.

The text of this book is composed in Janson, with display type set in Caslon. Composition by The Haddon Craftsmen, Inc.

Library of Congress Cataloging in Publication Data
Ekman, Paul.
    Telling Lies.
    Includes bibliographical references and index.
    1. Truthfulness and falsehood. Psychology. I. Title.
BJ1421.E36 1985 153.6 84–7994

ISBN 0-393-30872-3

W. W. Norton & Company, Inc.
500 Fifth Avenue, New York, N. Y. 10110
W. W. Norton & Company Ltd
10 Coptic Street, London WC1A 1PU

5 6 7 8 9 0

In Memory of
Erving Goffman,
Extraordinary Friend and Colleague

and for my wife,
Mary Ann Mason,
Critic and Confidante

When the situation seems to be exactly what it appears to be, the closest likely alternative is that the situation has been completely faked; when fakery seems extremely evident, the next most probable possibility is that nothing fake is present.—Erving Goffman, Strategic Interaction

The relevant framework is not one of morality but of survival. At every level, from brute camouflage to poetic vision, the linguistic capacity to conceal, misinform, leave ambiguous, hypothesize, invent is indispensable to the equilibrium of human consciousness and to the development of man in society. . . .—George Steiner, After Babel

If falsehood, like truth, had only one face, we would be in better shape. For we would take as certain the opposite of what the liar said. But the reverse of truth has a hundred thousand shapes and a limitless field.—Montaigne, Essays

Contents

Acknowledgments

I AM GRATEFUL to the Clinical Research Branch of the National Institute of Mental Health for supporting my research on nonverbal communication from 1963 through 1981 (MH11976). The Research Scientist Award Program of the National Institute of Mental Health has supported both the development of my research program over most of the past twenty years and the writing of this book (MH 06092). I wish to thank the Harry F. Guggenheim Foundation and the John D. and Catherine T. MacArthur Foundation for supporting some of the research described in chapters 4 and 5. Wallace V. Friesen, with whom I have worked for more than twenty years, is equally responsible for the research findings that I report in those chapters; many of the ideas developed in the book came up first in our two decades of dialogue.

I thank Silvan S. Tomkins, friend, colleague, and teacher, for encouraging me to write this book, and for his comments and suggestions about the manuscript. I benefited from the criticisms of a number of friends who read the manuscript from their different vantage points: Robert Blau, a physician; Stanley Caspar, a trial lawyer; Jo Carson, a novelist; Ross Mullaney, a retired FBI agent; Robert Pickus, a political activist; Robert Ornstein, a psychologist; and Bill Williams, a management consultant. My wife,

Mary Ann Mason, my first reader, was patient and constructively critical.

I discussed many of the ideas in the book with Erving Goffman, who had been interested in deceit from quite a different angle and enjoyed our contrasting but not contradictory views. I was to have had the benefit of his comments on the manuscript, but he died quite unexpectedly just before I was to send it. The reader and I lose by the unfortunate fact that our dialogue could only occur in my mind.

Telling Lies

ONE

Introduction

*I*T IS September 15, 1938, and one of the most infamous and deadly of deceits is about to begin. Adolf Hitler, the chancellor of Germany, and Neville Chamberlain, the prime minister of Great Britain, meet for the first time. The world watches, aware that this may be the last hope of avoiding another world war. (Just six months earlier Hitler's troops had marched into Austria, annexing it to Germany. England and France had protested but done nothing further.) On September 12, three days before he is to meet Chamberlain, Hitler demands to have part of Czechoslovakia annexed to Germany and incites rioting in that country. Hitler has already secretly mobilized the German Army to attack Czechoslovakia, but his army won't be ready until the end of September.

If he can keep the Czechs from mobilizing their army for a few more weeks, Hitler will have the advantage of a surprise attack. Stalling for time, Hitler conceals his war plans from Chamberlain, giving his word that peace can be preserved if the Czechs will meet his demands. Chamberlain is fooled; he tries to persuade the Czechs not to mobilize their army while there is still a chance to negotiate with Hitler. After his meeting with Hitler, Chamberlain writes to his sister, ". . . in spite of the hardness and ruthlessness I thought I saw in his face, I got the impression that here was a man who could be relied upon when he had given his word. ...."[1] Defending his policies against those who doubt Hitler's word, Chamberlain five days later in a speech to Parliament explains that his personal contact with Hitler allows him to say that Hitler "means what he says."[2]

When I began to study lies fifteen years ago I had no idea my work would have any relevance to such a lie. I thought it would be useful only for those working with mental patients. My study of lies began when the therapists I was teaching about my findings—that facial expressions are universal while gestures are specific to each culture—asked whether these nonverbal behaviors could reveal that a patient was lying.[3] Usually that is not an issue, but it becomes one when patients admitted to the hospital because of suicide attempts say they are feeling much better. Every doctor dreads being fooled by a patient who commits suicide once freed from the hospital's restraint. Their practical concern raised a very fundamental question about human communication: can people, even when they are very upset, control the messages they give off, or will their nonverbal behavior leak what is concealed by their words?

I searched my films of interviews with psychiatric patients for an instance of lying. I had made these films for another purpose—to isolate expressions and gestures that might help in diagnosing the severity and type of mental disorders. Now that I was focusing upon deceit, I thought I saw signs of lying in a number of films. The problem was how to be certain. In only one case was there no doubt—because of what happened after the interview.

Mary was a forty-two-year-old housewife. The last of her three suicide attempts was quite serious. It was only an accident that someone found her before an overdose of sleeping pills killed her. Her history was not much different from that of many other women who suffer a midlife depression. The children had grown up and didn't need her. Her husband seemed preoccupied with his work. Mary felt useless. By the time she had entered the hospital she no longer could handle the house, could not sleep well, and sat by herself crying much of the time. In her first three weeks in the hospital she received medication and group therapy. She seemed to respond very well: her manner brightened, and she no longer talked of committing suicide. In one of the interviews we filmed, Mary told the doctor how much better she felt and asked for a weekend pass. Before receiving the pass, she confessed that she had been lying to get it. She still desperately wanted to kill herself. After three more months in the hospital Mary had genuinely improved, although there was a relapse a year later. She has been out of the hospital and apparently well for many years.

The filmed interview with Mary fooled most of the young and even many of the experienced psychiatrists and psychologists to whom I showed it.[4] We studied it for hundreds of hours, going over it again and again, inspecting each gesture and expression in slow-motion to uncover any possible clues to deceit. In a moment's pause before replying to her doctor's question about her plans for the future, we saw in slow-motion a fleeting facial expression of despair, so quick that we had missed seeing it the first few times we examined the film. Once we had the idea that concealed feelings might be evident in these very brief *micro expressions,* we searched and found many more, typically covered in an instant by a smile. We also found a *micro gesture.* When telling the doctor how well she was handling her problems Mary sometimes showed a fragment of a shrug—not the whole thing, just a part of it. She would shrug with just one hand, rotating it a bit. Or, her hands would be quiet but there would be a momentary lift of one shoulder.

We thought we saw other nonverbal clues to deceit, but

we could not be certain whether we were discovering or imagining them. Perfectly innocent behavior seems suspicious if you know someone has lied. Only objective measurement, uninfluenced by knowledge of whether a person was lying or telling the truth, could test what we found. And, many people had to be studied for us to be certain that the clues to deceit we found are not idiosyncratic. It would be simpler for the person trying to spot a lie, the lie catcher, if behaviors that betray one person's deceit are also evident when another persons lies; but the signs of deceit might be peculiar to each person. We designed an experiment modeled after Mary's lie, in which the people we studied would be strongly motivated to conceal intense negative emotions felt at the very moment of the lie. While watching a very upsetting film, which showed bloody surgical scenes, our research subjects had to conceal their true feelings of distress, pain, and revulsion and convince an interviewer, who could not see the film, that they were enjoying a film of beautiful flowers. (Our findings are described in chapters 4 and 5).

Not more than a year went by—when we were still at the beginning stages of our lying experiments—before people interested in quite different lies sought me out. Could my findings or methods be used to catch Americans suspected of being spies? Over the years, as our findings on behavioral clues to deceit between patient and doctor were published in scientific journals, the inquiries increased. How about training those who guard cabinet officers so they could spot a terrorist bent on assassination from his gait or gestures? Can we show the FBI how to train police officers to spot better whether a suspect is lying? I was no longer surprised when asked if I could help summit negotiators spot their opponents' lies, or if I could tell from the photographs of Patricia Hearst taken while she participated in a bank hold-up if she was a willing or unwilling robber. In the last five years the interest has become international. I have been approached by representatives of two countries friendly to the United States; and, when I lectured in the Soviet Union, by officials who said they were from an "electrical institute" responsible for interrogations.

I was not pleased with this interest, afraid my findings would be misused, accepted uncritically, used too eagerly. I felt that nonverbal clues to deceit would not often be evident in most criminal, political, or diplomatic deceits. It was only a hunch. When asked, I couldn't explain why. To do so I had to learn why people *ever do* make mistakes when they lie. Not all lies fail. Some are performed flawlessly. Behavioral clues to deceit—a facial expression held too long, a missing gesture, a momentary turn in the voice—don't have to happen. There need be no telltale signs that betray the liar. Yet I knew that there can be clues to deceit. The most determined liars may be betrayed by their own behavior. Knowing when lies will succeed and when they will fail, how to spot clues to deceit and when it isn't worth trying, meant understanding how lies, liars, and lie catchers differ.

Hitler's lie to Chamberlain and Mary's to her doctor both involved deadly serious deceits, in which the stakes were life itself. Both people concealed future plans, and both put on emotions they didn't feel as a central part of their lie. But the differences between their lies are enormous. Hitler is an example of what I later describe as a natural performer. Apart from his inherent skill, Hitler was also much more practiced in deceit than Mary.

Hitler also had the advantage of deceiving someone who wanted to be misled. Chamberlain was a willing victim who wanted to believe Hitler's lie that he did not plan war if only the borders of Czechoslovakia were redrawn to meet his demands. Otherwise Chamberlain would have had to admit that his policy of appeasement had failed and in fact weakened his country. On a related matter, the political scientist Roberta Wohlstetter made this point in her analysis of cheating in arms races. Discussing Germany's violations of the Anglo-German Naval Agreement of 1936, she said: ". . . the cheater and the side cheated . . . have a stake in allowing the error to persist. They both need to preserve the illusion that the agreement has not been violated. The British fear of an arms race, manipulated so skillfully by Hitler, led to a Naval Agreement, in which the British (without consulting the French or the Italians) tacitly revised the Versailles Treaty; and London's fear of an arms race prevented it from recognizing or acknowledging violations of the new agreement."[5]

In many deceits the victim overlooks the liar's mistakes, giving ambiguous behavior the best reading, collusively helping to maintain the lie, to avoid the terrible consequences of uncovering the lie. By overlooking the signs of his wife's affairs a husband may at least postpone the humiliation of being exposed as a cuckold and the possibility of divorce. Even if he admits her infidelity to himself he may cooperate in not uncovering her lies to avoid having to acknowledge it to her or to avoid a showdown. As long as nothing is said he can still have the hope, no matter how small, that he may have misjudged her, that she may not be having an affair.

Not every victim is so willing. At times, there is nothing to be gained by ignoring or cooperating with a lie. Some lie catchers gain only by exposing a lie and if they do so lose nothing. The police interrogator only loses if he is taken in, as does the bank loan officer, and both do their job well only by uncovering the liar and recognizing the truthful. Often, the victim gains *and* loses by being misled or by uncovering the lie; but the two may not be evenly balanced. Mary's doctor had only a small stake in believing her lie.

If she was no longer depressed he could take some credit for effecting her recovery. But if she was not truly recovered he suffered no great loss. Unlike Chamberlain, the doctor's entire career was not at stake; he had not publicly committed himself, despite challenge, to a judgment that could be proven wrong if he uncovered her lie. He had much more to lose by being taken in than he could gain if she was being truthful. In 1938 it was too late for Chamberlain. If Hitler were untrustworthy, if there was no way to stop his aggression short of war, then Chamberlain's career was over, and the war he thought he could prevent would begin.

Quite apart from Chamberlain's motives to believe Hitler, the lie was likely to succeed because no strong emotions had to be concealed. Most often lies fail because some sign of an emotion being concealed leaks. The stronger the emotions involved in the lie, and the greater the number of different emotions, the more likely it is that the lie will be betrayed by some form of behavioral leakage. Hitler certainly would not have felt guilt, an emotion that is doubly problematic for the liar—not only may signs of it leak, but the torment of guilt may motivate the liar to make mistakes so as to be caught. Hitler would not feel guilty about lying to the representative of the country that had in his lifetime imposed a humiliating military defeat on Germany. Unlike Mary, Hitler did not share important social values with his victim; he did not respect or admire him. Mary had to conceal strong emotions for her lie to succeed. She had to suppress the despair and anguish motivating her suicide wish. And, Mary had every reason to feel guilty about lying to her doctors: she liked them, admired them, and knew they only wanted to help her.

For all these reasons and more it usually will be far easier to spot behavioral clues to deceit in a suicidal patient or a lying spouse than in a diplomat or a double agent. But not every diplomat, criminal, or intelligence agent is a perfect liar. Mistakes are sometimes made. The analyses I have made allow one to estimate the chances of being able to spot clues to deceit or being misled. My message to those interested in catching political or criminal lies is not to ignore behavioral clues but to be more cautious, more aware of the limitations and the opportunities. While there is some evidence about the behavioral clues to deceit, it is not yet firmly established. My analyses of how and why people lie and when lies fail fit the evidence from experiments on lying and from historical and fictional accounts. But there has not yet been time to see how these theories will weather the test of further experiment and critical argument. I decided not to wait until all the answers are in to write this book, because those trying to catch liars are not waiting. Where the stakes for a mistake are the highest, attempts already are being made to spot nonverbal clues to deceit. "Experts" unfamiliar with all the evidence and arguments are offering their services as lie spotters in jury selection and employment interviews. Some policemen and professional polygraphers using the "lie detector" are taught about the nonverbal clues to deceit. About half the information in the training materials I have seen is wrong. Customs officials attend a special course in spotting the nonverbal clues of smuggling. I am told that my work is being used in this training, but repeated inquiries to see the training materials have only brought repeated promises of "we'll get right back to you." It is also impossible to know what the intelligence agencies are doing, for their work is secret. I know they are interested, for the Defense Department six years ago invited me to explain to them what I thought were the opportunities and the hazards. Since then I have heard rumors that work is proceeding, and I have picked up the names of some of the people who may be involved. My letters to them have gone unanswered, or the answer given is that I can't be told anything. I worry about "experts" who go unchallenged by public scrutiny and the carping critics of the scientific community. This book will make clear to them and those for whom they work my view of both the hazards and the opportunities.

My purpose in writing this book is not to address only those concerned with deadly deceits. I have come to believe that examining how and when people lie and tell the truth can help in understanding many human relationships. There are few that do not involve deceit or at least the possibility of it. Parents lie to their children about sex to spare them knowledge they think their children are not ready for, just as their children, when they become adolescents, will conceal sexual adventures because the parents won't understand. Lies occur between friends (even your best friend won't tell you), teacher and student, doctor and patient, husband and wife, witness and jury, lawyer and client, salesperson and customer.

Lying is such a central characteristic of life that better understanding of it is relevant to almost all human affairs. Some might shudder at that statement, because they view lying as reprehensible. I do not share that view. It is too simple to hold that no one in any relationship must ever lie; nor would I prescribe that every lie be unmasked. Advice columnist Ann Landers has a point when she advises her readers that truth can be used as a bludgeon, cruelly inflicting pain. Lies can be cruel too, but all lies aren't. Some lies, many fewer than liars will claim, are altruistic. Some social relationships are enjoyed because of the myths they preserve. But no liar should presume too easily that a victim desires to be misled. And no lie catcher should too easily presume the right to expose every lie. Some lies are harmless, even humane. Unmasking certain lies may humiliate the victim or a third party. But all of this must be considered in more detail, and after many other issues have been discussed. The place to begin is with a definition of lying, a description of the two basic forms of lying, and the two kinds of clues to deceit.

TWO

Lying, Leakage,
and Clues to Deceit

*E*IGHT YEARS AFTER RESIGNING as president, Richard Nixon denied *lying* but acknowledged that he, like other politicians, had *dissembled*. It is necessary to win and retain public office, he said. "You can't say what you think about this individual or that individual because you may have to use him. . . . you can't indicate your opinions about world leaders because you may have to deal with them in the future."[1] Nixon is not alone in avoiding the term *lie* when not telling the truth can be justified.* As the *Oxford English Dictionary* tells us: "in modern use, the word [lie] is normally a violent expression of moral reprobation, which in polite conversation tends to be avoided,

---

*Attitudes may be changing. Jody Powell, former President Carter's press secretary, justifies certain lies: "From the first day the first reporter asked the first tough question of a government official, there has been a debate about whether government has the right to lie. It does. In certain circumstances, government not only has the right but a positive obligation to lie. In four years in the White House I faced such circumstances twice." He goes on to describe an incident in which he lied to spare "great pain and embarrassment for a number of perfectly innocent people." The other lie he acknowledged was in covering the military plans to rescue the American hostages from Iran (Jody Powell, *The Other Side of the Story*, New York: William Morrow & Co., Inc., 1984).

the synonyms *falsehood* and *untruth* being often substituted as relatively euphemistic."[2] It is easy to call an untruthful person a liar if he is disliked, but very hard to use that term, despite his untruthfulness, if he is liked or admired. Many years before Watergate, Nixon epitomized the liar to his Democratic opponents—"would you buy a used car from this man?"—while his abilities to conceal and disguise were praised by his Republican admirers as evidence of political savvy.

These issues, however, are irrelevant to my definition of lying or deceit. (I use the words interchangeably.) Many people—for example, those who provide false information unwittingly—are untruthful without lying. A woman who has the paranoid delusion that she is Mary Magdalene is not a liar, although her claim is untrue. Giving a client bad investment advice is not lying unless the advisor knew when giving the advice that it was untrue. Someone whose appearance conveys a false impression is not necessarily lying. A praying mantis camouflaged to resemble a leaf is not lying, any more than a man whose high forehead suggested more intelligence than he possessed would be lying.*

A liar can *choose* not to lie. Misleading the victim is deliberate; the liar intends to misinform the victim. The lie may or may not be justified, in the opinion of the liar or the community. The liar may be a good or a bad person, liked or disliked. But the person who lies could choose to lie or

---

*It is interesting to guess about the basis of such stereotypes. The high forehead presumably refers, incorrectly, to a large brain. The stereotype that a thin-lipped person is cruel is based on the accurate clue that lips do narrow in anger. The error is in utilizing a sign of a temporary emotional *state* as the basis for judging a personality *trait*. Such a judgment implies that thin-lipped people look that way because they are narrowing their lips in anger continuously; but thin lips can also be a permanent, inherited facial feature. The stereotype that a thick-lipped person is sensual in a similar way misconstrues the accurate clue that lips thicken, engorged with blood during sexual arousal, into an inaccurate judgment about a permanent trait; but again, thick lips can be a permanent facial feature.[3]

to be truthful, and knows the difference between the two.[4] Pathological liars who know they are being untruthful but cannot control their behavior do not meet my requirement. Nor would people who do not even know they are lying, those said to be victims of self-deceit.* A liar may come over time to believe in her own lie. If that happens she would no longer be a liar, and her untruths, for reasons I explain in the next chapter, should be much harder to detect. An incident in Mussolini's life shows that belief in one's own lie may not always be so beneficial: ". . . in 1938 the composition of [Italian] army divisions had been reduced from three regiments to two. This appealed to Mussolini because it enabled him to say that fascism had sixty divisions instead of barely half as many, but the change caused enormous disorganisation just when the war was about to begin; and because he forgot what he had done, several years later he tragically miscalculated the true strength of his forces. It seems to have deceived few other people except himself."[5]

It is not just the liar that must be considered in defining a lie but the liar's target as well. In a lie the target has not asked to be misled, nor has the liar given any *prior notification* of an intention to do so. It would be bizarre to call actors liars. Their audience agrees to be misled, for a time; that is why they are there. Actors do not impersonate, as does the con man, without giving notice that it is a pose put on for a time. A customer would not knowingly follow the advice of a broker who said he would be providing convincing but false information. There would be no lie if the psychiatric patient Mary had told her doctor she would be claiming feelings she did not have, any more than Hitler

---

*While I do not dispute the existence of pathological liars and individuals who are victims of self-deceit, it is difficult to establish. Certainly the liar's word cannot be taken as evidence. Once discovered, any liar might make such claims to lessen punishment.

could have told Chamberlain not to trust his promises.
In my definition of a lie or deceit, then, one person
intends to mislead another, doing so deliberately, without
prior notification of this purpose, and without having been
explicitly asked to do so by the target.* There are two
primary ways to lie: to *conceal* and to *falsify*.⁶ In concealing,
the liar withholds some information without actually saying anything untrue. In falsifying, an additional step is
taken. Not only does the liar withhold true information,
but he presents false information as if it were true. Often
it is necessary to combine concealing and falsifying to pull
off the deceit, but sometimes a liar can get away just with
concealment.

Not everyone considers concealment to be lying; some
people reserve that word only for the bolder act of falsifica-
tion.⁷ If the doctor does not tell the patient that the illness
is terminal, if the husband does not mention that he spent
his lunch hour at a motel with his wife's best friend, if the
policeman doesn't tell the suspect that a "bug" is recording
the conversation with his lawyer, no false information has
been transmitted, yet each of these examples meets my
definition of lying. The targets did not ask to be misled; and
the concealers acted deliberately without giving prior
notification of their intent to mislead. Information was
withheld wittingly, with intent, not by accident. There are
exceptions, times when concealment is not lying because
prior notification was given or consent to be misled was
obtained. If the husband and wife agree to have an open

---

*My focus is on what Goffman called barefaced lies, ones "for which there can
be unquestionable evidence tht the teller knew he lied and willfully did so."
Goffman did not focus upon these but upon other misrepresentations, in which
the distinction between the true and the false is less tenable: ". . . there is hardly
a legitimate everyday vocation or relationship whose performers do not engage
in concealed practices which are incompatible with fostered impressions." (Both
quotes are from *The Presentation of Self in Everyday Life* [New York: Anchor Books,
1959], pp. 59, 64.

marriage in which each will conceal affairs unless directly asked, concealing the assignation at the motel will not be a lie. If the patient asks the doctor not to be told if the news is bad, concealing that information is not a lie. By legal definition, however, a suspect and attorney have the right to private conversation; concealing the violation of that right will always be a lie.

When there is a choice about *how* to lie, liars usually prefer concealing to falsifying. There are many advantages. For one thing, concealing usually is easier than falsifying. Nothing has to be made up. There is no chance of getting caught without having the whole story worked out in advance. Abraham Lincoln is reported to have said that he didn't have a good enough memory to be a liar. If a doctor gives a false explanation of a patient's symptoms in order to conceal that the illness is terminal, the doctor will have to remember his false account in order not to be inconsistent when asked again a few days later.

Concealment may also be preferred because it seems less reprehensible than falsifying. It is passive, not active. Even though the target may be equally harmed, liars may feel less guilt about concealing than falsifying.* The liar can maintain the reassuring thought that the target really knows the truth but does not want to confront it. Such a liar could think, "My husband must know I am playing around, because he never asks me where I spend my afternoons. My discretion is a kindness; I certainly am not lying to him about what I am doing. I am choosing not to humiliate him, not forcing him to acknowledge my affairs."

Concealment lies are also much easier to cover afterward if discovered. The liar does not go as far out on a limb.

---

*Eve Sweetser makes the interesting point that the target may feel more outraged by being told a concealment than a falsification lie: "[T]hey can't complain that they were lied to, and thus feel rather as if their opponent has slid through a legal loophole."[8]

There are many available excuses—ignorance, the intent to reveal it later, memory failure, and so on. The person testifying under oath who says "to the best of my recollection" provides an out if later faced with something he has concealed. The claim not to remember what the liar does remember and is deliberately withholding is intermediate between concealment and falsification. It happens when the liar can no longer simply not say anything; a question has been raised, a challenge made. By falsifying only a failure to remember, the liar avoids having to remember a false story; all that needs to be remembered is the untrue claim to a poor memory. And, if the truth later comes out, the liar can always claim not to have lied about it, that it was just a memory problem.

An incident from the the Watergate scandal that led to President Nixon's resignation illustrates the memory failure strategy. As evidence grows of their involvement in the break-in and cover-up, presidential assistants H. R. Haldeman and John Ehrlichman are forced to resign. Alexander Haig takes Haldeman's place as the pressure on Nixon mounts. "Haig had been back in the White House for less than a month when, on June 4, 1973, he and Nixon discussed how to respond to serious allegations being made by John W. Dean, the former White House counsel. According to a tape recording of the Nixon-Haig discussion that became public during the impeachment investigation, Haig advised Nixon to duck questions about the allegations by saying 'you just can't recall.' "[9]

A memory failure is credible only in limited circumstances. The doctor asked if the tests were negative can't claim not to remember, nor can the policeman if asked by the suspect whether the room is bugged. A memory loss can be claimed only for insignificant matters, or something that happened some time ago. Even the passage of time may not justify a failure to remember extraordinary events, which anyone would be expected to recall no matter when they happened.

A liar loses the choice whether to conceal or falsify once challenged by the victim. If the wife asks her husband why she couldn't reach him at lunch, the husband has to falsify to maintain his secret affair. One could argue that even the usual dinner table question—"How was your day?"—is a request for information, but it can be dodged. The husband can mention other matters concealing the assignation unless a directed inquiry forces him to choose between falsifying or telling the truth.

Some lies from the outset require falsification; concealment alone will not do. The psychiatric patient Mary not only had to conceal her distress and suicide plans, she also had to falsify feeling better and the wish to spend the weekend with her family. Lying about previous experience to obtain a job can't be done by concealment alone. Not only must inexperience be concealed, but the relevant job history must be fabricated. Escaping a boring party without offending the host requires not only concealing the preference to watch TV at home but the falsification of an acceptable excuse, an early-morning appointment, babysitter problems, or the like.

Falsification also occurs, even though the lie does not directly require it, to help the liar cover evidence of what is being concealed. This use of falsification to mask what is being concealed is especially necessary when emotions must be concealed. It is easy to conceal an emotion no longer felt, much harder to conceal an emotion felt at the moment, especially if the feeling is strong. Terror is harder to conceal than worry, just as rage is harder to conceal than annoyance. The stronger the emotion, the more likely it is that some sign of it will leak despite the liar's best attempt to conceal it. Putting on another emotion, one that is not felt, can help disguise the felt emotion being concealed.

Falsifying an emotion can cover the leakage of a concealed emotion.

An incident in John Updike's novel *Marry Me* illustrates this and a number of other points I have described. Ruth's telephone conversation with her lover is overheard by her husband. Up until this point in the book Ruth has been able to conceal her affair without having to falsify, but now, directly questioned by her husband, she must falsify. While the object of her lie has been to keep her husband ignorant of her affair, this incident also shows how easily emotions can become involved in a lie and how, once involved, emotions add to the burden of what must be concealed.

"Jerry [Ruth's husband] had frightened her by over-hearing the tag end of a phone conversation with Dick [her lover]. She had thought he was raking in the back yard. Emerging from the kitchen he asked her, "Who was that?' "She panicked. 'Oh somebody. Some woman from the Sunday school asking if we were going to enroll Joanna and Charlie.' "[10]

Panic itself is not proof of lying, but it would make Jerry suspicious, if he noticed it, because, he would think, Ruth wouldn't panic if she had nothing to hide. While perfectly innocent people may become fearful when interrogated, interrogators often don't take heed of that. Ruth is in a difficult position. Not anticipating the need to falisfy, she did not prepare her line. Caught in that predicament, she panics about being discovered, and since panic is very hard to conceal, this increases the chance Jerry will catch her. One ploy she might try would be to be truthful about how she feels, since she isn't likely to be able to hide that, lying instead about what has caused her feelings. She could admit feeling panicked, claiming that she feels that way because she fears Jerry won't believe her, not because she has anything to hide. This would not be likely to work unless there has been a long history in which Jerry has often disbelieved Ruth, and later events had always proved her to have been innocent, so that mention now of his unreasonable accusations might deflect his pursuit of her. Ruth probably won't succeed if she tries to look cool, poker faced, totally unaffected. When hands begin to tremble it is much easier to do something with them—make a fist or fold them—than just let them lie still. When lips are tightening and stretching, and the upper eyelids and brows are being pulled up in fear, it is very hard to keep a still face. Those expressions can be better concealed by adding other muscle movements—gritting the teeth, pressing the lips, lowering the brow, glaring.

The best way to conceal strong emotions is with a mask. Covering the face or part of it with one's hand or turning away from the person one is talking to usually can't be done without giving the lie away. The best mask is a false emotion. It not only misleads, but it is the best camouflage. It is terribly hard to keep the face impassive or the hands inactive when an emotion is felt strongly. Looking unemotional, cool, or neutral is the hardest appearance to maintain when emotions are felt. It is much easier to put on a pose, to stop or counter with another set of actions those actions that are expressions of the felt emotion.

A moment later in Updike's story, Jerry tells Ruth he does not believe her. Presumably her panic would increase, making it even harder to conceal. She could try to use anger, amazement, or surprise to mask her panic. She could angrily challenge Jerry for disbelieving her, for snooping. She could even appear amazed that he doesn't believe her, surprised that he was listening to her conversations.

Not every situation allows the liar to mask the felt emotion. Some lies require the much more difficult task of concealing emotions without falsifying. Ezer Weizman, a former Israeli minister of defense, described such a difficult situation. Talks were held between the Israeli and Egyptian military delegations to initiate negotiations after Anwar Sadat's dramatic visit to Jerusalem. During a negotiating session, Mohammed el-Gamasy, the head of the Egyptian delegation, tells Weizman he has just learned that the Israelis are erecting another settlement in the Sinai. Weizman knows that this could jeopardize the negotiations, since the issue of whether Israel can even keep any of the already existing settlements is still a matter of dispute.

"I was outraged, though I could not vent my anger in public. Here we were, discussing security arrangements, trying to give the wagon of peace one more little shove forward—and my colleagues in Jerusalem, instead of learning the lesson of the phony settlements, were erecting yet another one at the very hour that negotiations were in progress."[11]

Weizman could not allow his anger at his colleagues in Jerusalem to show. Concealing his anger would also allow him to conceal that his colleagues in Jerusalem had not consulted with him. He had to conceal a strongly felt emotion without being able to use any other emotion as a mask. It would not do to look happy, afraid, distressed, surprised, or disgusted. He had to look attentive but impassive, giving no clue that Gamasy's information was news of any consequence. His book gives no hint of whether he succeeded.

Poker is another situation in which masking cannot be used to conceal emotions. When a player becomes excited about the prospect of winning a large pot because of the superb hand he has drawn, he must conceal any sign of his excitement so the other players do not fold. Masking with the sign of any other emotion will be dangerous. If he tries to hide his excitement by looking disappointed or irritated, others will think he drew badly and will expect him to fold, not stay in. He must look blankly poker faced. If he decides to conceal his disappointment or irritation at a bad draw by bluffing, trying to force the others to fold, he might be able to use a mask. By falsifying happiness or excitement he could hide his disappointment and add to the impression that he has a good hand. It won't be believable to the other players unless they consider him a novice. An experienced poker player is supposed to have mastered the talent of not showing any emotion about his hand.* (Incidentally, untruths in poker—concealing or bluffing—do not fit my definition of lying. No one expects poker players to reveal the cards they have drawn. The game itself provides prior notification that players will attempt to mislead each other).

Any emotion can be falsified to help conceal any other emotion. The smile is the mask most frequently employed. It serves as the opposite of all the negative emotions—fear, anger, distress, disgust, and so on. It is selected often because some variation on happiness is the message required to pull off many deceits. The disappointed employee must smile if the boss is to think he isn't hurt or angry about being passed over for promotion. The cruel friend should pose as well-meaning as she delivers her cutting criticism with a concerned smile.

Another reason why the smile is used so often to mask is because smiling is part of the standard greeting and is required frequently throughout most polite exchanges. If a person feels terrible, it usually should not be shown or acknowledged during a greeting exchange. Instead, the unhappy person is expected to conceal negative feelings, put-

---

*In his study of poker players, David Hayano describes another style used by professionals: the "animated players constantly chat throughout the game to make their opponents anxious and nervous. . . . Truths are told as lies and lies are told as truths. Coupled with chattery verbal performance [are] animated and exaggerated gestures. . . . As one such player was described: 'He's got more moves than a belly dancer.' " ("Poker Lies and Tells," *Human Behavior*, March 1979, p. 20).

ting on a polite smile to accompany the "Just fine, thank you, and how are you?" reply to the "How are you today?" The true feelings will probably go undetected, not because the smile is such a good mask but because in polite exchanges people rarely care how the other person actually feels. All that is expected is a pretense of amiability and pleasantness. Others rarely scrutinize such smiles carefully. People are accustomed to overlooking lies in the context of polite greetings. One could argue that it is wrong to call these lies, because the implicit rules of polite greetings provide notification that true accounts of emotions will not be given.

Still another reason for the popularity of the smile as a mask is that it is the easiest of the facial expressions of emotions to make voluntarily. Well before the age of one, infants can deliberately smile. It is one of the very earliest expressions used by the infant in a deliberate fashion to please others. Throughout life social smiles falsely present feelings not felt but required or useful to show. Mistakes may be made in the timing of these unfelt smiles; they may be too quick or too slow. Mistakes may be evident also in the location of the smiles; they may occur too soon before or too long after the word or phrase they should accompany. But the smiling movements themselves are easy to make, which is not so for the expression of all the other emotions.

The negative emotions are harder for most people to falsify. My research, described in chapter 5, found that most people cannot voluntarily move the particular muscles needed to realistically falsify distress or fear. Anger and disgust are a little easier to display when they are not felt, but mistakes are often made. If the lie requires falsifying a negative emotion rather than a smile, the deceiver may have difficulty. There are exceptions; Hitler evidently was a superb performer, easily able to convincingly falsify negative emotions. In a meeting with the British ambassador, Hitler appeared to be totally enraged, not capable of discussing matters any further. A German official present at the scene reported: "Hardly had the door shut behind the Ambassador than Hitler slapped himself on the thigh, laughed and said: 'Chamberlain won't survive that conversation; his Cabinet will fall this evening.' "[12]

There are a number of other ways to lie, in addition to concealment and falsification. I suggested one way already, in considering what Ruth could do to maintain her deceit despite her panic in the incident quoted from John Updike's novel *Marry Me*. Rather than trying to conceal her panic, which is hard to do, she could acknowledge the feeling but lie about what brought it about. Misidentifying the cause of her emotion, she could claim she is perfectly innocent and is panicked only because she fears he won't believe her. If the psychiatrist had asked the patient Mary why she seemed a bit nervous, she could similarly acknowledge the emotion but misidentify what caused it—"I'm nervous because I want so much to be able to spend time with my family again." Truthful about the felt emotion, the lie misleads about what was the cause of the emotion.

Another, related technique is to tell the truth but with a twist, so the victim does not believe it. It is telling the truth . . . falsely. When Jerry asked who Ruth was talking to on the telephone she could have said: "Oh I was talking to my lover, he calls every hour. Since I go to bed with him three times a day we have to be in constant touch to arrange it!" Exaggerating the truth would ridicule Jerry, making it difficult for him to pursue his suspicious line. A mocking tone of voice or expression would also do the trick.

Another example of telling the truth falsely was described in Robert Daley's book, and the film based on it, *Prince of the City: The True Story of a Cop Who Knew Too Much*. As the subtitle proclaims, reportedly this is a true account,

not fiction. Robert Leuci is the cop who became an undercover informant, working for federal prosecutors to obtain
evidence of criminal corruption among policemen, attorneys, bail bondsmen, and dope pushers and Mafia members. He obtained most of the evidence on a tape recorder
concealed in his clothing. At one point Leuci is suspected
of being an informant. If he is caught wearing a wire his
life will be in jeopardy. Leuci speaks to DeStefano, one of
the criminals about whom he is obtaining evidence.

" 'Lets not sit next to the jukebox tonight, because I am
not getting any kind of recording.' [Leuci speaking]

" 'That's not funny,' said DeStefano.

"Leuci began to brag that he was indeed working for
the government, and so was that barmaid across the room,
whose transmitter was stuffed in her—

"They all laughed, but DeStefano's laugh was dry."[13]

Leuci ridicules DeStefano by brazenly telling the truth
—he really can't make a good recording near the jukebox,
and he is working for the government. By admitting it so
openly, and by joking about the waitress also wearing a
concealed recorder in her crotch or bra, Leuci makes it
difficult for DeStefano to pursue his suspicions without
seeming foolish.

A close relative of telling the truth falsely is a half-
concealment. The truth is told, but only partially. Under-
statement, or leaving out the crucial item, allows the liar to
maintain the deceit while not saying anything untrue.
Shortly after the incident I quoted from *Marry Me*, Jerry
joins Ruth in bed and, snuggling, asks her to tell him who
she likes.

" 'I like you,' she said, 'and all the pigeons in that tree,
and all the dogs in town except the ones that tip over our
garbage cans, and all the cats except the one that got Lulu
pregnant. And I like the lifeguards at the beach, and the
policemen downtown except the one who bawled me out

for my U-turn, and I like some of our awful friends, especially when I'm drunk . . .'
" 'How do you like Dick Mathias?' [Dick is Ruth's lover].
" 'I don't mind him.' "[14]
Another technique that allows the liar to avoid saying anything untrue is the incorrect-inference dodge. A newspaper columnist gave a humorous account of how to use this dodge to solve the familiar problem of what to say when you don't like a friend's work. You are at the opening of your friend's art exhibition. You think the work is dreadful, but before you can sneak out your friend rushes over and asks you what you think. " 'Jerry,' you say (assuming the artist in question is named Jerry), gazing deep into his eyes as though overcome by emotion, 'Jerry, Jerry, Jerry.' Maintain the clasp; maintain the eye contact. Ten times out of ten Jerry will finally break your grip, mumble a modest phrase or two, and move on. . . . There are variations. There's the high-tone artcrit third-person-invisible two-step, thus: 'Jerry. *Jer*-ry. What can one say?' Or the more deceptively low-key: 'Jerry. Words fail me.' Or the somewhat more ironic: 'Jerry. Everyone, *everyone*, is talking about it.' "[15] The virtue of this gambit, like the half-concealment and telling the truth falsely, is that the liar is not forced to say anything untrue. I consider them lies nevertheless, because there is a deliberate attempt to mislead the target without prior notification given to the target.

Any of these lies can be betrayed by some aspect of the deceiver's behavior. There are two kinds of clues to deceit. A mistake may reveal the truth, or it may only suggest that what was said or shown is untrue without revealing the truth. When a liar mistakenly reveals the truth, I call it *leakage*. When the liar's behavior suggests he or she is lying without revealing the truth, I call it a *deception clue*. If Mary's doctor notes that she is wringing her hands as she tells him she feels fine, he would have a deception clue, reason to suspect she is lying. He would not know how she really felt—she might be angry at the hospital, disgusted with herself, or fearful about her future—unless he obtained leakage. A facial expression, tone of voice, slip of the tongue, or certain gestures could leak her true feelings.

A deception clue answers the question of whether or not the person is lying, although it does not reveal what is being concealed. Only leakage would do that. Often it does not matter. When the question is whether or not a person is lying, rather than what is being concealed, a deception clue is good enough. Leakage is not needed. What information is being held back can be figured out or is irrelevant. If the employer senses through a deception clue that the applicant is lying, that may be sufficient, and no leakage of what is being concealed may be needed for the decision not to hire a job applicant who lies.

But it is not always enough. It may be important to know exactly what has been concealed. Discovering that a trusted employee embezzled may be insufficient. A deception clue could suggest that the employee lied; it might have led to a confrontation and a confession. Yet even though the matter has been settled, the employee discharged, the prosecution completed, the employer might still seek leakage. He might still want to know how the employee did it, and what he did with the money he embezzled. If Chamberlain had detected any deception clues he would have known Hitler was lying, but in that situation it would also have been useful to obtain leakage of just what his plans for conquest were, how far Hitler intended to go.

Sometimes leakage provides only part of the information the victim wants to know, betraying more than a deception clue but not all that is being concealed. Recall the incident in *Marry Me* quoted earlier, when Ruth panicked, uncertain how much her husband Jerry had heard of her telephone conversation with her lover. When Jerry asks her about it Ruth could have done something that would have betrayed her panic—a tremble in her lip or raised upper eyelid. Given the context, such a hint of panic would imply that Ruth might be lying. For why else should she be worried about his question? But such a deception clue would not tell Jerry what she was lying about, nor to whom she was talking. Jerry obtained part of that information from leakage in Ruth's voice:

" '. . . it was your tone of voice.' [Jerry is explaining to Ruth why he does not believe her account of who she was talking to on the telephone.]

" 'Really? How?' She wanted to giggle.

"He stared off into space as if at an aesthetic problem. He looked tired and young and thin. His haircut was too short. 'It was different,' he said. 'Warmer. It was a woman's voice.'

" 'I am a woman.'

" 'Your voice with me,' he said, 'is quite girlish.' "[16]

The sound of her voice does not fit talking to the Sunday school but to a lover. It leaks that the deceit is probably about an affair, but it does not tell him the whole story. Jerry does not know if it is an affair about to begin or in the middle; nor does he know who the lover is. But he knows more than he would from just a deception clue that would only suggest that she is lying.

I defined lying as a deliberate choice to mislead a target without giving any notification of the intent to do so. There are two major forms of lying: concealment, leaving out true information; and falsification, or presenting false information as if it were true. Other ways to lie include: misdirecting, acknowledging an emotion but misidentifying what caused it; telling the truth falsely, or admitting the truth but with such exaggeration or humor that the target remains uniformed or misled; half-concealment, or admitting only part of what is true, so as to deflect the target's interest in what remains concealed; and the incorrect-inference dodge, or telling the truth but in a way that implies the opposite of what is said. There are two kinds of clues to deceit: leakage, when the liar inadvertently reveals the truth; and deception clues, when the liar's behavior reveals only that what he says is untrue.

Both leakage and deception clues are mistakes. They do not always happen. Not all lies fail. The next chapter explains why some do.

THREE

Why Lies Fail

*L*IES FAIL for many reasons. The victim of deceit may accidentally uncover the evidence, finding hidden documents or a telltale lipstick stain on a handkerchief. Someone else may betray the deceiver. An envious colleague, an abandoned spouse, a paid informer, all are major sources for the detection of deception. What concerns us, however, are those mistakes made during the act of lying, mistakes the deceiver makes despite himself, lies that fail because of the liar's behavior. Deception clues or leakage may be shown in a change in the expression on the face, a movement of the body, an inflection to the voice, a swallowing in the throat, a very deep or shallow breath, long pauses between words, a slip of the tongue, a micro facial expression, a gestural slip. The question is: Why can't liars prevent these behavioral betrayals? Sometimes they do. Some lies are performed beautifully; nothing in what the liar says or does betrays the lie. Why not always? There are two reasons, one that involves thinking and one that involves feeling.

Bad Lines

Liars do not always anticipate when they will need to lie. There is not always time to prepare the line to be taken, to rehearse and memorize it. Ruth, in the incident I quoted from Updike's novel *Marry Me*, did not anticipate that her husband, Jerry, would overhear her speaking on the telephone to her lover. The cover story she invents on the spot —that it is the Sunday school calling about their children —betrays her because it does not fit with what her husband overheard her say.

Even when there has been ample advance notice, and a false line has been carefully devised, the liar may not be clever enough to anticipate all the questions that may be asked and to have thought through what his answers must be. Even cleverness may not be enough, for unseen changes in circumstances can betray an otherwise effective line. During the Watergate grand jury investigation federal judge John J. Sirica described such a problem in explaining his reactions to the testimony of Fred Buzhardt, special counsel to President Nixon: "The first problem Fred Buzhardt faced in trying to explain why the tapes were missing was to get his story straight. On the opening day of the hearing, Buzhardt said there was no tape of the president's April 15 meeting with Dean because a timer . . . had failed. . . . But before long revised his first explanation. [Buzhardt had learned that other evidence might become known that would show that the timers were in fact working.] He now said that the April 15 meeting with Dean . . . hadn't been recorded because both of the available tapes had been filled up during a busy day of meetings."[1] Even when a liar is not forced by circumstances to change lines, some liars have trouble recalling the line they have previously committed themselves to, so that new questions cannot be consistently answered quickly.

Any of these failures—in anticipating when it will be necessary to lie, in inventing a line adequate to changing circumstances, in remembering the line one has adopted— produce easily spotted clues to deceit. What the person says is either internally inconsistent or discrepant with other incontrovertible facts, known at the time or later revealed.

Such obvious clues to deceit are not always as reliable and straightforward as they seem. Too smooth a line may be the sign of a well-rehearsed con man. To make matters worse, some con men, knowing this, purposely make slight mistakes in order not to seem too smooth. James Phelan, an investigative reporter, described a fascinating instance of this trick in his account of the Howard Hughes biography hoax.

No one had seen Hughes for years, which only added to the public's fascination with this billionaire, who also made movies and who owned an airline and the largest gambling house in Las Vegas. Hughes had not been seen for so long that some doubted he was alive. It was astonishing that a person who was so reclusive would authorize anyone to write his biography. Yet that is what Clifford Irving claimed to have produced. McGraw-Hill paid Irving $750,000 to publish it; *Life* magazine paid $250,000 to publish three excerpts; and it turned out to be a fake! Clifford Irving was ". . . a great con man, one of the best. Here's an example. When we cross examined him, trying to break down his story, he never made the mistake of telling his story the same way each time. There would be little discrepancies in it, and when we'd catch him up, he'd freely admit them. The average con man will have his story down letter-perfect, so he can tell it over and over without deviation. An honest man usually makes little mistakes, particularly in relating a long, complex story like Cliff's. Cliff was smart enough to know this, and gave a superb impersonation of an honest man. When we'd catch him up on something that looked incriminating, he'd freely say, 'Gee, that makes it look bad for me, doesn't it? But that's the way it happened.' He conveyed the picture of being candid, even to his own detriment—while he was turning lie after lie after lie."[2] There is no protection against such cleverness; the most skillful con men *do* succeed. Most liars are not so devious.

Lack of preparation or a failure to remember the line one has adopted may produce clues to deceit in *how* a line is spoken, even when there are no inconsistencies in *what* is said. The need to think about each word before it is spoken—weighing possibilities, searching for a word or idea—may be obvious in pauses during speech or, more subtly, in a tightening of the lower eyelid or eyebrow and certain changes in gesture (explained in more detail in chapters 4 and 5). Not that carefully considering each word before it is spoken is always a sign of deceit, but in some circumstances it is. When Jerry asks Ruth who she has been talking with on the phone, any signs that she was carefully selecting her words would suggest she was lying.

Lying about Feelings

A failure to think ahead, plan fully, and rehearse the false line is only one of the reasons why mistakes that furnish clues to deceit are made when lying. Mistakes are also made because of difficulty in concealing or falsely portraying emotion. Not every lie involves emotions, but those that do cause special problems for the liar. An attempt to conceal an emotion at the moment it is felt could be betrayed in words, but except for a slip of the tongue, it usually isn't. Unless there is a wish to confess what is felt, the liar doesn't have to put into words the feelings being concealed. One has less choice in concealing a facial expression or rapid breathing or a tightening in the voice.

When emotions are aroused, changes occur automatically without choice or deliberation. These changes begin in a split second. In *Marry Me*, when Jerry accuses Ruth of lying, Ruth has no trouble stopping the words "Yes, it's true!" from popping out of her mouth. But panic about her affair being discovered seizes her, producing visible and audible signs. She does not choose to feel panic; nor can she choose to stop feeling it. It is beyond her control. That, I believe, is fundamental to the nature of emotional experience.

People do not actively select when they will feel an emotion. Instead, they usually experience emotions more passively as happening to them, and, in the case of negative emotions such as fear or anger, it may happen to them despite themselves. Not only is there little choice about when an emotion is felt, but people often don't feel they have much choice about whether or not the expressive signs of the emotion are manifest to others. Ruth could not simply decide to eliminate any signs of her panic. There is no relax button she could press that would interrupt her emotional reactions. It may not even be possible to control one's actions if the emotion felt is very strong. A strong emotion explains, even if it does not always excuse, improper actions—"I didn't mean to yell (pound the table, insult you, hit you), but I lost my temper. I was out of control."

When an emotion begins gradually rather than suddenly, if it starts at a very low level—annoyance rather than fury—the changes in behavior are small and are relatively easy to conceal if one is aware of what one is feeling. Most people are not. When an emotion begins gradually and remains slight, it may be more noticeable to others than to the self, not registering in awareness unless it becomes more intense. Once an emotion is strong, however, it is much harder to control. Concealing the changes in face, body, and voice requires a struggle. Even when the concealment is successful and there is no leakage of the feelings, sometimes the struggle itself will be noticeable as a deception clue.

While concealing an emotion is not easy, neither is falsifying the appearance of an unfelt emotion, even when there is no other emotion that must be concealed. It requires more than just saying "I am angry" or "I am afraid." The deceiver must look and sound as if he is angry or afraid if his claim is to be believed. It is not easy to assemble the right movements, the particular changes in voice, that are required for falsifying emotions. There are certain movements of the face, for example, that very few people can perform voluntarily. (These are described in chapter 5). These difficult-to-perform movements are vital to successful falsification of distress, fear, and anger.

Falsifying becomes much harder just when it is needed most, to help conceal another emotion. Trying to look angry is not easy, but if fear is felt when the person tries to look angry the person will be torn. One set of impulses arising out of the fear pulls one way, while the deliberate attempt to seem angry pulls the other way. The brows, for example, are involuntarily pulled upward in fear. But to falsify anger the person must pull them down. Often the signs of this internal struggle between the felt and the false emotion themselves betray the deceit.

What about lies that don't involve emotions, lies about actions, plans, thoughts, intentions, facts, or fantasies? Are these lies betrayed by the liar's behavior?

Feelings about Lying

Not all deceits involve concealing or falsifying emotions. The embezzler conceals the fact that she is stealing money. The plagiarist conceals the fact that he has taken the work of another and pretends it is his own. The vain middle-aged man conceals his age, dying his gray hair and claiming he is seven years younger than he is. Yet even when the lie is about something other than emotion, emotions may become involved. The vain man might be embarrassed about his vanity. To succeed in his deceit he must conceal not only his age but his embarrassment as well.

The plagiarist might feel contempt toward those he misleads. He would thus not only have to conceal the source of his work and to pretend ability that is not his, he would also have to conceal his contempt. The embezzler might feel surprise when someone else is accused of her crime. She would have to conceal her surprise or at least the reason for it.

Thus emotions often become involved in lies that were not undertaken for the purpose of concealing emotions. Once involved, the emotions must be concealed if the lie is not to be betrayed. Any emotion may be the culprit, but three emotions are so often intertwined with deceit as to merit separate explanation: fear of being caught, guilt about lying, and delight in having duped someone.

Fear of Being Caught

Such fear in its milder forms is not disruptive but instead may help the liar avoid mistakes by keeping him alert. A moderate level of fear can produce behavioral signs noticeable to the skilled lie catcher, and when strong, the liar's fear of being caught produces just what he fears. If a liar could estimate how much *detection apprehension* he would feel if he were to embark on a lie, he could better decide whether it is worth the likely risk. Even if he is already committed, an estimate of how much detection apprehension he is likely to feel could help him to plan countermeasures to reduce or conceal his fear. A lie catcher can also be helped by this information. He could be alerted to search for signs of fear if he expects a suspect would be very fearful of being caught.

Many factors influence how much detection apprehension will be felt. The first determinant to consider is the liar's beliefs about his target's skill as a lie catcher. If the target is known to be a pushover, a pussy-cat, there usually won't be much detection apprehension. On the other hand, someone known to be tough to fool, who has a reputation as an expert lie catcher, will instill detection apprehension. Parents often convince their children that they are such masterful detectors of deceit. "I can tell from looking in your eyes whether or not you are lying to me." The untruthful child becomes so afraid of being caught that her fear betrays her, or she confesses because she thinks that there is so little chance of success.

In Terence Rattigan's play *The Winslow Boy*, and the 1950 film based on it, the father used this ploy quite carefully. His adolescent son, Ronnie, had been discharged from the naval training school, accused of stealing a postal money order:

"ARTHUR. [father] In this letter it says you stole a postal order. (RONNIE *opens his mouth to speak.* ARTHUR *stops him.*) Now I don't want you to say a word until you've heard what I've got to say. If you did it, you must tell me. I shan't be angry with you, Ronnie —provided you tell me the truth. But if you tell me a lie, I shall know it, because a lie between you and me can't be hidden. I shall know it, Ronnie—so remember that before you speak. *(He pauses.)* Did you steal this postal order?

RONNIE. *(With hesitation.)* No, Father. I didn't.

(Arthur *takes step towards him.*)

ARTHUR. *(Staring into his eyes.)* Did you steal this postal order?

RONNIE. No, Father. I didn't. (Arthur *continues to stare into his eyes for a second, then relaxes*).[3]

Arthur believes Ronnie, and the play tells the story of the enormous sacrifices the father and the rest of the family make to vindicate Ronnie.

A parent can't always use Arthur's strategy to obtain the truth. A boy who has lied many times in the past and succeeded in fooling his father won't have any reason to think he can't succeed again. A parent may not be willing to offer amnesty for confession of a misdeed, or the offer may not, because of past incidents, be believed. The boy must trust the father, certain that his father is capable of trusting him. A father who has been suspicious and distrusting, who previously did not believe his son when he was being truthful, will arouse fear in an innocent boy. This raises a crucial problem in detecting deception: it is next to impossible to distinguish the innocent boy's *fear of being disbelieved* from the guilty boy's detection apprehension. The signs of fear would be the same.

These problems are not specific to the detection of deceit between parent and child. It is always a problem to distinguish between the innocent's fear of being disbelieved and the guilty person's detection apprehension. The difficulty is magnified when the lie catcher has a reputation for being suspicious and has not accepted the truth before. Each successive time, it will be harder for the lie catcher to distinguish fear of disbelief from detection apprehension. Practice in deceiving and success in getting away with it should always reduce detection apprehension. The husband who is having his fourteenth affair won't worry much about getting caught. He is practiced in deceit. He knows what to anticipate and how to cover it. Most importantly, he knows he can get away with it. Self-confidence deflates detection apprehension. If it goes on too long a liar may make careless errors. Some detection apprehension is probably useful to the liar.

The polygraph lie detector works on the same principles as detecting behavioral betrayals of deceit, and it is vulnerable to the same problems. The polygraph exam does not detect lies, just signs of emotion. Wires from the polygraph are attached to the suspect to measure changes in sweating, respiration, and blood pressure. Increases in blood pressure or sweating are not in themselves signs of deceit. Hands get clammy and hearts beat faster when emotion is aroused. Before giving the polygraph test most poly-

graph operators try to convince the suspect that the polygraph never fails to catch a liar, giving what is known as
a "stimulation," or "stim," test. The most common technique is to demonstrate to the suspect that the machine will
be able to tell which card the suspect picks from a deck.
After the suspect has picked a card and returned it to the
deck, he is asked to say no each time the polygraph operator
asks him if it is a particular card. Some of those using this
technique make no mistakes, because they don't trust the
polygraph record to catch the lie but use a marked set of
cards. They justify deceiving the suspect on two grounds.
If he is innocent it is important that he think the machine
will make no mistake; otherwise, he might show fear of
being disbelieved. If he is guilty it is important to make him
afraid of being caught; otherwise, the machine really won't
work. Most polygraph operators don't engage in this deceit
but rely upon the polygraph record to spot which card was
taken.[4]

It is the same as in *The Winslow Boy*—the suspect must
believe in the ability of the lie catcher. Signs of fear would
be ambiguous unless matters can be arranged so that only
the liar, not the truth teller, will be afraid. The polygraph
exams fail not only because some innocents still fear being
falsely accused or for other reasons are upset when tested
but also because some criminals don't believe in the magic
of the machine. They know they can get away with it, and
if they know it, they are more likely to be able to do so.*

Another parallel with *The Winslow Boy* is the polygraph
operator's attempt to extract a confession. Just as the father
claimed special powers to detect lies in order to induce his
son to confess if he was guilty, so some polygraph operators

---

*Some polygraph experts think that the suspect's beliefs about the accuracy of
the machine don't matter much. This and other issues about polygraph testing
and how it compares to behavioral clues in detecting deceit are discussed in
chapter 7.

attempt to extract a confession by convincing their suspects that they can't beat the machine. When a suspect does not confess, some polygraph operators will browbeat the suspect, telling the suspect that the machine has shown that the suspect is not telling the truth. By increasing detection apprehension, the hope is to make the guilty confess. The innocent suffer the false accusations but supposedly will be vindicated. Unfortunately, under such pressures some innocents will confess in order to obtain relief.

Polygraph operators usually do not have the parents' option of inducing confession by offering amnesty for the crime if it is admitted. Criminal interrogators may approximate this by suggesting that the punishment may be less severe if the suspect confesses. Although usually not able to offer total amnesty, interrogators may offer a psychological amnesty, hoping to extract a confession by implying the suspect need not feel ashamed of, or even responsible for, committing the crime. An interrogator may sympathetically explain that he finds it very understandable, that he might have done it himself had he been in the same situation. Another variation is to offer the suspect a face-saving explanation of the motive for the crime. The following example is taken from a tape-recorded interrogation of a suspected murderer, who, incidentally, was innocent. The police interrogator is speaking to the suspect:

"There are times when due to environment, due to illness, due to many reasons, people don't follow the straight and narrow path. . . . Sometimes we can't help what we do. Sometimes we do things in a moment of passion, a moment of anger and maybe because things just aren't clicking off right up here in our heads. Normal human beings want to get things straightened out, where we know we have done wrong."[5]

So far we have been considering how the lie catcher's reputation may influence detection apprehension in the liar and fear of being disbelieved in the innocent. Another factor influencing detection apprehension is the personality of the liar. Some people have a very hard time lying, while other people can do so with alarming ease. Much more is known about people who lie easily than about those who can't. I have found out a bit about these people in my research on the concealment of negative emotions.

I began a series of experiments in 1970 to verify the clues to deceit I had discovered when I had analyzed the film of the psychiatric patient Mary, whose lie I describe in the first chapter. Recall that Mary had concealed her anguish and despair so her doctor would give her a weekend pass and she, free of supervision, could then commit suicide. I had to examine similar lies by other people to learn whether or not the clues to deceit I found in her film would be shown by others. I had little hope of finding enough clinical examples. Although often one may suspect a patient has lied, rarely can one be certain, unless, like Mary, the patient confesses. My only choice was to create an experimental situation modeled after Mary's lie, in which I could examine the mistakes other people make when they lie.

To be relevant to Mary's lie, the experimental subjects would have to feel very strong negative emotions and be very motivated to conceal those feelings. I produced the strong negative emotions by showing films of gruesome medical scenes to the subjects, asking them to hide any sign of their feelings as they watched. At first my experiment failed; no one tried very hard to succeed. I had not anticipated how difficult it would be to induce people to lie in a laboratory. People become embarrassed knowing that scientists are watching them misbehave. Often so little is at stake that even when they do lie, they don't try as hard as they might in real life, when it matters. I selected student nurses as my experimental subjects because there was a great deal at stake for them in succeeding in just this kind of lie. Nurses must be able to conceal any negative emotions they feel when they see surgical or other bloody scenes. My experiment offered these nursing students a chance to practice this career-relevant skill. Another reason for selecting nurses was to avoid the ethical problem of exposing just anyone to such gory scenes. By their career choice nurses elect to confront such material. The instructions I gave them were:

"If you are working in an emergency room and a mother rushes in with a badly mangled child, you can't show your distress, even if you know the child is in terrible pain and has little chance to survive. You have to hold your own feelings in and calm the mother down until the doctor comes. Or, imagine what you will do when you have to clean up the feces for a patient who no longer can control his bowel movements. He is already embarrassed or ashamed of being reduced to an infantile state. You'll probably feel disgusted, but you have to conceal that feeling. This experiment offers you the chance to test out and practice your ability to control the expression of your feelings. First you will see a pleasant film showing colorful ocean scenes, and while you watch it you are to describe your feelings frankly to an interviewer who cannot see which film you are seeing. Then you will see some of the very worst scenes you may ever encounter in years of nursing experience. While you watch those scenes you will have to conceal your real feelings so that the interviewer will think you are seeing another pleasant film; you can say it is showing pretty flowers in [San Francisco's] Golden Gate Park. Try as hard as you can."

We selected the very worst films we could find. In preliminary studies we found that some people were extremely upset by a film showing severe burns, since they knew that a burn victim's terrible pain can't be much relieved by medication. Others were more upset by an amputation scene, partly by seeing all the blood gush out but also by the thought of how that person would feel afterward when he awoke and realized he was without a limb. We edited the two films together so that it appeared as if the burn victim also had an amputation. By using these terrible films we could find out how well people can conceal very, very strong emotions when they want to or must.

Because the competition for admission to the nursing school at my university is very intense, these young students all had top scores on various achievement tests, very high grades, and excellent character references. Despite being such a select group, they differed markedly in their ability to hide their feelings. Some did so superbly, while others could not do so at all. I found out in interviews with them afterward that an inability to lie while watching my gruesome films was not specific to my experiment. Some of the student nurses always had trouble lying about their feelings. Some people are especially vulnerable to detection apprehension. They have a great fear of being caught in a lie. They are certain that everyone who looks at them can tell if they are lying, and this becomes a self-fulfilling prophecy. I gave all these students many objective personality tests and to my surprise found that those who had great trouble lying did not differ on the tests from the rest of their group. Apart from this one quirk they seem no different than anyone else. Their families and friends know about this characteristic and forgive them for being too truthful.

I also tried to learn more about their opposites; those who lied easily and with great success. *Natural liars* know about their ability, and so do those who know them well. They have been getting away with things since childhood, fooling their parents, teachers, and friends when they wanted to. They feel no detection apprehension. Just the opposite. They are confident in their ability to deceive. Such confidence, not feeling much detection apprehension when lying, is one of the hallmarks of the psychopathic personality. But it is the only characteristic these natural liars shared with psychopaths. Unlike psychopaths, the natural liars did not show poor judgment; nor did they fail to learn from experience. They also did *not* have these other psychopathic characteristics: ". . . superficial charm . . . lack of remorse or shame; antisocial behavior without apparent compunction; and pathologic egocentricity and incapacity for love."[6] (I'll explain more about how remorse and shame may betray deceit later when I consider deception guilt.)

The natural liars in my experiment did not differ from the others in their scores on a variety of objective personality tests. Their tests showed no trace of the psychopathic personality. There was nothing anti-social in their make-up. Unlike psychopaths, they did not use their ability to lie to harm others.* Natural liars, highly skilled in deceit but not without conscience, should be able to capitalize upon their talent in certain professions—as actors, salesmen, trial lawyers, negotiators, spies, or diplomats.

Students of military deceits have been interested in the characteristics of those who can lie most skillfully: "He must have a flexible combinatorial mind—a mind which

---

*Criminal psychopaths fool the experts. "Robert Resllser, a supervisor of the FBI's Behavioral Science Unit . . . who has interviewed 36 multiple murderers . . . [said:] The majority are normal in appearance and conversation. . . . [Ann] Rule, a former police officer, psychology student and author of five books on serial killers . . . gained fleeting glances into the mind of a serial killer when, in a horrifying coincidence, she found herself working with Ted Bundy. [Bundy later was convicted for murders, some of which he committed during the time he worked with Rule]. They fast became friends. [Rule said:] Ted was such a manipulator, you never knew whether he was putting you on or not. . . . The anti-social personality always sounds sincere, the façade is absolutely perfect. I thought I knew what to look for, but when I was working with Ted, there wasn't one signal or giveaway" (Edward Iwata, "The Baffling Normalcy of Serial Murders," *San Francisco Chronicle*, May 5, 1984).

works by breaking down ideas, concepts, or 'words' into their basic components, and then recombining them in a variety of ways. (One example of this type of thinking may be found in the game of Scrabble.) . . . the greatest past users of deception . . . are highly individualistic and competitive; they would not easily fit into a large organization . . . and tend to work by themselves. They are often convinced of the superiority of their own opinions. They do in some ways fit the supposed character of the lonely, eccentric bohemian artist, only the art they practice is different. This is apparently the only common denominator for great practitioners of deception such as Churchill, Hitler, Dayan, and T. E. Lawrence."[7]

Such "great practitioners" may need to have two very different skills—the skill needed to plan a deceptive strategy and the skill needed to mislead an opponent in a face-to-face meeting. Hitler apparently had both, but presumably one could excel at one skill and not the other. Regrettably, there has been little study of the characteristics of successful deceivers; no work that has asked whether the personality characteristics of successful deceivers differ depending upon the arena in which the deceit is practiced. I suspect the answer is no, and that those who lie successfully in the military arena could do quite well in large businesses as well.

It is tempting to damn any political enemy known to have lied as an anti-social, psychopathic personality. While I have no evidence to dispute that, I am suspicious of such judgments. Just as Nixon is a hero or a villain depending upon one's politics, so too foreign leaders can appear to be psychopathic or shrewd depending upon whether or not their lies further one's own values. I expect that psychopaths rarely survive in bureaucratic structures long enough to achieve a position of national leadership.

So far I have described two determinants of detection

apprehension: the personality of the liar and, before that, the reputation and character of the lie catcher. Equally important are the *stakes*. There is a simple rule: the greater the stakes, the more the detection apprehension. Applying this simple rule can be complicated, because it isn't always so easy to figure out what is at stake.

Sometimes it is easy. Since nursing students are highly motivated to succeed in their careers, especially when they begin their training, the stakes in our experiment were high. Therefore the nurses should have had high detection apprehension, which could leak or otherwise betray their deceit. The detection apprehension would have been weaker if their careers did not seem to be involved. For example, most of them probably would have cared less about failing if they had been asked to conceal their feelings about the morality of shoplifting. The stakes would have been increased if they had been led to believe that those who failed in our experiment would be denied admission to the school of nursing.*

A salesman misleading his customer should care more about a sale involving a large than a small commission. The larger the reward, the greater should be the detection apprehension. There is more at stake. Sometimes the obvious reward is not the important one to the deceiver. The salesman may be after the admiration of his fellow salesmen. Suckering a tough customer may involve high rewards in terms of their admiration, even if the commission earned is small. The stakes could be very high in the penny ante poker game if a poker player wanted to trounce a rival for his girlfriend's affection. For some people winning is everything. It does not matter whether it is pennies or dollars; for them the stakes are very high in any competition.

---

*Our research did show that those who did best in our experiment, who were most able to control their emotions, did the best over the next three years of their training.

What is at stake may be so idiosyncratic that no outside observer would readily know. The philanderer may enjoy fooling his wife, repeating some compulsion to hide things from Mommy, more than satisfying a burning lust.

Detection apprehension should be greater when the stakes involve avoiding punishment, not just earning a reward. When the decision to deceive is first made, the stakes usually involve obtaining rewards. The liar thinks most about what he might get. An embezzler may think only about the "wine, women, and song" when he first begins his deceit. Once deceit has been under way for some time, the rewards may no longer be available. The company may become aware of its losses and suspicious enough that the embezzler can take no more. Now he maintains his deceit to avoid being caught, as only punishment is now at stake. Avoiding punishment may be at stake right from the start if the target is suspicious or the deceiver has little confidence.

Two kinds of punishment are at stake in deceit: the punishment that lies in store if the lie fails and the punishment for the very act of engaging in deception. Detection apprehension will be greater if both kinds of punishment are at stake. Sometimes the punishment for being caught deceiving is far worse than the punishment the lie was designed to avoid. The *Winslow Boy*'s father made it known that this was the case. If the lie catcher can make it clear before questioning the suspect that the punishment for lying will be worse than the punishment for the crime, there is a better chance of discouraging the suspect from embarking on a lie.

Parents should know that the severity of their punishments is one of the factors that influence whether their children confess or lie about transgressions. The classic description comes from Mason Locke Weems's somewhat fictionalized account, *The Life and Memorable Actions of*

George Washington. The father is speaking to young George: "Many parents, indeed, even compel their children to this vile practice [lying], by barbarously beating them for every little fault: hence, on the next offense, the little terrified creature slips out a *lie!* Just to escape the rod. But as to yourself George, you know I have *always* told you, and now tell you again, that, whenever by accident, you do anything wrong, which must often be the case, as you are but a poor little boy yet, without *experience* or *knowledge,* you must never tell a falsehood to conceal it; but come *bravely* up, my son, like a *little* man, and tell me of it: and, instead of beating you, George, I will but the more honor and love you for it, my dear." The cherry-tree story shows that George trusted his father's claim.

It is not just children who may lose more by the very act of lying than they could have lost by being truthful. A husband may tell his wife that, although hurt, he could have excused her affair if she had not lied about it. The loss of trust, he would be claiming, is greater than the loss of belief in her fidelity. His wife might not have known this, and it may not be true. Confessing an affair may be construed as cruelty, and the offended spouse may claim that a truly considerate mate would be discreet about indiscretions. Husband and wife often may not agree. Feelings may change over the course of a marriage. Attitudes may change radically once there has been an extramarital affair, may differ from what they were when the matter was hypothetical.

Even if the transgressor knows that the damage done if he is caught lying will be greater than the loss from admitting the transgression, the lie may be very tempting, since telling the truth brings immediate, certain losses, while a lie promises the possibility of avoiding any loss. The prospect of being spared immediate punishment may be so attractive that the wish to take this course causes the liar to underestimate the likelihood and the costs of being caught. Recognition that confession would have been a better policy comes too late, when the deceit has been maintained so long and with such elaboration that confession no longer wins a lesser punishment.

Sometimes there is little ambiguity about the relative costs of confession versus continued concealment. There are actions that are themselves so bad that confessing them wins little approval for having come forward and concealing them adds little to the punishment that awaits the offender. Such is the case if the lie conceals child abuse, incest, murder, treason, or terrorism. Unlike the rewards possible for some repentant philanderers, forgiveness is not to be expected by those who confess these crimes (although confession with contrition may lessen the punishment). Nor is there much chance that there will be moral outrage over their concealment once it is discovered. It is not only nasty or cruel people who may be in this situation. The Jew in a Nazi-occupied country who was concealing his identity, the spy during wartime, gain little by confessing and lose nothing by attempting to maintain their deceits. When there is no chance of winning a lesser punishment, a liar may still confess to relieve the burden of having to maintain the deceit, to extinguish the suffering from a high level of detection apprehension, or to relieve guilt.

Another factor to consider about how the stakes influence detection apprehension is what is gained or lost by the target, not just by the deceiver. Usually the deceiver's gains are at the expense of the target. The embezzler gains what the employer loses. It is not always equal. A salesman's commission gained by misrepresenting a product may be much smaller than the loss suffered by the gullible customer. The stakes for the liar and the target can differ not just in amount but in kind. A philanderer may gain adventure, while the cuckolded spouse loses self-respect. When the stakes for the liar and target differ, the stakes for either might be the determinant of the liar's detection apprehension. It depends upon whether the liar recognizes the difference.

Liars are not the most trustworthy source for estimating what is at stake for their targets. They have a vested interest in believing what serves their ends. Deceivers find it comfortable to think that their targets are benefiting from their deceits as much as or more than the liars. That can happen. Not all lies harm the target. There are altruistic lies:

"A pale, slight 11-year-old boy, injured but alive, was pulled yesterday from the wreckage of a small plane that crashed Sunday in the mountains of Yosemite National Park. The boy had survived days of raging blizzards and nights of sub-zero temperatures at the 11,000-foot-high crash site, swaddled in a down sleeping bag in the rear seat of the snow-buried wreckage. Alone. 'How is my mom and dad?' asked the dazed fifth-grader. 'Are they all right?' Rescuers did not tell the boy that his stepfather and his mother were dead, still strapped into their seats in the airplane's shattered cockpit, only inches from where he lay."[8]

Few would deny that this is an altruistic lie, benefiting the target, not providing any gains to the rescuers. The fact that the target benefits does not mean there may not be very high detection apprehension. If the stakes are high, there will be great detection apprehension, no matter who is the beneficiary. Worried about whether the boy could withstand the shock, the rescuers should be very concerned that their concealment succeed.

To summarize, detection apprehension is greatest when:

- the target has a reputation for being tough to fool;
- the target starts out being suspicious;
- the liar has had little practice and no record of success;
- the liar is specially vulnerable to the fear of being caught;
- the stakes are high;
- both rewards and punishments are at stake; or, if it is only one or the other, punishment is at stake;
- the punishment for being caught lying is great, or the punishment for what the lie is about is so great that there is no incentive to confess;
- the target in no way benefits from the lie.

Deception Guilt

Deception guilt refers to a feeling about lying, not the legal issue of whether someone is guilty or innocent. Deception guilt must also be distinguished from feelings of guilt about the content of a lie. Suppose in *The Winslow Boy* Ronnie actually had stolen the postal money order. He might have had guilty feelings about the theft itself— judged himself to be a terrible person for what he did. If Ronnie had concealed his theft from his father he would also have felt guilty about lying; that would be deception guilt. It is not necessary to feel guilty about the content of a lie to feel guilty about lying. Suppose Ronnie had stolen from a boy who had cheated to defeat Ronnie in a school contest. Ronnie might not feel guilty about stealing from such a nasty schoolmate; it might seem like appropriate revenge. But he could still feel deception guilt about concealing his theft from the schoolmaster or his father. The psychiatric patient Mary did not feel guilty about her plan to commit suicide, but she did feel guilty about lying to her doctor.

Like detection apprehension, deception guilt can vary in strength. It may be very mild, or so strong that the lie will fail because the deception guilt produces leakage or deception clues. When it becomes extreme, deception guilt is a torturing experience, undermining the sufferer's most fundamental feelings of self-worth. Relief from such severe deception guilt may motivate a confession despite the likelihood of punishment for misdeeds admitted. In fact, the punishment may be just what is needed, and why the person confesses, to alleviate the tortured feelings of guilt.

When the decision to lie is first made, people do not always accurately anticipate how much they may later suffer from deception guilt. Liars may not realize the impact of being thanked by their victims for their seeming helpfulness, or how they will feel when they see someone else blamed for their misdeeds. While such scenes typically arouse guilt, for others it is catnip, the spice that makes a lie worth undertaking. I'll discuss that reaction below as *duping delight*. Another reason why liars underestimate how much deception guilt they will feel is that it is only with the passage of time that a liar may learn that one lie will not suffice, that the lie has to be repeated again and again, often with expanding fabrications in order to protect the original deceit.

Shame is closely related to guilt, but there is a key qualitative difference. No audience is needed for feelings of guilt, no one else need know, for the guilty person is his own judge. Not so for shame. The humiliation of shame requires disapproval or ridicule by others. If no one ever learns of a misdeed there will be no shame, but there still might be guilt. Of course, there may be both. The distinction between shame and guilt is very important, since these two emotions may tear a person in opposite directions. The wish to relieve guilt may motivate a confession, but the wish to avoid the humiliation of shame may prevent it.

Suppose that in *The Winslow Boy* Ronnie had stolen the money, that he felt extremely guilty about having done it and also felt deception guilt about having concealed his misdeed. Ronnie might want to confess to get relief from the torture of his guilty conscience. Yet the shame he feels as he imagines how his father will react might stop him. In order to encourage him to confess, his father, remember, offers amnesty—no punishment if he confesses. Reducing Ronnie's fear of punishment should lessen his detection apprehension, but the father still needs to reduce shame if Ronnie is to confess. The father tries to do so by telling Ronnie he will forgive him, but he could have strengthened the shame reduction, increasing the likelihood of confession, if he had added something like the ploy used by the interrogator I quoted a few pages back, who was trying to extract a confession from a suspected murderer. He could have told Ronnie: "I can understand stealing, I might have done it myself if I had been in your situation, tempted as you were. Everyone makes mistakes in his life and does things that later he realizes are wrong. Sometimes you just can't help yourself." Of course, a proper English father might not be able to honestly say that, and unlike the criminal's interrogator, he might not be willing to lie to extract a confession.

Some people are especially vulnerable to shame about lying and deception guilt. This would include those who have been very strictly brought up to believe that lying is one of the most terrible of sins. The upbringing of others may not have particularly condemned lying but more generally have instilled strong, pervasive guilt feelings. Such guilty people appear to seek experiences in which they can intensify their guilt and stand shamefully exposed to others. Unfortunately, there has been very little research about guilt-prone individuals. A little more is known about their opposite.

Jack Anderson, the newspaper columnist, gave an account of a liar who felt neither shame nor guilt in a column attacking the credibility of Mel Weinberg, the FBI's chief witness in the Abscam prosecutions. Anderson described Weinberg's reaction to his wife's discovery that he had been concealing an extramarital affair for the past fourteen years. "When Mel finally came home, he shrugged off Marie's demand for an explanation. 'So I got caught,' he said. 'I always told you I'm the world's biggest liar.' Then he nestled into his favorite armchair, ordered some Chinese food—and asked Marie to give him a manicure."[9]

A failure to feel any guilt or shame about his misdeeds is considered the mark of a psychopath, if the lack of guilt or shame pervades all or most aspects of his life. (Obviously no one can make such a diagnosis from a newspaper account.) Experts disagree about whether the lack of guilt and shame is due to upbringing or some biological determinants. There is agreement that neither guilt about lying nor fear of being caught will cause a psychopath to make mistakes when he lies.

Whenever the deceiver does not share social values with the victim, there won't be much deception guilt. People feel less guilty about lying to those they think are wrongdoers. A philanderer whose marital partner is cold and unwilling in bed might not feel guilty in lying about an affair. A revolutionary or terrorist rarely feels guilty about deceiving the agents of the state. A spy won't feel guilty about misleading his victim. A former CIA agent put that succinctly—"Peel away the claptrap of espionage and the spy's job is to betray trust."[10] When I advised security officials who wanted to catch people trying to assassinate a highly placed government official, I could not count on deception guilt to produce any telltale signs. Assassins might be afraid of being caught if they are not professionals, but they are not likely to be guilty about what they planned. A professional criminal does not feel guilt about deceiving an outsider. The same principle is at work to explain why a diplomat or spy does not feel guilty about misleading the other side. Values are not shared. The liar is doing good, for his side.

Lying is *authorized* in most of these examples—each of these individuals appeals to a well-defined social norm that legitimates deceiving an opponent. There is little guilt about such authorized deceits when the targets are from an opposing side and hold different values. There also may be authorization to deceive targets who are not opponents, who share values with the deceiver. Physicians may not feel guilty about deceiving their patients if they think it is for the patient's own good. Giving a patient a placebo, a sugar pill identified as a useful drug, is an old, time-honored medical deceit. If the patient feels better, or at least stops hassling the doctor for an unneeded drug that might actually be harmful, many physicians believe that the lie is justified. Hippocrates' oath does not call for honesty with the patient. The doctor is supposed to do what helps the patient.* The priest who conceals a criminal's confession when the police ask him if he knows anything about who did it should not feel deception guilt. His vows authorize his deceit. He does not benefit from the deceit; the benefit is to the criminal, whose identity remains unknown. The nursing students in my experiment had no deception guilt about concealing their feelings. De-

---

*While 30 to 40 percent of patients gain relief from placebos, some medical workers and philosophers believe that the use of placebos jeopardizes the trust required in medical relationships and paves the way for more dangerous deceits. See Lindsey Gruson's article "Use of Placebos Being Argued on Ethical Grounds," *New York Times,* February 13, 1983, p. 19 for references and a discussion of the two sides of this issue.

ceit was authorized by my examples that explained when a nurse must conceal to do her job of relieving a patient's suffering.

Liars may not realize or admit that often they too benefit from deceits that are represented as altruistic. A senior vice president of a national insurance company explained that telling the truth can be ignoble when the ego of another person is involved—"Sometimes, it's hard to say to a guy, "No, you'll never be chairman.' "[11] The guy's feelings are spared, but so are the feelings of the vice president. It might be "hard" to deal with the guy's disappointment, let alone the possibility of protest, especially if the guy might hold the vice president responsible for the negative judgment of him. The lie spares both of them. One could, of course, argue that the guy is harmed by the lie, deprived of information that, though unpleasant, might lead him to improve his performance or seek employment elsewhere. In a similar way one can argue that the placebo-giving doctor, while being altruistic, also gains from the lie. He does not have to deal with the patient's frustration or disappointment that there is no medicine for patient's illness, or the patient's anger if the patient were to learn that the doctor gives placebos because he thinks the patient is a hypochondriac. Again, it is arguable whether the lie actually benefits or harms the patient.

Nevertheless, there are totally altruistic lies—the priest who conceals the criminal's confession, the rescuers who don't tell the injured eleven-year-old boy that his parents died in the airplane crash—in which the liar obtains no benefits. If a liar thinks he is not gaining from the lie, he probably won't feel any deception guilt.

Even selfish deceits may not produce deception guilt when the lie is authorized. Poker players don't feel deception guilt about bluffing. The same is true about bargaining, whether in a Middle East bazaar, on Wall Street, or in the local real estate agent's office. An article about industrial lies said: "Perhaps the most famous lie of all is: 'That's my final offer.' Such language is not only accepted in the business world, it's expected. . . . During collective bargaining, for example, no one is expected to put all his cards on the table at the outset."[12] The homeowner who asks more for his house then he will actually sell it for won't feel guilty if he gets his asking price. His lie is authorized. Because the participants expect misinformation, not the truth, bargaining and poker don't meet any definition of lying. These situations by their nature provide prior notification that no one will be truthful. Only a fool shows his hand in poker or asks the lowest price he will accept when he first puts his house up for sale.

Deception guilt is most likely when lying is *not* authorized. Deception guilt should be most severe when the target is trusting, not expecting to be misled because honesty is authorized between liar and target. In such *opportunistic* deceits, guilt about lying will be greater if the target suffers at least as much as the liar gains. Even then there won't be much (if there is any) deception guilt, unless there are at least some shared values between target and liar. The adolescent who conceals smoking marijuana from her parents may not feel any deception guilt if she thinks her parents are foolish to say that dope is harmful, if she believes that she knows from experience that their judgment is wrong. If she were also to think that they are hypocrites, boozing but not allowing her to use the recreational drug of her choice, there is even less chance she will feel deception guilt. Even though she disagrees with her parents about marijuana, and other matters as well, if she still is attached to them, cares about them, she may feel shame if they discover her lies. Shame requires some respect for those who disapprove; otherwise disapproval brings forth anger or contempt, not shame.

Liars feel less guilty when their targets are impersonal or totally anonymous. A customer who conceals from the check-out clerk that she was undercharged for an expensive item in her shopping cart will feel less guilty if she does not know the clerk. If the clerk is the owner, or a member of the owner's family, if it is a small, family-owned store, the lying customer will feel more guilty than she will if it is one of a large chain of supermarkets. It is easier to indulge the guilt-reducing fantasy that the target is not really hurt, doesn't really care, won't even notice the lie, or even deserves or wants to be misled, if the target is anonymous.[13]

Often there will be an inverse relationship between deception guilt and detection apprehension. What lessens guilt about the lie increases fear of being caught. When deceits are authorized there should be less deception guilt, yet the authorization usually increases the stakes, thus making detection apprehension high. It was because the concealment was relevant to their careers—authorized—that the nursing students cared enough to be afraid of failing in my experiment. They had high detection apprehension and low deception guilt. The employer who lies to his employee whom he has come to suspect of embezzling, concealing his suspicions to catch him in the crime, is likely to feel high detection apprehension but low deception guilt.

The very factors that heighten deception guilt also may lessen detection apprehension. A liar may feel guilty misleading a trusting target, but he may be less afraid of being caught by someone who doesn't expect to be exploited. Of course, it is possible for a person to feel both very guilty about lying and very afraid of being caught, or to feel very little of either. It depends upon the particulars of the situation, the liar, and the lie catcher.

Some people wallow in deception guilt. Part of their motivation for lying might even be to have an opportunity to feel guilty about what they have done. Most people, however, find the experience of guilt so toxic that they seek ways to diminish it. There are many ways to justify deceit. It can be considered retaliation for injustice. A nasty or mean target can be said not to deserve honesty. "The boss was so stingy, he didn't reward me for all the work I did, so I took some myself." Victims may be seen as so gullible that the liar considers it their fault, not his. A sitting duck asks for it.

Two other justifications for lying, which reduce deception guilt, were mentioned earlier. A noble purpose or job requirement is one—recall Nixon's failure to call his untruths lies because he said they were necessary to win and retain office. The other justification is to protect the target. Sometimes the liar may go so far as to claim that the target was willing. If the target cooperated in the deceit, knew the truth all along but pretended not to, then in a sense there was no lie, and the liar is free of any responsibility. A truly willing target helps the deceiver maintain the deceit, overlooking any behavioral betrayals of the lie. An unwilling target, of course, will, if suspicious, attempt to uncover deceit.

An interesting example of when a target may be willing is contained in recent revelations about Robert Leuci, the policeman turned undercover informant, whose story I quoted near the end of chapter 2. Leuci was glamorized in Robert Daley's book *Prince of the City*, and the film based on it, which claimed to be true accounts of how Leuci helped federal prosecutors obtain evidence of corruption among policemen and lawyers. When Leuci went to work for the federal prosecutors, they asked him what crimes he had himself committed. He admitted to only three crimes. Those whom he later exposed claimed that Leuci had committed many more crimes than he had admitted, and because he had lied about his own criminality, they argued, his testimony against them should be discredited. These allegations were never proven, and many people were convicted on the basis of Leuci's testimony. Alan Dershowitz, the lawyer who defended one of the people convicted on Leuci's testimony, described a conversation after the trial in which Leuci admitted he had indeed committed more crimes.

"I [Dershowitz] told him [Leuci] that it was hard for me to believe that Shaw [the federal prosecutor] didn't know about the other crimes prior to the Rosner [the man Dershowitz defended] trial. 'I'm convinced that in his heart he knew that I had committed more crimes,' Leuci said. 'He had to. Mike [Shaw] is no fool.'

" 'Then how could he sit there and watch you lie on the witness stand?' I asked.

" 'He didn't consciously know for sure I was lying,' Leuci continued. 'He certainly suspected it and he probably believed it, but I had told him not to press me and he didn't. I said "three crimes" '—Leuci raised three fingers and smiled broadly—'and he had to accept that. Prosecutors suborn perjury every day, Alan. You know that.' "[14]

Dershowitz later learned that this confession of lying was also a lie. A law enforcement official, present when Leuci first met with the federal prosecutors, told Dershowitz that Leuci from the start openly admitted to many more than the three crimes that were later publicly acknowledged. The federal prosecutors joined Leuci in concealing the full story of his criminal acts in order to preserve Leuci's credibility as a witness—juries might believe a policemen who had committed only three crimes, but not one who had committed multitudes. After the trials, when it became widely known that Leuci had committed more crimes, Leuci lied to Dershowitz, claiming that the prosecutors were only willing victims, not admitting that they had explicitly colluded to conceal his criminal record

to hold up his part of their deal, protecting them as long as they protected him. Not trusting to honor among thieves, Leuci reportedly had made and kept a tape recording of his confession to the prosecutors. That way the prosecutors could never claim innocence, and because Leuci could always expose their perjury about his testimony, Leuci could trust that the prosecutors would always remain loyal to him, protecting him from any criminal prosecution.

No matter what the truth is about Leuci, his conversation with Alan Dershowitz provides an excellent example of how a willing target who profits from a lie can make it easy for a liar to pull off the deceit. People may cooperate with being misled for less malevolent reasons. In politeness, the target of the deceit is often willing. The hostess accepts the excuse for the guest's early departure without scrutinizing too carefully. The important thing is an absence of rudeness, a pretense delivered to spare the hostess's feelings. Because the target is not only willing but has in a sense given consent to be misled, the untruths called for by politeness etiquette do not fit my definition of lying.

Romance is another instance of a benign deceit, in which the target cooperates with being misled, both parties cooperating in maintaining each other's lies. Shakespeare wrote:

> When my love swears that she is made of truth,
> I do believe her, though I know she lies,
> That she might think me some untutored youth,
> Unlearned in the world's false subtleties.
> Thus vainly thinking that she thinks me young,
> Although she knows my days are past the best,
> Simply I credit her false-speaking tongue.
> On both sides thus is simple truth suppressed.
> But wherefore says she not she is unjust?
> And wherefore say not I that I am old?

Oh, love's best habit is in seeming trust,
And age in love loves not to have years told.
Therefore I lie with her and she with me,
And in our faults by lies we flattered be.[15]

Of course not all romantic deceits are so benign; nor are the targets always so willing to be misled. Deceivers can't be trusted for an honest opinion about whether or not their targets were willing. They are biased towards willingness because it makes them feel less guilty. If they can get their target to admit being suspicious they are at least partially off the hook.

An unwilling target may after a time become a willing one in order to avoid the costs of discovering deceit. Imagine the plight of the government official who begins to suspect that the lover to whom he has been trusting information about his work is a spy. A job recruiter may similarly become the willing victim of a fraudulent job applicant, once the applicant is hired, rather than acknowledge his own mistaken judgment. Roberta Wohlstetter describes numerous instances in which national leaders have become willing victims of their adversaries—Chamberlain was not an isolated case. "In all of these instances of error persisting over a long period of time, in the face of increasing and sometimes rather bald contrary evidence, a very significant role is played by cherished beliefs and comforting assumptions about the good faith of a potential adversary and the common interests supposedly shared by that antagonist. . . . An adversary may only have to help the victim along somewhat; the latter will tend to explain away what might otherwise look like a rather menacing move."[16]

To summarize, deception guilt will be greatest when:

- the target is unwilling;
- the deceit is totally selfish, and the target derives no

benefit from being misled and loses as much as or more than the liar gains;
- the deceit is unauthorized, and the situation is one in which honesty is authorized;
- the liar has not been practicing the deceit for a long time;
- the liar and target share social values;
- the liar is personally acquainted with the target;
- the target can't easily be faulted as mean or gullible;
- there is reason for the target to expect to be misled; just the opposite, the liar has acted to win confidence in his trustworthiness.

Duping Delight

So far I have discussed only negative feelings that may be aroused when someone lies: fear of being caught and guilt about misleading the target. Lying can also produce positive feelings. The lie may be viewed as an accomplishment, which feels good. The liar may feel excitement, either when anticipating the challenge or during the very moment of lying, when success is not yet certain. Afterward there may be the pleasure that comes with relief, pride in the achievement, or feelings of smug contempt toward the target. Duping delight refers to all or any of these feelings that can, if not concealed, betray the deceit. An innocent example of duping delight occurs when kidding takes the form of misleading a gullible friend. The kidder has to conceal his duping delight even though his performance may in large part be directed to others who are appreciating how well the gullible person is being taken in.

Duping delight can vary in strength. It may be totally absent, almost insignificant compared to the amount of detection apprehension that is felt, or duping delight may be so great that some behavioral sign of it leaks. People may confess their deception in order to share their delight in having put one over. Criminals have been known to reveal their crime to friends, strangers, even to the police in order to be acknowledged and appreciated as having been clever enough to pull off a particular deceit.

Like mountain climbing or chess, lying may be enjoyable only if there is some risk of loss. When I was a college student at the University of Chicago in the early fifties, it was the fashion to steal books from the university bookstore. Almost an initiation rite for a new student, the theft was limited usually to a few books, and the accomplishment widely shown and acknowledged. Deception guilt was low. The student culture held that a university bookstore should be run as a cooperative, and since it was instead run for profit it deserved to be abused. Nearby private bookstores were held inviolate. Detection apprehension was also low because there were no security measures at the bookstore. Only one person was caught during my days there, and he was betrayed by his duping delight. Bernard was not satisfied with the challenge posed by the usual thefts. He had to increase the risks in order to take pride, show his contempt toward the bookstore, and earn the admiration he sought from his fellow students. He stole only large art books, which were very hard to conceal. After a while that paled, and he upped the ante by taking three or four art books at a time. Still it was too easy. He began to tease the bookstore clerks. Lingering around the cash register with his prizes under his arm, he made no attempt to conceal the books. He dared the clerks to question him. Duping delight motivated him to increasingly tempt fate. The behavioral signs of his duping delight provided part of the tip-off. He was caught. Almost five hundred stolen books were found in his dormitory room. Bernard later became a millionaire in a perfectly respectable business.

There are other ways to enhance duping delight. If the person being deceived has the reputation of being difficult to fool, this may add spice, facilitating duping delight. The presence of others who know what is going on can also increase the likelihood of duping delight. The audience need not be present, as long as it is attentive and appreciative. When the audience is present, enjoying the liar's performance, the liar may have the most duping delight and the hardest time suppressing any sign of it. When one kid lies to another while others watch, the liar may so enjoy observing how he is entertaining his buddies that his delight bursts forth, ending the whole matter. A skillful poker player manages to control any sign of duping delight. Dealt a very strong hand, his actions must mislead the others to think his hand is not very good, so they will raise the ante and stay in the game. Even when kibitzers know what he is doing, he must inhibit any sign of duping delight. This may be easiest by avoiding any eye contact with the kibitzers.

Some people may be much more prone to duping delight. No scientist has yet studied such people or even verified that they do exist. Yet it seems obvious that some people boast more than others, and that braggarts might more than others be vulnerable to duping delight.

While lying, a person may feel duping delight, deception guilt, and detection apprehension—all at once or in succession. Consider poker again. In a bluff, where a player has a poor hand but is pretending to have such a good one that the others will fold, there maybe detection apprehension if the pot has gotten very high. As the bluffer watches each player cave in, he may also feel duping delight. Since misinformation is authorized there should be no deception guilt as long as the poker player does not cheat. An embezzler might feel all three emotions: delight in how she has fooled her fellow employees and employer; apprehension at any moments when she thinks there might be some suspicion; and, perhaps, guilt about having broken the law and violated trust shown in her by her company.

To summarize, duping delight will be greatest when:

- the target poses a challenge, having a reputation for being difficult to fool;
- the lie is a challenge, because of either what must be concealed or the nature of what must be fabricated;
- others are watching or know about the lie and appreciate the liar's skillful performance.

Guilt, fear, delight, all can be shown in facial expression, the voice, or body movement, even when the liar is trying to conceal them. Even if there is no nonverbal leakage, the struggle to prevent it may produce a deception clue. The next two chapters explain how to detect deceit from the words, voice, body, and face.

FOUR

Detecting Deceit from Words, Voice, or Body

"And how can you possibly know that I have told a lie?'
"Lies, my dear boy, are found out immediately, because they are of
two sorts. There are lies that have short legs, and lies that have long noses.
Your lie, as it happens, is one of those that have a long nose."—Pinocchio,
1892

P EOPLE WOULD LIE less if they thought there was any
such certain sign of lying, but there isn't. *There is no*
sign of deceit itself—no gesture, facial expression, or
muscle twitch that in and of itself means that a person is
lying. There are only clues that the person is poorly prepared and clues of emotions that don't fit the person's line.
These are what provide leakage or deception clues. The lie
catcher must learn how emotion is registered in speech,
voice, body, and face, what traces may be left despite a liar's
attempts to conceal feelings, and what gives away false
emotional portrayals. Spotting deceit also requires understanding how these behaviors may reveal that a liar is making up his line as he goes along.

It is not a simple matter to catch lies. One problem is

the *barrage* of information. There is too much to consider at once. Too many sources—words, pauses, sound of the voice, expressions, head movements, gestures, posture, respiration, flushing or blanching, sweating, and so on. And all of these sources may transmit information simultaneously or in overlapping time, competing for the lie catcher's attention. Fortunately, the lie catcher does not need to scrutinize with equal care everything that can be heard and seen. Not every source of information during a conversation is reliable. Some leak much more than others. Strangely enough, most people pay most attention to the least trustworthy sources—words and facial expressions—and so are easily misled.

Liars usually do not monitor, control, and disguise all of their behavior. They probably couldn't even if they wanted to. It is not likely that anyone could successfully control everything he did that could give him away, from the tip of his toes to the top of his forehead. Instead liars conceal and falsify what they expect others are going to watch most. Liars tend to be most careful about their choice of words. Everyone learns in the process of growing up that most people listen closely to what is said. Words receive such great attention because they are, obviously, the richest, most differentiated way to communicate. Many more messages can be transmitted, far more quickly, by words than by the face, voice, or body. Liars censor what they say, carefully concealing messages they do not want to deliver, not only because they have learned that everyone pay attention to this source but also because they know that they will be held more accountable for their words than for the sound of their voice, facial expressions, or most body movements. An angry expression or a harsh tone of voice can always be denied. The accuser can be put on the defensive: "You heard it that way. There was no anger in my voice." It is much harder to deny having said an angry word. It stands there, easily repeated back, hard to disavow totally.

Another reason why words are carefully monitored and so often the chief target for disguise is that it is easy to falsify—to state things that are not true—in words. Exactly what is to be said can be written down and reworded ahead of time. Only a highly trained actor could so precisely plan each facial expression, gesture, and voice inflection. Words are easy to rehearse, again and again. The speaker has continual feedback, hearing what he says, and thus is able to fine-tune his message. The feedback from the face, body, and voice channel is much less accurate.

After words, the face receives the greatest amount of attention from others. People receive commentary about the appearance of their face: "Wipe that look off your face!" "Smile when you say that!" "Don't look sassy at me." The face receives attention partly because it is the mark and symbol of the self. It is the chief way we distinguish one person from another. Faces are icons, celebrated in photographs hung on walls, placed on desks, and carried in wallets and purses.[1] Recent research has found that one part of the brain is specialized for recognizing faces.[2]

There are a number of other reasons why people pay such attention to faces. The face is the primary site for the display of emotions. Together with the voice, it may tell the listener how the speaker feels about what is being said—but not always accurately, since faces can lie about feelings. If there is difficulty hearing, watching the speaker's lips can help the listener figure out the words being spoken. Attending to the face can also provide an important signal necessary for conversations to proceed. Speakers want to know whether their listeners are listening. Looking at the speaker's face implies that, but it isn't the most trustworthy signal. Bored but polite listeners can watch a speaker's face while their minds are elsewhere. Listeners also encourage the speaker with head nods and "mm-hmms," but these too can be faked.*

Compared to the attention lavished on the words and face, the body and voice don't receive much. Not much is lost, since usually the body provides much less information than the face, the voice much less than the words. Hand gestures could provide many messages, as they do in the sign language of the deaf, but hand gestures are not common in conversations among northern Europeans and Americans of that background, unless speech is prohibited.† The voice, like the face, can show whether someone is emotional or not, but it is not known yet whether the voice can provide as much information as the face about precisely which emotions are felt.

Liars usually monitor and try to control their words and face—what they know others focus upon—more than their voice and body. They will have more success with their words than with their face. Falsifying is easier with words than with facial expression because, as mentioned earlier, words can be rehearsed more readily than facial actions. Concealing also is easier. People can more readily monitor their words than their face, censoring anything that could betray them. It is easy to know what one is saying; much harder to know what one's face is showing. The only parallel to the clarity of feedback given by hearing words as they are spoken would be a mirror always in

---

*Most people, when they talk, are dependent upon these listener responses and if deprived will quickly ask, "Are you listening?" There are a few people who are closed systems, talking heedless of whether their listeners provide any encouragement responses.

†Among sawmill workers, for example, who must communicate but can't do so with words because of the noise, a very elaborate system of hand gestures is used. Pilots and landing crews for the same reason use an elaborate system of gestures.

place showing each expression. While there are sensations in the face that could provide information about when muscles are tensing and moving, my research has shown that most people don't make much use of this information. Few are aware of the expressions emerging on their face until the expressions are extreme.*

There is still another, more important reason why there are more clues to deceit in the face than in words. The face is directly connected to those areas of the brain involved in emotion, and words are not. When emotion is aroused, muscles on the face begin to fire involuntarily. It is only by choice or habit that people can learn to interfere with these expressions, trying, with varying degrees of success, to conceal them. The initial facial expressions that begin when emotion is aroused are not deliberately chosen, unless they are false. Facial expressions are a dual system—voluntary and involuntary, lying and telling the truth, often at the same time. That is why facial expressions can be so complex, confusing, and fascinating. In the next chapter I will explain more about the neural basis for the distinction between voluntary and involuntary expressions.

Suspicious people should pay more attention to the voice and body than they do. The voice, like the face, is tied to the areas of the brain involved in emotion. It is very difficult to conceal some of the changes in voice that occur when emotion is aroused. And the feedback about what the voice sounds like, necessary for a liar to monitor how he sounds, is probably not as good for hearing the voice as it is for the words. People are surprised the first time they hear themselves on a tape recorder, because self-monitor-

---

*Neuroscientists are not certain about the circuitry that provides us with information about changes in our own expression or about whether it is changes in muscle or in the skin that are registered. Psychologists disagree about how well people can feel their own facial expressions as they emerge. My studies suggest that we don't feel the expressions we make very well and that most of the time we don't pay much attention to the sensations in our face.

ing of the voice comes partly through bone conduction, and it sounds different.

The body is also a good source of leakage and deception clues. Unlike the face or voice, most body movements are not directly tied to the areas of the brain involved in emotion. Monitoring of body movements need not be difficult. A person can feel and often see what his body is doing. Concealment of body movement could be much easier than concealing facial expressions or voice changes in emotion. But most people don't bother. They have grown up having learned it was not necessary to do so. Rarely are people held accountable for what they reveal in their bodily actions. The body leaks because it is ignored. Everyone is too busy watching the face and evaluating the words.

While we all know that words can lie, my research has found that people take others at their word and are often misled. I am not suggesting that the words be totally ignored. People do make verbal mistakes that can provide both leakage and deception clues. And even if there are no mistakes in the words, it is the discrepancy between the verbal line and what is revealed by the voice, body, and face that often betrays a lie. But most of the clues to deceit in the face, body, and voice are ignored or misinterpreted. I found this out in a number of studies in which I asked people to judge others shown to them on videotape.

Some saw just the face, others just the body, still others heard the speech run through a filter that made the words unintelligible but left the sound intact, and the rest heard or read the words. Everyone saw the same people—the nursing students, described in the last chapter, who told the truth or lied about their feelings while they watched films. Remember that in the honest interviews these students had seen a pleasant film showing the ocean and had been instructed to describe their feelings frankly. In the dishonest interviews they had seen a film showing gory medical scenes and had been instructed to convince the interviewer they were looking at another pleasant film, this time showing flowers. The interviewer couldn't see which film the nursing student was watching. These students tried very hard to mislead the interviewer, for the stakes were very high. They believed our experiment tested how well they would be able to control their emotional reactions in the emergency or operating room.

In our studies of how well people can detect when these students were lying, we were interested not only in which source was the best—face, body, voice, or words—but also whether suspicious people did better than those not expecting to be misled. We divided the people who were to see or hear the videotape into two groups. Some we made suspicious by what we told them about the people they were to judge, and some we tried to keep unsuspecting. The unsuspecting group were not told anything about the experiment; no mention was made of possible deceit or lying. We just told them they would be seeing or hearing people talking about a film they were watching. In order not to arouse their suspicion, we buried the judgment they were to make about honesty in a long list of judgments they had to make about friendliness, extroversion, dominance, awkwardness, calmness, and so on.

Although a few nursing students were terrible liars and were easily detected, most of the students misled the unsuspecting judges. Those who saw just the face or heard just the words did the worst: they rated the nursing students as more honest when they were, in fact, lying. Suspicious people did not do much better. These judges were told all about the instructions given to the nursing students, and they were told that the people they were to judge would be either lying or telling the truth. They were asked to make only one judgment—honesty or deceit. Very few did better than chance in spotting which was which. Those who saw just the body did the best, but even they were right on only about 65 percent of their judgments, when chance would be 50 percent.[3] A few people did very well, correctly identifying 85 percent of the liars. Some of these accurate judges were highly experienced psychotherapists with reputations for being expert clinicians. Some were just extraordinarily sensitive people in other professions.*

It is not necessary to be so misled. People who have been told some of what is in this and the next chapter did very well in judging when the nursing students were lying, as well as the most experienced psychotherapists were able to do. Clues to some deceits can be learned. The lie catcher has a better chance if the deceit involves emotion, and the liar is not a psychopath, highly practiced, or a natural liar. There are three goals: to spot a liar more often; to misjudge the truthful less often; and, most importantly, to realize when it may not be possible to do either.

The Words

Surprisingly, many liars are betrayed by their words because of carelessness. It is not that they couldn't disguise what they said, or that they tried to and failed, but simply that they neglected to fabricate carefully. The head of an executive search firm described a fellow who applied to his agency under two different names within the same year. When asked the fellow which name should he be called, "The man, who first called himself Leslie D'Ainter, but later switched to Lester Dainter, continued his prevaricating ways without skipping a beat. He explained that he

---

*Many psychologists have attempted to identify what it is that makes someone a good or bad judge of people. Not much progress has been made. For a review of this research, see Maureen O'Sullivan, "Measuring the Ability to Recognize Facial Expressions of Emotion," in *Emotion in the Human Face*, ed. Paul Ekman (New York: Cambridge University Press, 1982).

changed his first name because Leslie sounded too femi-
nine, and he altered his last name to make it easier to
pronounce. But his references were the real giveaway. He
presented three glowing letters of recommendation. Yet all
three 'employers' misspelled the same word."[4]

Even a careful liar may be betrayed by what Sigmund
Freud first identified as a slip of the tongue. In *The Psychopathology of Everyday Life* Freud showed how the faulty
actions of everyday life, such as slips of the tongue, the
forgetting of familiar names, and mistakes in reading and
writing were not accidents but meaningful events revealing internal psychological conflicts. Slips express, he
said, ". . . something one did not wish to say: it becomes a
mode of self-betrayal."[5] Freud was not specifically concerned with deceit, but one of his examples was of a
slip that betrayed a lie. The example describes the experience of Dr. Brill, one of Freud's early and well-known
followers:

I went for a walk one evening with Dr. Frink, and we discussed some of the business of the New York Psychoanalytic
Society. We met a colleague, Dr. R., who I had not seen for years
and of whose private life I knew nothing. We were very pleased
to meet again, and on my invitation he accompanied us to a café,
where we sat two hours in lively conversation. He seemed to
know some details about me, for after the usual greetings he
asked after my small child and told me that he heard about me
from time to time from a mutual friend and had been interested
in my work every since he had read about in in the medical press.
To my question as to whether he was married he gave a negative
answer, and added: "Why should a man like me marry?"

On leaving the café, he suddenly turned to me and said: "I
should like to know what you would do in a case like this: I know
a nurse who was named as co-respondent in a divorce case. The
wife sued the husband and named her as co-respondent, and *he*

got the divorce." I interrupted him, saying: "You mean *she* got the divorce." He immediately corrected himself, saying: "Yes, of course, *she* got the divorce,' and continued to tell how the nurse had been so affected by the divorce proceedings and the scandal that she had taken to drink, had become very nervous, and so on; and he wanted me to advise him how to treat her.

As soon as I had corrected his mistake I asked him to explain it, but I received the usual surprised answers: had not everyone a right to make a slip of the tongue? It was only an accident, there was nothing behind it, and so on. I replied that there must be a reason for every mistake in speaking, and that, had he not told me earlier that he was unmarried, I would be tempted to suppose he himself was the hero of the story; for in that case the slip could be explained by his wish that he had obtained the divorce rather than his wife, so that he should not have (by our matrimonial laws) to pay alimony, and so that he could marry again in New York State. He stoutly denied my conjecture, but the exaggerated emotional reaction which accompanied it, in which he showed marked signs of agitation followed by laughter, only strengthened my suspicions. To my appeal that he should tell the truth in the interests of science, he answered: "Unless you wish me to lie you must believe that I was never married, and hence your psycho-analytic interpretation is wrong." He added that someone who paid attention to every triviality was positively dangerous. Then he suddenly remembered that he had another appointment and left us.

Both Dr. Frink and I were still convinced that my interpretation of his slip of the tongue was correct, and I decided to corroborate or disprove it by further investigation. Some days later I visited a neighbour, an old friend of Dr. R., who was able to confirm my explanation in every particular. The divorce proceedings had taken place some weeks before, and the nurse was cited as co-respondent.[6]

Freud said that *"the suppression of the speaker's intention to say something is the indispensable condition for the occurrence of a slip of the tongue* [italics in original]."[7] The suppression could be deliberate if the speaker was lying, but Freud was more interested in instances in which the speaker is not aware of the suppression. Once the slip occurs, the speaker may recognize what has been suppressed; or, even then, the speaker may not become aware of it.

The lie catcher must be cautious, not assuming that any slip of the tongue is evidence of lying. Usually the context in which a slip occurs should help in figuring out whether or not the slip is betraying a lie. The lie catcher must also avoid the error of considering someone truthful just because there are no slips of the tongue. Many lies do not contain any. Freud did not explain why some lies are betrayed by slips while most are not. It is tempting to think that slips occur when the liar wants to be caught, when there is guilt about lying. Certainly Dr. R. should have felt deception guilt about lying to his esteemed colleague. But there has been no study—or even much speculating— that would explain why only certain lies are betrayed by slips.

Tirades are a third way liars may betray themselves in words. A tirade is different from a slip of the tongue. The speech blunder is more than a word or two. The information doesn't slip out, it pours out. The liar is carried away by emotion, not realizing until afterward the consequences of what he is revealing. Often, if the liar had remained cool, he would not have revealed the damaging information. It is the pressure of overwhelming emotion—fury, horror, terror, or distress—that causes the liar to give away information.

Tom Brokaw, when he was the interviewer on NBC-TV's "Today Show," described a fourth source of deception clues. "Most of the clues I get from people are verbal, not physical. I don't look at a person's face for signs that he is lying. What I'm after are convoluted answers or sophisticated evasions."[8] A few studies of deceit support Brokaw's hunch, finding that some people when they lied were indirect in their reply, circumlocutious, and gave more information than was requested. Other research studies have shown just the opposite: most people are too smart to be evasive and indirect in their replies.* Tom Brokaw might miss those liars. A worse hazard would be to misjudge a truthful person who happens to be convoluted or evasive in his speech. A few people always speak this way. For them it is not a sign of lying; it is just the way they talk. Any behavior that is a useful clue to deceit will for some few people be a usual part of their behavior. The possibility of misjudging such people I will call the *Brokaw hazard.* Lie catchers are vulnerable to the *Brokaw hazard* when they are unacquainted with the suspect, not familiar with idiosyncrasies in the suspect's typical behavior. I will discuss ways to avoid the Brokaw hazard in chapter 6.

No other sources of leakage and deception clues in words have been uncovered as yet by research. I suspect that not many more will be found. It is too easy, as I de-

---

*It is hard to know what to make of this and other contradictions in the research literature on deceit, since the experiments are not themselves too trustworthy. Almost all have examined students, who lied about trivial matters, with little at stake. Most of the experiments on lying have shown little thought about just what type of lie they might be examining. Usually the lie studied is one selected because it is easy to arrange in a laboratory. For example, students have been asked to argue convincingly an opinion about capital punishment or abortion contrary to their own. Or, students were asked to say whether they would like or dislike a person shown to them in a photograph and then were asked to pretend that they have the opposite attitude. Typically these experiments fail to consider the liar's relationship to the target, and how this might influence how hard the liar tries to succeed. Usually the liar and target were not acquainted and had no reason to think they would ever meet each other again. Sometimes there was no actual target, but instead the liar spoke in a misleading fashion to a machine. For a recent, but not sufficiently critical, review of these experiments, see Miron Zuckerman, Bella M. DePaulo, and Robert Rosenthal, "Verbal and Nonverbal Communication of Deception," in *Advances in Experimental Social Psychology*, vol. 14 (New York: Academic Press, 1981).

scribed earlier, for a deceiver to conceal and falsify words, although errors do occur—careless errors, slips, tirades, and circumlocutious or indirect speech.

The Voice

The voice refers to everything involved in speech other than the words themselves. The most common vocal deception clues are pauses. The pauses may be too long or too frequent. Hesitating at the start of a speaking turn, particularly if the hesitation occurs when someone is responding to a question, may arouse suspicion. So may shorter pauses during the course of speaking if they occur often enough. Speech errors may also be a deception clue. These include nonwords, such as "ah," "aaa," and "uhh"; repetitions, such as "I, I, I mean I really . . . "; and partial words, such as "I rea-really liked it."

These vocal clues to deceit—speech errors and pauses—can occur for two related reasons. The liar may not have worked out her line ahead of time. If she did not expect to lie, or if she was prepared to lie but didn't anticipate a particular question, she may hesitate or make speech errors. But these can also occur when the line is well prepared. High detection apprehension may cause the prepared liar to stumble or forget her line. Detection apprehension may also compound the errors made by the poorly prepared liar. Hearing how badly she sounds may make a liar more afraid of being caught, which only increases her pauses and speech errors.

Deceit may be revealed also by the sound of the voice. While most of us believe that the sound of the voice tells us what emotion a person feels, scientists studying the voice are still not certain. They have discovered a number of ways to distinguish unpleasant from pleasant voices but don't yet know whether the sound of the voice differs for each of the unpleasant emotions: anger, fear, distress, disgust, or contempt. I believe such differences will, with time, be found. For now, I will describe what is known, and what looks promising.

The best-documented vocal sign of emotion is pitch. For about 70 percent of the people who have been studied, pitch becomes higher when the subject is upset. Probably this is most true when the upset is a feeling of anger or fear. There is some evidence that pitch drops with sadness or sorrow, but that is not as certain. Scientists have not yet learned whether pitch changes with excitement, distress, disgust, or contempt. Other signs of emotion, not as well established, but promising, are louder, faster speech with anger or fear and softer, slower speech with sadness. Breakthroughs are likely to occur measuring other aspects of voice quality, the timber, the energy spectrum in different frequency bands, and changes related to respiration.[9]

Changes in the voice produced by emotion are not easy to conceal. If the lie is principally about emotions felt at the very moment of the lie, then there is a good chance for leakage. If the aim of the lie was to conceal fear or anger, the voice should sound higher and louder, and the rate of talk may be faster. Just the opposite pattern of voice changes could leak feelings of sadness a deceiver is trying to conceal.

The sound of the voice can also betray lies that were not undertaken to conceal emotion if emotion has become involved. Detection apprehension will produce the voice sounds of fear. Deception guilt might be shown to produce the same changes in the sound of the voice as sadness, but that is only a guess. It is not clear whether duping delight can be isolated and measured in the voice. I believe that excitement of any kind has a particular vocal signature, but that is yet to be established.

Our experiment with the student nurses was one of the

first to document a change in pitch with deceit.[10] We found that pitch went up during deceit. We believe this occurred because the nurses felt afraid. There were two reasons why they felt this emotion. We had done everything possible to make the stakes very high so they would feel strong detection apprehension. And, watching the gory medical scenes generated empathic fear in some of the nurses. We might not have found this result if either source of fear was lessened. Suppose we had studied people whose career choice was not involved, for whom it was only an experiment. With little at stake, there might not have been enough fear to cause any change in pitch. Or, suppose we had shown the nursing students a film of a child dying, which would be more likely to arouse sadness than fear. While their fear of being caught would have acted to raise their pitch, this reaction could have been canceled out by sad feelings lowering their pitch.

Raised pitch is not a sign of deceit. It is a sign of fear or anger, perhaps also of excitement. In our experiment, a sign of those emotions betrayed the student's claim that she was feeling happily contented in response to a film showing flowers. There is a danger in interpreting any of the vocal signs of emotion as evidence of deceit. A truthful person who is worried she won't be believed may out of that fear show the same raised pitch a liar may manifest because she is afraid of being caught. The problem for the lie catcher is that innocents also are sometimes emotionally aroused, not just liars. In discussing how this problem confuses the lie catcher's interpretation of other potential clues to deceit, I will refer to it as the *Othello error*. In chapter 6 I will discuss this error in detail, explaining how the lie catcher can guard against making it. It is, unfortunately, not easy to avoid. The voice changes that may betray deceit are also vulnerable to the Brokaw hazard (individual differences in emotional behavior), mentioned earlier in regard to pauses and speech errors.

Just as a vocal sign of an emotion, such as pitch, does not always mark a lie, so the absence of any vocal sign of emotion does not necessarily prove truthfulness. The credibility of John Dean's testimony during the nationally televised Senate Watergate hearings hinged in part on how the absence of emotion in his voice—his remarkably flat tone of voice—was interpreted. It was twelve months after the break-in at the Watergate Democratic National Committee headquarters when John Dean, counsel to President Nixon, testified. Nixon had finally admitted, a month earlier, that his aides had tried to cover up the Watergate burglary, but Nixon denied that he had known about it.

In the words of federal judge John Sirica: "The small fry in the cover-up had been pretty well trapped, mostly by each other's testimony. What remained to be determined was the real guilt or innocence of the men at the top. And it was Dean's testimony that was to be at the heart of that question. . . . Dean alleged [in his Senate testimony] that he told Nixon again that it would take a million dollars to silence the [Watergate burglary] defendants, and Nixon responded that the money could be obtained. No shock, no outrage, no refusals. This was Dean's most sensational charge. He was saying Nixon himself had approved the pay-offs to the defendants."[11]

The next day the White House disputed Dean's claims. In his memoirs, published five years later, Nixon said, "I saw John Dean's testimony on Watergate as an artful blend of truth and untruth, of possible sincere misunderstandings and clearly conscious distortions. In an effort to mitigate his own role, he transplanted his own total knowledge of the cover-up and his own anxiety onto the words and actions of others."[12] At the time the attack on Dean was much rougher. Stories, reputedly from the White House, were leaked to the press, claiming that Dean was lying, attacking the president because he was afraid of being homosexually attacked if he went to jail.

It was Dean's word against Nixon's, and few knew for certain which one was telling the truth. Judge Sirica, describing his doubts, said: "I must say I was skeptical of Dean's allegations. He was obviously a key figure himself in the cover-up. . . . He had a lot to lose. . . . It seemed to me at the time that Dean might well be more interested in protecting himself by involving the President than in telling the truth."[13]

Sirica goes on to describe how Dean's voice impressed him: "For days after he read his statement, the committee members peppered him with hostile questions. But he stuck to his story. He didn't appear upset in any way. His flat, unemotional tone of voice made him believable."[14] To other people, someone who speaks in a flat tone of voice may seem to be controlling himself, which may suggest he has something to hide. Not misinterpreting Dean's flat voice would require knowing whether or not this tone of voice is characteristic of him.

The failure to show a sign of emotion in the voice is not necessarily evidence of truthfulness; some people never show emotion, at least not in their voice. And even people who are emotional may not be about a particular lie. Judge Sirica was vulnerable to the Brokaw hazard. Recall that newscaster Tom Brokaw said he interprets circumlocutiousness as a sign of lying, and that I explained how he could be mistaken because some individuals are always circumlocutious. Now Judge Sirica could be making the opposite mistake—judging someone to be truthful because he fails to show a clue to deceit, not recognizing that some people never do.

Both mistakes arise from the fact that individuals differ in their emotional expressiveness. The lie catcher is vulnerable to errors unless he knows what the suspect's usual emotional behavior is like. There would not be a Brokaw hazard if there were *no* reliable behavioral clues to deceit.

Then lie catchers would have nothing to go on. And, there would not be a Brokaw hazard if behavioral clues were perfectly reliable for *all*, rather than for *most*, people. *No clue to deceit is reliable for all human beings*, but singly and in combination they can help the lie catcher in judging most people. John Dean's spouse, friends, and co-workers would know whether he is like most people in showing emotion in his voice, or is unusually able to control his voice. Judge Sirica, having no prior acquaintance with Dean, was vulnerable to the Brokaw hazard.

Dean's flat-voiced testimony provides another lesson. A lie catcher must always consider the possibility that a suspect might be an unusually gifted performer, so able to disguise his behavior that it is not possible to know whether or not he is lying. According to his own account, John Dean was such a gifted performer. He seemed to know in advance just how Judge Sirica and others would interpret his behavior. He reports the following thoughts as he planned how he would act when he testified: "It would be easy to overdramatize, or to seem too flip about my testimony. . . . I would, I decided, read evenly, unemotionally, as coldly as possibly, and answer questions the same way. . . . People tend to think that somebody telling the truth will be calm about it."[15] After he finished his testimony and cross examination began, Dean said he became quite emotional. "I knew I was choking up, feeling alone and impotent in the face of the President's power. I took a deep breath to make it look as if I were thinking; I was fighting for control. . . . You *cannot* show emotion I told myself. The press will jump all over it as a sign of unmanly weakness".[16] The fact that Dean's performance was contrived, that he was so talented in controlling his behavior, does not necessarily mean that he was a liar, only that others should have been wary of interpreting his behavior. In fact, the subsequent evidence suggests that Dean's testimony was largely true, and that Nixon, who, unlike Dean, is not a very talented performer, was lying.

The last topic to consider before leaving the voice is the claim that there are machines that can automatically and accurately detect lies from the voice. These include the Psychological Stress Evaluator (PSE), the Mark II Voice Analyzer, the Voice Stress Analyzer, the Psychological Stress Analyzer (PSA), the Hagoth, and the Voice Stress Monitor. The manufacturers of these devices claim that they can detect a lie from the voice, even over the telephone. Of course, as their names suggest, they are detecting stress, not lying. There is no voice sign of lying per se, only of negative emotions. The manufacturers of these rather expensive gadgets have not been too forthright in cautioning the user about missing liars who feel no negative emotions and misjudging innocent people who are upset. Scientists specializing in the study of voice and those who specialize in the use of other techniques for detecting lies have found that these machines do no better than chance in detecting lies, and not even very well at the easier task of telling whether or not someone is upset.[17] That does not seem to have affected sales. The possibility of a sure-fire, unobtrusive way to detect lies is too intriguing.

The Body

I learned one way body movements leak concealed feelings in an experiment done during my student days more than twenty-five years ago. There was not much scientific evidence then as to whether body movements accurately reflect emotions or personality. A few psychotherapists thought so, but their claims were dismissed as unsubstantiated anecdotes by the behaviorists, who dominated academic psychology at the time. Many studies from 1914 to 1954 had failed to find support for the claim that nonverbal behavior provides accurate information about emotion and personality. Academic psychology took some pride in how scientific experiments had exposed as a myth the layman's belief that he could read emotion or personality from the face or body. Those few social scientists or therapists who continued to write about body movement were regarded, like those who were interested in ESP and graphology, as naïve, tender-minded, or charlatans.

I could not believe this was so. Watching body movement during group therapy sessions, I was convinced I could tell who was upset about what. With all the optimism of a first-year graduate student I set out to make academic psychology change its view of nonverbal behavior. I devised an experiment to prove that body movements change when someone is under stress. The source of the stress was my senior professor, who agreed to follow a plan I devised in questioning my fellow students about matters on which I knew we all felt vulnerable. While the hidden camera recorded their behavior, the professor asked these budding psychologists what they planned to do when they finished their training. Those who mentioned research were attacked for hiding in the laboratory and shirking their responsibility to help people suffering from mental illness. Those who planned to give such help by practicing psychotherapy were criticized for wanting only to make money and shirking their responsibility to do the research needed to find a cure for mental illness. He also asked if the student had ever been a patient in psychotherapy. Those who said yes were asked how they hoped to help others if they were sick themselves. If they had not obtained psychotherapy he attacked them for trying to help others without first knowing themselves. It was a no-win situation. To make matters worse, I had instructed the professor to interrupt, never letting the student complete a reply to one of his barbs.

The students had volunteered for this miserable experience to help me, their fellow student. They knew it was a research interview, and that stress would be involved, but that did not make it any easier for them once it began. Outside of the experiment this professor, who was now acting so unreasonably, had enormous power over them. His evaluations were crucial for their graduation, and the enthusiasm of his recommendations determined what job they might get. Within a few minutes the students floundered. Unable to leave or to defend themselves, seething with frustrated anger, they were reduced to silence or inarticulate groans. Before five minutes went by I instructed the professor to end their misery by explaining what he had been doing and why, praising the student for taking the stress so well.

I watched through a one-way mirror and operated a camera to record permanently the body movements. I could not believe what I saw in the very first interview. After the third attack, the student was giving the professor the finger! She kept her hand in that position about one full minute. And yet she didn't look mad, and the professor was acting as if he didn't see it. I rushed in when the interview was over. Both of them claimed I had made it up. She admitted she had been angry but denied expressing it. The professor agreed that I must have imagined it because, he said, he would not miss an obscene gesture. When the film was developed my proof was there. This gestural slip, the finger, was not expressing an unconscious feeling. She knew she was mad, but the expression of those feelings was not conscious. She did not know she was giving him the finger. The feelings she was deliberately trying to conceal had leaked.

Fifteen years later I saw the same type of nonverbal leakage, another gestural slip, in the experiment in which nursing students tried to conceal their reactions to the gory medical films. It was not the finger gesture that slipped this time, but a shrug. Nursing student after nursing student gave away her lie by a slight shrug when the interviewer

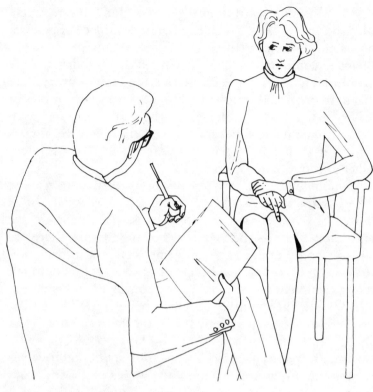

Figure 1

asked "Do you want to see more?" or "Would you show this film to a young child?"

The shrug and the finger are two examples of actions that are called *emblems*, to distinguish them from all of the other gestures that people show. Emblems have a very precise meaning, known to everyone within a cultural group. Everyone knows that the finger means "fuck you" or "up yours" and that the shrug means "I don't know," "I'm helpless," or "What does it matter?" Most other gestures don't have such a precise definition, and their meaning is vague. Without words most gestures don't mean much. Not so for emblems—they can be used in place of a word, or when words can't be used. There are about sixty emblems in common usage in the United States today. (There are different emblem vocabularies for each country and, often, for regional groups within a country.) Examples of other well-known emblems are the head-nod yes, headshake no, come-here beckon, wave hello/goodbye, finger-on-finger shame on you, hand-to-ear louder request, hitchhiker's thumb, and so on.[18]

Emblems are almost always performed deliberately. The person who makes an emblem knows what she is doing. She has chosen to state a message. But there are exceptions. Just as there are slips of the tongue, there are slips in body movement—emblems that leak information the person is trying to conceal. There are two ways to tell that an emblem is a slip, revealing concealed information, and not a deliberate message. One is when only a fragment of the emblem is performed, not the entire action. The shrug can be performed by raising both shoulders, or by turning the palms up, or by a facial movement that involves raising the brows and drooping the upper eyelid and making a horseshoe-shaped mouth, or by combining all of these actions and, sometimes, throwing in a sideways head tilt. When an emblem is leakage, only one element will be shown, and even it won't be complete. Only one shoulder may be raised, and not very high; or only the lower lip may be pushed up; or the palms may be turned up only slightly. The finger emblem not only involves a particular arrangement of the five fingers, but the hand is thrust forward and upward, often repeatedly. When the finger emblem was not performed deliberately but leaked a student's stifled fury, the movement component was not there, only the arrangement of the fingers.

The second tip-off that the emblem is a slip rather than a deliberate action is that it is performed out of the usual presentation position. Most emblems are performed right out in front of the person, between the waist and the neck area. An emblem can't be missed when it is in the presentation position. A leakage emblem is never performed in the presentation position. In the stress interview when the student gave the professor the finger, it was not shoved out in space but instead was lying on the student's knee, out of the presentation position. In the experiment with the nursing students, the shrugs that leaked their feelings of helplessness and inability to conceal their feelings were small rotations of the hands, while the hands stayed in the lap. If the emblem was not fragmented and out of the presentation position, the liar would realize what was happening and would censor the emblem. Of course, these characteristics that distinguish the leakage emblem—fragmentation and out-of-presentation position—also make it hard for others to notice. A liar can show these leakage emblems again and again, and usually neither the liar nor her victim will notice them.

There is no guarantee that every liar will make an emblematic slip. There are no such sure-fire signs of deceit. There has been too little research to yet estimate how often emblematic slips will occur when people lie. Subjected to the hostile professor, two of the five students showed an emblematic slip. A little more than half of the nursing students showed an emblematic slip when they were lying. I don't know why some people had this form of leakage while others did not.*

While not every liar shows an emblematic slip, when emblematic slips occur they are quite reliable. The emblematic slip can be trusted as a genuine sign of a message that the person does not want to reveal. Their interpreta-

---

*Unfortunately, none of the other investigators who have studied deceit have checked to see if they could replicate our finding on emblematic slips. I feel optimistic that they would, having twice over a twenty-five-year period found leakage through emblematic slips.

tion is less vulnerable than most other signs of deceit to either the Brokaw hazard or the Othello error. Some people always talk in a circumlocutious fashion, but few people make emblematic slips regularly. Speech errors may signify stress of many kinds, not necessarily just the stresses involved in lying. Because the emblem has a very specific message, much like words, emblematic slips are usually not so ambiguous. If the person slips the message "fuck you" or "I'm mad" or "I don't mean it" or "over there"—all of which can be shown by an emblem—there shouldn't be much of a problem in interpreting what is meant.

What emblem will slip during a lie, which message will leak out, will depend upon what is being concealed. The students in my hostile professor experiment were concealing anger and outrage, so the emblematic slips were the finger and a fist. In the medical training film experiment the nursing students were not feeling angry, but many felt they were not adequately concealing their feelings. The helpless shrug was the emblematic slip. No adult needs to be taught the vocabulary of emblems. Everyone knows the emblems shown by members of their own culture. What many people do need to learn is that emblems may occur as slips. Unless lie catchers are alert to this possibility, they won't spot the emblematic slips that will escape their notice, because they are fragmented and out of the presentation position.

Illustrators are another type of body movement that can provide deception clues. Illustrators are often confused with emblems, but it is important to distinguish between them, for these two kinds of body movements may change in opposite ways when people lie. While emblematic slips may increase, illustrators usually will decrease.

Illustrators are called by that name because they illustrate speech as it is spoken. There are many ways to do so:

emphasis can be given to a word or phrase, much like an accent mark or underlining; the flow of thought can be traced in the air, as if the speaker is conducting her speech; the hands can draw a picture in space or show an action repeating or amplifying what is being said. It is the hands that usually illustrate speech, although brow and upper eyelid movements often provide emphasis illustrators, and the entire body or upper trunk can do so also.

Social attitudes toward the propriety of illustrators have gone back and forth over the last few centuries. There have been times when illustrating was the mark of the upper classes, and also times when they have been considered the mark of the uncouth. Books on oratory have usually depicted the illustrators required for successful public speaking.

The pioneering scientific study of illustrators was not undertaken to uncover clues to deceit but to challenge the claims of the Nazi social scientists. The results of that study can help the lie catcher avoid mistakes due to a failure to recognize national differences in illustrators. During the 1930s, many articles appeared that claimed illustrators were inborn and that the "inferior races," such as the Jews or gypsies, made many large, sweeping illustrators compared to the "superior," less gesturally expansive Aryans. No mention was made of the grand illustrators shown by Germany's Italian ally! David Efron,[19] an Argentinian Jew studying at Columbia University with the anthropologist Franz Boas, examined the illustrators of people living on the Lower East Side of New York City. He found that immigrants from Sicily used illustrators that draw a picture or show an action, while Jewish Lithuanian immigrants used illustrators that give emphasis or trace the flow of thought. Their offspring born in the United States who attended integrated schools did not differ from one another in the use of illustrators. Those of Sicilian parentage used illustrators similar to those used by children of Jewish Lithuanian parents.

The style of illustrators is acquired, Efron showed, not inborn. People from different cultures not only use different types of illustrators, but some illustrate very little while others illustrate a lot. Even within a culture, individuals differ in how many illustrators they typically show.* It is not the sheer number of illustrators or their type, then, that can betray a lie. The clue to deceit comes from noting a decrease in the number of illustrators shown, when a person illustrates less than usual. More needs to be explained about when people *do* illustrate, to avoid misinterpreting why someone shows a decrease.

First consider why people illustrate at all. Illustrators are used to help explain ideas that are difficult to put into words. We found that people were more likely to illustrate when asked to define zigzag than chair, more likely to illustrate when explaining how to get to the post office than when explaining their occupational choice. Illustrators also are used when a person can't find a word. Snapping the fingers or reaching in the air seems to help the person find the word, as if the word floats above the person captured by the illustrator movement. Such word-search illustrators at least let the other person know that a search is under way and that the first person hasn't given up his turn to speak. Illustrators may have a self-priming function, helping people put words together into reasonably coherent speech. Illustrators increase with involvement with what is being said. People tend to illustrate more than usual when they are furious, horrified, very agitated, distressed, or excitedly enthused.

---

*Immigrant families from cultures that make frequent use of illustrators often train their children not to speak with their hands. Their children are cautioned that if they illustrate they will look like they are from the old country. Not illustrating will make them resemble the northern European, older American stock.

Now consider why people show less than their usual level of illustrating, for this will make clear when such decreases can be a clue to deceit. The first reason is a lack of emotional investment in what is being said. People illustrate less than usual when they are uninvolved, bored, disinterested, or deeply saddened. People who feign concern or enthusiasm can be betrayed by the failure to accompany their speech with increased illustrators.

Illustrators also decrease when a person is having trouble deciding exactly what to say. If someone weighs each word carefully, considering what is said before it is said, there is not much illustrating. When giving a talk for the first or second time, whether it be a lecture or sales pitch, there will not be as many illustrators as there later will be when not much effort has to be spent finding words. Illustrators decrease whenever there is caution about speech. It may have nothing to do with deceit. There may be caution because the stakes are high: the first impression made on a boss, the answer to a question that could bring a prize, the first words to a person passionately admired previously from a distance. Ambivalence also makes for caution about what to say. A timorous person may be terribly tempted by a much more lucrative job offer but be afraid to take the risks involved in a new work situation. Torn by whether he should or shouldn't, he is afflicted with the ponderous problem of what to say and how to say it.

If a liar has not adequately worked out her line in advance she also will have to be cautious, carefully considering each word before it is spoken. Deceivers who are not rehearsed, who have had little practice in the particular lie, who failed to anticipate what would be asked or when, will show a decrease in illustrators. Even if the liar has worked out and practiced her line, her illustrators may decrease because of the interference of her emotions. Some emotions, especially fear, can interfere with speaking coherently. The burden of managing almost any strong emotion distracts from the processes involved in stringing words together. If the emotion has to be concealed, not just managed, and if it is a strong emotion, then it is likely that even the liar with a well-prepared line may have trouble speaking it, and illustrators will decrease.

The student nurses in our experiment illustrated less when they were trying to conceal their reactions to the amputation-burn film than when they honestly described their feelings about the flower film. This decrease in illustrators occurred for at least two reasons: the students were not practiced in making the required lie and had been given no time to prepare their line, and strong emotions were aroused, both detection apprehension and emotions in response to the gory film they were watching. Many other investigators have also found illustrators less apparent when someone is lying as compared to when someone is telling the truth. In these studies little emotion was involved, but the liars were ill prepared.

In introducing illustrators I said that it is important to distinguish them from emblems, for opposite changes may occur in each when someone lies: emblematic slips increase and illustrators decrease. The crucial differences between emblems and illustrators are in the precision of movement and message. For the emblem both are highly prescribed: not any movement will do; only a highly defined movement conveys the quite precise message. Illustrators, by contrast, can involve a wide variety of movements and may convey a vague rather than a precise message. Consider the thumb-to-first-finger A-OK emblem. There is only one way to do it. If the thumb goes to the middle finger or pinky it would not be very clear. And, the meaning is very specific—"OK," "that's good," "all right."* Illustrators don't have much meaning independent of the words. Watching someone il-

---

*This emblem has a quite different, obscene meaning in some southern European countries. Emblems are not universal. Their meaning varies with culture.

lustrate without hearing the words doesn't reveal much about the conversation; that is not so if the person makes an emblem. Another difference between emblems and illustrators is that although both are shown when people converse, emblems can be used in place of a word or when people cannot or do not speak. Illustrator movements, by definition, occur only during speech, not to replace it or when people don't talk.

The lie catcher must be more cautious in interpreting illustrators than emblematic slips. As described earlier, both the Othello error and the Brokaw hazard influence illustrators but not emblematic slips. If the lie catcher notes a decrease in illustrating, he must rule out all the other reasons (apart from lying) for someone wanting to carefully choose each word. There is less ambiguity about the emblematic slip; the message conveyed is usually sufficiently distinct to make it easier for the lie catcher to interpret. And, the lie catcher does not need previous acquaintance with the suspect to interpret an emblematic slip. Such an action, in and of itself, has meaning. Since individuals differ enormously in their usual rate of illustrating, no judgment can be made about them unless the lie catcher has some basis for comparison. Interpreting illustrators, like most of the other clues to deceit, requires previous acquaintance. Spotting deceit is very difficult in first meetings. Emblematic slips offer one of the few possibilities.

The reason for explaining the next type of body movement, *manipulators,* is to warn the lie catcher about the risk of interpreting them as signs of deceit. We have found that lie catchers often mistakenly judge a truthful person to be lying because they show many manipulators. While manipulators can be a sign that someone is upset, they are not always so. An increase in manipulator activity is not a reliable sign of deceit, but people think it is.

Manipulators include all those movements in which one part of the body grooms, massages, rubs, holds, pinches, picks, scratches, or otherwise manipulates another body part. Manipulators may be of very short duration or they may go on for many minutes. Some of the brief ones appear to have a purpose: the hair is rearranged, matter is removed from the ear canal, a part of the body is scratched. Other manipulators, particularly those that last a long time, seem to be purposeless: hair is twisted and untwisted, fingers rubbed, a foot tapped. Typically the hand is the manipulator. The hand may also be the recipient, as can any other part of the body. Common recipients are the hair, ears, nose, or crotch. Manipulator actions also can be performed within the face—tongue against cheeks, or teeth slightly biting lips—and by leg against leg. Props may become part of a manipulator act—match, pencil, paper clip, or cigarette.

While most people were brought up not to perform these bathroom behaviors in public, they haven't learned to stop doing them, only to stop noticing that they do them. It is not that people are completely unconscious of their manipulators. If we realize someone is looking at one of our manipulator acts, we will quickly interrupt, diminish, or disguise it. A larger gesture often will deftly cover a fleeting one. Even this elaborate strategy to conceal a manipulator is not done with much awareness. Manipulators are on the edge of consciousness. Most people cannot stop doing them for very long even when they try deliberately to do so. People are accustomed to manipulating themselves.

People are much more proper as observers than as performers. The person making a manipulator movement is given the privacy to complete this act, even when the manipulator begins right in the midst of a conversation. Others look away when a manipulator is performed, looking back only when it is over. If the manipulator is one of those seemingly pointless activities, like hair twisting, which goes on and on, then of course others don't look away forever, but people won't look for long directly at the manipulator act. Such polite inattention to manipulators is an overlearned habit, operating without thought. It is the manipulator watcher rather than the performer who, like a Peeping Tom, creates the offense to manners. When two cars pull up at a stop sign, it is the person who glances over at the person in the adjacent car who commits the offense, not the person who is vigorously cleaning his ear.

I and others studying manipulators have wondered why people engage in one manipulator rather than another. Does it mean anything if it is a rub rather than a squeeze, a pick rather than a scratch? And, is there some message that can be read from whether it is the hand, ear, or nose that is scratched? Part of the answer is idiosyncrasy. People have their favorites, a particular type of manipulator that is their hallmark. For one person it may be twisting a ring, for another picking cuticles, and for another twisting a mustache. No one has tried to discover why people have one versus another favorite manipulator, or why some people have no special idiosyncratic manipulator. There is a bit of evidence to suggest that certain manipulator actions reveal more than just discomfort. We found picking manipulators in psychiatric patients who were not expressing anger. Covering the eyes was common among patients who felt shame. But this evidence is tentative, compared to the more general finding that manipulators increase with discomfort.[20]

Scientists have reasonably well substantiated the layman's belief that people fidget, make restless movements, when they are ill at ease or nervous. Body scratching, squeezing, picking, and orifice cleaning and grooming manipulators increase with any type of discomfort. I believe that people also show many manipulators when they are quite relaxed and at ease, letting their hair down. When with their chums, people don't worry as much about being proper. Some people will be more likely than others to burp, manipulate, and indulge in behaviors that in most situations are at least partially managed. If this is correct, then manipulators are discomfort signs only in more formal situations, with people who are not so familiar.

Manipulators are unreliable as signs of deceit because they may indicate opposite states—discomfort and relaxation. Also, liars know they should try to squelch their manipulators, and most will succeed part of the time. Liars do not have any special knowledge of this; it is part of the general folklore that manipulators are discomfort signs, nervous behavior. Everyone thinks that liars will fidget, that restlessness is a deception clue. When we asked people how they would tell if someone were lying, squirming and shifty eyes were the winners. *Clues that everyone knows about, that involve behavior that can be readily inhibited, won't be very reliable if the stakes are high and the liar does not want to be caught.*

The student nurses did not show more manipulator actions when lying than when telling the truth. Other studies have found an increase in manipulators during deceits. I believe it is differences in the stakes that account for this contradiction in findings. When the stakes are high the manipulator actions may be intermittent, for contrary forces may be at work. High stakes make the liar monitor and control accessible and known clues to deceit, such as manipulators, but those high stakes may make the liar afraid of being caught, and that discomfort should increase this behavior. Manipulators may increase, be monitored, squelched, disappear for a time, reappear, and then after a time again be noticed and suppressed. Since the stakes were high, the nursing students worked hard to control their manipulator actions. There was not much at stake in studies that found manipulators increased during lying. The situation was a bit strange—being asked to lie in an experiment is unusual—and so there could have been enough discomfort to increase manipulator actions. But there were no important gains or losses for success or failure in these deceits, little reason for the liar to expend the effort to monitor and suppress manipulator actions. Even if my explanation of why contradictory results were obtained is incorrect (and such after-the-fact interpretations must be viewed as tentative until confirmed by further studies), the contradictory findings themselves are sufficient reason for the lie catcher to be cautious about interpreting manipulators.

In our study of how well people can catch lies, we found that people judged those who showed many manipulators as liars. It didn't matter whether the person showing the manipulator was actually telling the truth or lying; those who saw them labeled them as dishonest if they showed many. It is important to recognize the likelihood of making this error. Let me review the multiple reasons why manipulators are an unreliable sign of deceit.

People vary enormously in how many manipulators and what kinds of manipulators they usually show. This individual difference problem (the Brokaw hazard) can be countered if the lie catcher has some previous acquaintance and can make behavioral comparisons.

The Othello error also interferes with the interpretation of manipulators as deception clues, since manipulators increase when people are uncomfortable about anything. This is a problem with other signs of deceit also, but it is especially acute with manipulators, since they are not just discomfort signs but sometimes, with buddies, comfort signs.

Everyone believes that showing many manipulators betrays deceit, and so a motivated liar will try to squelch them. Unlike facial expression, which people also try to control, manipulators are fairly easy to inhibit. Liars will succeed in inhibiting manipulators at least part of the time if the stakes are high.

Another aspect of the body—posture—has been exam-

ined by a number of investigators, but little evidence of
leakage or deception clues has been found. People know
how they are supposed to sit and stand. The posture appropriate for a formal interview is not the posture assumed
when talking with a friend. Posture seems well under control and successfully managed when someone is deceiving.
I and others studying deceit have found no differences in
posture when people lie or tell the truth.* Of course, we
might not have measured that aspect of posture that does
change. A possibility is the tendency to move forward with
interest or anger and backward with fear or disgust. A
motivated liar should, however, be able to inhibit all but
the most subtle signs of postural clues to those emotions.

Autonomic Nervous System Clues

So far I have discussed bodily actions produced by the
skeletal muscles. The autonomic nervous system (ANS)
also produces some noticeable changes in the body with
emotional arousal: in the pattern of breathing; in the frequency of swallowing; and in the amount of sweating.
(ANS changes registered in the face, such as blushing,
blanching, and pupil dilation, are discussed in the next
chapter.) These changes occur involuntarily when emotion
is aroused, are very hard to inhibit, and for that reason can
be very reliable clues to deceit.

The polygraph lie detector measures these ANS
changes, but many of them will be visible without the use
of a special apparatus. If a liar feels afraid, angry, excited,
distressed, guilty, or ashamed there may well be rapid

---

*One study of deceit found that people believe that those who shift their posture
frequently are lying. In fact, though, posture proved to be unrelated to truthfulness. See Robert E. Kraut and Donald Poe, "Behavioral Roots of Person Perception: The Deception Judgments of Custom Inspectors and Laymen," *Journal of
Personality and Social Psychology* 39 (1980): 784–98.

breathing, heaving chest, frequent swallowing, or the smell or appearance of sweating. For decades psychologists have disagreed about whether or not each emotion has a distinctive set of these ANS changes. Most psychologists think there is not; they believe that one breathes more rapidly, sweats, and swallows when *any* emotion becomes aroused. ANS changes mark how strong an emotion is, not which emotion it is. This view contradicts most people's experience. People feel different bodily sensations when they are afraid, for example, as compared to when they are angry. That, many psychologists say, is because people interpret the same set of bodily sensations differently if they are afraid than if they are angry. It is not proof that the ANS activity itself actually differs for fear versus anger.[21]

My most recent research, begun when I had almost finished writing this book, challenges this view. If I am correct, and ANS changes are not the same for, but instead are specific to, each emotion, this could be quite important in detecting lies. It would mean that the lie catcher could discover, either with a polygraph and even to some extent just by watching and listening, not just whether a suspect is emotionally aroused but which emotion is felt—is the suspect afraid or angry, disgusted or sad? While such information is available from the face as well, as the next chapter explains, people are able to inhibit many of the facial signs. ANS activity is much harder to censor.

We have published only one study as of now (see page 117), and some eminent psychologists disagree with what we have found. My findings are considered controversial, not established, but our evidence is strong and in time I believe will be accepted by the scientific community.

Two problems had stood in the way, I thought, of discovering convincing evidence that emotions have different ANS activity, and I thought I had solutions to both. One problem is how to obtain pure samples of emotion. To contrast the ANS changes in fear with those in anger the scientist must be certain when his research subject experiences each emotion. Since the measurement of ANS changes requires elaborate equipment, the subject must provide the emotion samples in a laboratory. The problem is how to elicit emotions in a sterile, unnatural setting. How do you make people afraid and angry, and not both at the same time? That last question is very important—not making them afraid and angry at the same time in what I and others call an emotion *blend*. Unless the emotions are kept separate—unless the samples are pure—there would be no way to determine if the ANS activity differs for each emotion. Even if it did, if the anger samples always included some fear, and the fear sample some anger, the result would be that the ANS changes would appear to be the same. It is not easy to avoid blends, in the laboratory or in real life. Blends are more common than pure emotions.

The most popular technique for sampling emotions has been to ask the subject to remember or imagine something fearful. Let's suppose the subject imagines being attacked by a mugger. The scientist must be certain that in addition to fear the subject doesn't become a bit angry at the mugger, or angry at himself for having been made afraid or having been stupid enough to put himself in jeopardy. The same hazards of blends occurring rather than pure emotions happens with other techniques for arousing emotions. Suppose the scientist shows a fear-inducing movie, perhaps a scene from a horror movie like Alfred Hitchcock's *Psycho*, in which Tony Perkins suddenly attacks Janet Leigh with a knife while she is taking a shower. The subject might become angry at the scientist for making him afraid, angry at himself for getting afraid, angry at Tony Perkins for attacking Janet Leigh, disgusted by the blood, distressed by Janet Leigh's suffering, surprised by the action, and so on. It is not so easy to think of a way to obtain pure emotion samples. Most scientists who have studied the ANS simply assumed, I think incorrectly, that subjects did what they wanted when they wanted them to, producing with ease the desired pure emotion samples. They failed to take any steps to guarantee or verify that their emotion samples really were pure.

The second problem is produced by the need to sample emotions in a laboratory, and results from the impact of the research technology. Most research subjects are self-conscious about what is going to happen to them when they come in the door. Then it gets amplified. To measure ANS activity, wires have to be attached to different parts of the subject's body. Just to monitor respiration, heart rate, skin temperature, and sweating requires attaching many of these wires. Sitting there hooked up, having scientists scrutinize what is going on inside their body, and often having cameras record any visible changes, embarrasses most people. Embarrassment is an emotion, and if it produces ANS activity, those ANS changes would be smeared across every emotion sample the scientist is trying to obtain. He may think the subject is remembering a fearful event at one moment, and an angry memory at another point, but what actually may happen is embarrassment during both memories. No scientist took steps to reduce embarrassment, none checked to be certain that embarrassment did not spoil their pure emotion samples.

My colleagues and I eliminated embarrassment by selecting professional actors as our research subjects.[22] Actors are accustomed to being scrutinized, and they don't get upset when people watch their every move. Rather than being embarrassed, they liked the idea that we would attach wires to them and monitor the insides of their body. Studying actors also helped in solving the first problem—obtaining pure emotion samples. We could make use of the actors' years of training in the Stanislavski acting technique, which makes them skilled in remembering and re-experiencing emotions. Actors practice this technique so that they can use sense-memories in portraying a particular role. In our experiment we asked the actors, while they were hooked up, with video cameras trained on their faces, to remember and re-experience as strongly as they could a time when they had felt the most anger in their lives, and then a time when they had felt the most fear, sadness, surprise, happiness, and disgust. Other scientists have used this technique before, but we thought we had a better chance of success because we were using professionals, trained in the technique, who wouldn't be embarrassed. Furthermore, we didn't just take for granted that our subjects did what we asked; we verified that we had obtained pure samples, not blends. After each memory retrieval, we asked the actors to rate how strongly they had felt the requested emotion, and whether they had felt any other emotion. Any attempts in which they reported re-experiencing any other emotion nearly as strongly as the one requested was not kept in our sample.

Studying actors also made it easier for us to try a second technique for sampling pure emotions, one that had never before been used. We discovered this new technique for arousing emotions by accident, years earlier, when doing another study. To learn the mechanics of facial expressions —which muscles produce which expression—my colleagues and I systematically made thousands of facial expressions, filming and then analyzing how each combination of muscle movements change appearance. To our surprise, when we did the muscle actions that relate to emotions, we would suddenly feel changes in our bodies, changes due to ANS activity. We had no reason to expect that deliberately moving facial muscles could produce involuntary ANS changes, but it happened again and again. We still did not know whether or not the ANS activity

differed with each set of facial muscle movements. We told
the actors exactly which facial muscles to move. There
were six different instructions, one for each of six emotions. Not embarrassed by making facial expressions on
demand or by being watched when they did it, and skilled
in facial expression, they met most of our requests with
ease. Again, we didn't just trust them to produce pure
samples of emotion. We videotaped their facial performances and only used their attempts if measurements of the
videotapes showed they had produced each set of requested
facial actions.

Our experiment found strong evidence that ANS activity is *not* the same for all emotions. The changes in heart
rate, skin temperature, and sweating (which is all we had
measured) are not the same for every emotion. For example, when the actors made the muscle movements on their
face for anger and those for fear (and remember, they
weren't told to pose these emotions but instead just to make
specific muscle actions), their heart beat faster, but different things happened to their skin temperature. Their skin
became hot with anger and cold with fear. We have just
repeated our experiment with different subjects and obtained the same results.

If these results hold up when other scientists try to
repeat them in their laboratories, they could change what
the lie detector tries to learn from the polygraph. Instead
of just trying to know whether a suspect is feeling *any*
emotion, the polygraph operator could tell by measuring a
number of ANS activities *which* emotion. Even without a
polygraph machine, just by looking a lie catcher may be
able to notice changes in the pattern of breathing or in
sweating that could help to spot the occurrence of specific
emotions. Errors in catching lies—disbelieving-the-truthful and believing-the-liar-could be reduced if ANS activity,
which is very hard to inhibit, could reveal which emotion

a suspect feels. We don't yet know whether emotions can be distinguished just by the visible and audible signs of ANS activity, but now there is a reason to find out. How signs of specific emotions—whether they be from face, body, voice, words, or ANS—can help to determine whether someone is lying or truthful, and the hazards of making mistakes and precautions to avoid making them, is the topic of chapter 6.

Chapter 2 explained that there are two principal ways to lie—to conceal or to falsify. So far this chapter has considered how attempts to conceal feelings may be betrayed by the words, voice, or body. A liar may falsify when no emotion is felt but one is required, or to help cover a concealed feeling. For example, a fellow may falsify a look of sadness when he learns that his brother-in-law's business has failed. If he is totally unmoved, the false expression simply shows the proper countenance, but if he was secretly delighted by his brother-in-law's misfortune, the false look of sadness would also mask his true feelings. Can the words, voice, or body betray such false expressions, revealing that an emotional performance is not felt? No one knows. Defects in false performances of emotion have been investigated less thoroughly than leakage of concealed emotions. I can only give my observations, theories, and hunches.

While words are made for fabricating, it is not easy for anyone, truthful or not, to describe emotions in words. Only a poet conveys the nuances revealed by an expression. It may be no more difficult to claim in words a feeling not felt than one that is. Usually neither will be very eloquent, elaborate, or convincing. It is the voice, the body, the facial expression that give meaning to the verbal account of an emotion. I suspect that most people can put on the voice of anger, fear, distress, happiness, disgust, or surprise well enough to fool others. While it is very hard to conceal the changes in the sound of the voice that occur with these emotions, it is not so hard to falsify them. Most people probably are fooled by the voice.

Some of the changes produced by the autonomic nervous system are easy to falsify. While it is hard to conceal the signs of emotion in respiration or swallowing, it takes no special skill to falsify them, breathing more quickly or swallowing often. Sweating is a different matter, hard to conceal and hard to falsify. While a liar could use respiration and swallowing to falsely give the impression of negative emotions, I expect few do.

While a deceiver could increase manipulators in order to appear uncomfortable, most people probably won't remember to do so. The failure to include these actions, which could be easily performed, might by their absence betray an otherwise convincing claim to be feeling fear or distress.

Illustrators can be put on but probably not very successfully, to create the impression of involvement and enthusiasm for what is being said when none is felt. Newspaper accounts said that former presidents Nixon and Ford were both coached to increase their illustrators. Watching them on TV, I thought the coaching often made them look phony. It is hard to deliberately place an illustrator exactly where it should be in relation to the words; they tend to come in too early or late or stay on too long. It is much like trying to ski by thinking about each action as you do it; the coordination is rough and looks it.

I have described behavioral clues that may leak concealed information, indicate that the person has not prepared his line, or betray an emotion that does not fit the line being taken.

Slips of the tongue, emblematic slips, and tirades can

leak concealed information of any kind—emotions, past deeds, plans, intentions, fantasies, ideas, etc.

Indirect speech, pauses, speech errors, and a decrease in illustrators may indicate that the speaker is being very careful about what is said, not having prepared the line being taken. They are signs of any negative emotion. A decrease in illustrators also occurs with boredom.

Raised voice pitch and louder, faster speech occur with fear, anger, and perhaps excitement. The voice changes in the opposite way with sadness and perhaps with guilt.

Changes in breathing or sweating, increased swallowing, and a very dry mouth are signs of strong emotions, and it may be possible in the future to determine which emotion from the pattern of these changes.

FIVE

Facial Clues to Deceit

*T*HE FACE CAN be a valuable source for the lie catcher, because it can lie and tell the truth and often does both at the same time. The face often contains two messages—what the liar wants to show and what the liar wants to conceal. Some expressions serve the lie, providing untrue information. Yet others betray the lie because they look false, and feelings sometimes leak despite efforts to conceal them. False but convincing expressions may occur one moment and concealed expressions leak the very next moment. It is even possible for the felt and the false to be shown in different parts of the face within a single blend expression. I believe that the reason most people fail to detect lies from the face is that they don't know how to sort out the felt from the false expressions.

The true, felt expressions of emotion occur because facial actions can be produced involuntarily, without thought or intention. The false ones happen because there is voluntary control over the face, allowing people to interfere with the felt and assume the false. The face is a dual system, including expressions that are deliberately chosen and those that occur spontaneously, sometimes without the person even aware of what emerges on his own face. There is a ground in between the voluntary and the involuntary occupied by expressions that were once learned but come to operate automatically without choice, or even despite choice, and typically without awareness. Facial mannerisms and ingrained habits that dictate the management of certain expressions, such as being unable to show anger toward authority figures, are examples. My concern here, however, is with the voluntary, deliberate, false expressions, recruited as part of an effort to mislead, and the involuntary, spontaneous, emotional expressions that may occasionally leak feelings despite a liar's attempt to conceal them.

Studies of patients with different kinds of brain damage dramatically show that the voluntary and the involuntary expressions involve different parts of the brain. Patients who have damage to one part of the brain, involving what is called the pyramidal neural systems, are unable to smile if asked to do so but will smile when they hear a joke or otherwise enjoy themselves. The pattern is reversed for patients who have suffered damage to another part of the brain, involving nonpyramidal systems. They can produce a voluntary smile but are blank-faced when enjoying themselves. Patients with pyramidal system damage—those who cannot make expressions deliberately—should not be able to lie facially, for they should not be able to inhibit or put on false expressions. Patients with nonpryamidal system damage—those who do not show expressions when they do feel emotion—should be very good facial liars since they won't have to inhibit any true, felt emotional expressions.[1]

The involuntary facial expressions of emotion are the product of evolution. Many human expressions are the same as those seen on the faces of other primates. Some of the facial expressions of emotion—at least those indicating happiness, fear, anger, disgust, sadness, and distress, and perhaps other emotions—are universal, the same for all people regardless of age, sex, race, or culture.[2] These facial expressions are the richest source of information about emotions, revealing subtle nuances in momentary feelings. The face can reveal the particulars of emotional experience that only the poet can capture in words. The face can show:

- which emotion is felt—anger, fear, sadness, disgust, distress, happiness, contentment, excitement, surprise, and contempt can all be conveyed by distinctive expressions;
- whether two emotions are blended together—often two emotions are felt and the face registers elements of each;
- the strength of the felt emotion—each emotion can vary in intensity, from annoyance to rage, apprehension to terror, etc.

But, as I said, the face is not just an involuntary emotional signal system. Within the first years of life children learn to control some of these facial expressions, concealing true feelings and falsifying expressions of emotions not felt. Parents teach their children to control their expressions by example and, more directly, with statements such as: "Don't you give me that angry look"; "Look happy now when your aunt gives you a present"; "Don't look so bored." As they grow up people learn *display rules* so well that they become deeply ingrained habits. After a time many display rules for the management of emotional expression come to operate automatically, modulating expression without choice or even awareness. Even when people become aware of their display rules, it is not always possible, and certainly never easy, to stop following them. Once any habit becomes established, operating automatically, not requiring awareness, it is hard to undo. I believe that those habits involving the management of emotion—display rules—may be the most difficult of all to break.

It is display rules, some of which differ from culture to culture, that are responsible for the traveler's impression that facial expressions are not universal. I found that when Japanese watched emotion-arousing films their expressions were no different than those shown by Americans, *if* the Japanese were *alone*. When another person was present while they watched the films, a person in authority, the Japanese much more than most Americans followed display rules that led them to mask any expression of negative emotions with a polite smile.[3]

In addition to these automatically operating habitual controls of facial expressions, people can and do choose deliberately, quite consciously, to censor the expression of their true feelings or falsify the expression of an emotion not felt. Most people succeed in some of their facial deceits. Nearly everyone can remember being totally misled by someone's expression. Yet, almost everyone has also had the opposite experience, realizing that someone's words were false by the look that passed across the face. What couple cannot remember an instance in which one of them saw on the other's face an emotion (usually anger or fear), that the other was unaware of showing, and even denied feeling? Most people believe they can detect false expressions; our research has shown most cannot.

In the last chapter I described our experiment in which we found that people were not able to tell when the student nurses were lying and when they were telling the truth. Those who saw just the nurses' facial expressions did worse than chance, rating the nurses as most honest when they were, in fact, lying. They were taken in by the false expressions and ignored the expressions that leaked the true feelings. When people lie, their most evident, easy-to-see expressions, which people pay most attention to, are often the false ones. The subtle signs that these expressions are not felt, and the fleeting hints of the concealed emotions, are usually missed.

Most researchers have not measured the liar's facial

expressions but instead have focused on easier-to-measure behaviors, such as body illustrators or speech errors. The few who have measured the face have examined only the smile, and they measured smiling too simply. They found that people smile just as often when they lie or tell the truth. These researchers did not identify the kind of smile. Not all smiles are the same. Our technique for measuring the face can distinguish more than fifty different smiles. When the nursing students lied we found that they smiled in a different way than when they told the truth. I will describe those findings at the end of this chapter.

It is just because there are so many different expressions to be distinguished that those interested in nonverbal communication and lying have avoided measurement of the face. Until recently there was no comprehensive, objective way to measure all facial expressions. We set out to develop such a method because we knew, after looking at our videotapes of the student nurses lying, that uncovering facial signs of deceit would require precise measurement. We spent nearly ten years developing a technique to measure facial expression precisely.[4]

There are thousands of facial expressions, each different one from another. Many of them have nothing to do with emotion. Many expressions are what we call *conversational signals*, which, like body-movement illustrators, emphasize speech or provide syntax (such as facial question marks or exclamation points). There are also a number of facial emblems: the one-eye closure wink, the raised eyebrows-droopy upper eyelid-horseshoe mouth shrug, the one-eyebrow-raised skepticism, to mention a few. There are facial manipulators, such as lip biting, lip sucking, lip wiping, and cheek puffing. And then there are the emotional expressions, the true ones and the false.

There is not one expression for each emotion but dozens and, for some emotions, hundreds of expressions.

Every emotion has a family of expressions, each visibly different one from another. This shouldn't be surprising. There isn't one feeling or experience for each emotion, but a family of experiences. Consider the members of the anger family of experiences. Anger varies in:

- intensity, from annoyance to rage;
- how controlled it is, from explosive to fuming;
- how long it takes to begin (onset time), from short-fused to smoldering;
- how long it takes to end (offset time), from rapid to lingering;
- temperature, from hot to cold;
- genuineness, from real to the phony anger an amused parent shows a naughty, charming child.

If one includes the blends of anger with other emotions— such as enjoyable anger, guilty anger, self-righteous anger, contemptuous anger—there would be even more members of the angry family.

No one yet knows whether there are different facial expressions for each of those different anger experiences. I believe there are and more. Already we have evidence that there are more different facial expressions than there are different single words for any emotion. The face signals nuances and subtleties that language does not map in single words. Our work mapping the repertoire of facial expression, determining exactly how many expressions there are for each emotion, which are synonyms and which signal different but related internal states, has been under way only since 1978. Some of what I will describe about facial signs of deceit is based on systematic studies using our new facial measurement technique, and some on thousands of hours inspecting facial expressions. What I report is *tentative*, because no other scientist has yet tried to repeat our studies of how voluntary and involuntary expressions differ.

Let's begin with the most tantalizing source of facial leakage, micro expressions. These expressions provide a full picture of the concealed emotion, but so quickly that it is usually missed. A micro expression flashes on and off the face in less than one-quarter of a second. We discovered micro expressions in our first study of clues to deceit, nearly twenty years ago. We were examining a filmed interview with the psychiatric patient Mary, mentioned in chapter 1, who was concealing her plan to commit suicide. In the film, taken after Mary had been in the hospital for a few weeks, Mary tells the doctor she no longer feels depressed and asks for a weekend pass to spend time at home with her family. She later confesses that she had been lying so that she would be able to kill herself when freed from the hospital's supervision. She admits to still feeling desperately unhappy.

Mary showed a number of partial shrugs—emblematic slips—and a decrease in illustrator movements. We also saw a micro expression: using slow-motion repeated replay, we saw a complete sadness facial expression, but it was there only for an instant, quickly followed by a smiling appearance. Micro expressions are full-face emotional expressions that are compressed in time, lasting only a fraction of their usual duration, so quick they are usually not seen. Figure 2 (see next page) shows the sadness expression.* It is very easy to interpret, because it is frozen on the page. If you were to see it for only one-twenty-fifth of a second, and it was covered immediately by another expression, as it would be in a micro expression, you would be

---

*To protect privacy, I have not used photographs of the people we have studied. The drawings in this and other illustrations were made directly from photographs and are correct in all details, except for the features, which have been changed.

Figure 2

likely to miss it. Soon after we discovered the micro expression other investigators published their discovery of micros, saying they are the result of repression, revealing unconscious emotions.[5] Certainly for Mary the feelings were not unconscious; she was painfully aware of the sadness shown in her micro expressions.

We showed excerpts containing micro expressions from Mary's interview to people and asked them to judge how she was feeling. Untrained people were misled; missing the message in the micros, they thought she felt good. It was only when we used slow-motion projection that these people picked up the sadness message. Experienced clinicians, however, didn't need slow-motion. They spotted the sadness message from the micro expression when they saw the film at real time.

With about one hour's practice most people can learn to see such very brief expressions. We put a shutter over a projector lens so that a slide could be exposed very briefly. At first when an expression is flashed for one-fiftieth of a second, people claim they can't see it and never will. Yet very quickly they learn to do so. It becomes so easy that sometimes people think we have slowed down the shutter. After seeing a few hundred faces, everyone has been able to recognize the emotion despite the brief exposure. Anyone can learn this skill without the shutter device by flashing a photograph of a facial expression very rapidly, as fast as they can, in front of their eyes. They should try to guess what emotion was shown in the picture, then look carefully at the picture to verify what is there, and then try another picture. Such practice has to be continued for at least a few hundred pictures.[6]

Micros are tantalizing, because rich as they are, providing leakage of a concealed emotion, they don't occur very often. We found few micro expressions in the experiment in which the student nurses lied. Much more common were *squelched* expressions. As an expression emerges the person seems to become aware of what is beginning to show and interrupts the expression, sometimes also covering it with another expression. The smile is the most common cover or mask. Sometimes the squelch is so quick that it is hard to pick up the emotion message the interrupted expression would have conveyed. Even if the message does not leak, the squelch can be a noticeable clue that the person is concealing feelings. The squelched expression usually lasts longer but is not as complete as the micro. The micro is compressed in time, but the full display is there, shortened. The squelched expression is interrupted, the expression does not always reach a full display, but it lasts longer than a micro and the interruption itself may be noticeable.

Both micro and squelched expressions are vulnerable to the two problems that can cause difficulty in interpreting most clues to deceit. Recall from the last chapter the Brokaw hazard, in which the lie catcher fails to take account of individual differences in emotional expression. Not every individual who is concealing an emotion will show either a micro or squelched expression—so their absence is not evidence of truth. There are individual differences in the ability to control expression, and some people, what I call natural liars, do it perfectly. The second problem, what I called the Othello error, is caused by a failure to recognize that some truthful people become emotional when suspected of lying. Avoiding the Othello error requires that the lie catcher understand that even when someone shows a micro or squelched expression, that is not sufficient to be certain the person is lying. Almost any emotion leaked by these expressions can be felt by an innocent trying to conceal having those feelings. An innocent person might feel afraid of being disbelieved, guilty about something else, angry or disgusted at an unjust accusation, delighted at the opportunity to prove the accuser wrong, surprised at the charge, and so on. If that innocent person wanted to conceal having those feelings, a micro or squelched expression could occur. Ways to deal with these problems in interpreting micro and squelched expressions are discussed in the next chapter.

Not all of the muscles that produce facial expression are equally easy to control. Some muscles are more reliable than others. *Reliable* muscles are not available for use in false expressions; the liar cannot gain access to them. And, the liar has a difficult time concealing their action when trying to hide a felt emotion, as they are not readily inhibited or squelched.

We learned about which muscles cannot be easily controlled by asking people to move deliberately each of their facial muscles, and also to pose emotions on their faces.[7] There are certain muscle movements that very few people can make deliberately. For example, only about 10 percent of those we have tested can deliberately pull the corners of their lips downward without moving their chin muscle. Yet, we have observed that those difficult-to-control muscles do move when the person feels an emotion that calls forth the movement. For example, the same people who cannot deliberately pull their lip corners down will show this action when they feel sadness, sorrow, or grief. We have been able to teach people how to move these difficult-to-control muscles deliberately, although it usually takes hundreds of hours for people to learn. These muscles are reliable because the person does not know how to get a message to the muscle to deploy it in a false expression. I reason that if a person can't get a message to a muscle for false expression, then the person will have a hard time getting a "stop" or squelch message to interfere with that muscle's action when an emotion is felt that calls the muscle into play. If you can't deliberately move a muscle to falsify an expression, you won't be able to readily inhibit the muscle from moving to conceal part of an emotional expression.*

There are other ways to conceal a felt expression without being able to inhibit it. The expression may be masked, typically with a smile, but this won't cover the signs of the felt emotion in the forehead and upper eyelids. Alternatively, antagonistic muscles can be tightened to hold the real expression in check. A smile of pleasure, for example, can be diminished by pressing the lips together and pushing the chin muscle up. Often, however, the use of antagonistic muscles may itself be a deception clue, since the melding of the antagonistic muscles with the muscles involved in the expression of the felt emotion may make the face look unnatural, stiff, or controlled. The best way to conceal a felt emotion would be to inhibit the actions of the muscles involved in its expression totally. And that may be difficult to do if the emotion involves the reliable facial muscles.

*I have discussed this idea with a number of neuroscientists knowledgeable about the face or emotion, and they believe this is a reasonable and probable notion. It has not yet been tested and must be regarded as a hypothesis.

The forehead is the chief locus for reliable muscle movements. Figure 3A shows the reliable muscle movements that occur with sadness, grief, distress, and probably also with guilt. (It is the same expression as shown in figure 2, but it is easier in figure 3A to focus just on the forehead since the rest of the face is blank.) Note that the inner corners of the eyebrow are pulled upward. Usually this will also triangulate the upper eyelid and produce some wrinkling in the center of the forehead. Less than 15 percent of the people we tested could produce this movement deliberately. It should not be present in a false display of these emotions, and it should appear when a person feels sad or distressed (or perhaps with guilt), despite attempts to conceal those feelings. This and the other drawings of facial expression show an extreme version of the display to make the shape of the expression clear despite not being able to show the action move on and off the face. If a sad feeling was weak, the appearance of the forehead would be the same as in figure 3A but it would be smaller. Once the pattern of an expression is known, even slight versions are detectable, when, as in real life, the movement, not a static representation, is seen.

Figure 3B shows the reliable muscle movements that occur with fear, worry, apprehension, or terror. Note that the eyebrows are raised and pulled together. This combination of actions is extremely difficult to make deliberately. Less than 10 percent of the people we tested could produce it deliberately. The drawing also shows the raised upper eyelid and tensed lower eyelid that typically mark fear. These eyelid actions may drop out when a person attempts to conceal fear, for these are not difficult actions to control. The eyebrow position is more likely to remain.

Figures 3C and 3D show the eyebrow and eyelid actions that mark anger and those for surprise. There are no distinctive eyebrow and eyelid actions that mark other emo-

Figure 3A

Figure 3B

Figure 3C

Figure 3D

tions. The eyebrow and eyelid movements shown in figures 3C and 3D are not reliable. Everyone can do them, and therefore they should appear in false expressions and easily be concealed. They are included to round out the picture of how the eyebrows and eyelids signal emotions, so that the contrast in appearance with the reliable actions shown in figures 3A and 3B will be more evident.

The eyebrow actions shown in figures 3C and 3D— raising or lowering—are the most frequent facial expressions. These eyebrow actions are often used as conversational signals to accent or emphasize speech. Brow raises are also deployed as exclamation or question marks, and as disbelief and skepticism emblems. Darwin called the muscle that pulls the brows down and together the "muscle of difficulty." He was correct in asserting that this action occurs with difficulty of any kind, from lifting something heavy to solving a complex arithmetic problem. Lowering and drawing the brows together is common with perplexity and concentration as well.

There is another reliable facial action in the mouth area. One of the best clues to anger is a narrowing of the lips. The red area becomes less visible, but the lips are not sucked in or necessarily pressed. This muscle action is very difficult for most people to make, and I have noted it often appears when someone starts to become angry, even before the person is aware of the feeling. It is a subtle movement, however, and also one easily concealed by smiling actions. Figure 4 shows how this action changes the appearance of the lips.

The Othello error—failing to recognize that a truthful person suspected of lying may show the same signs of emotion as a liar—can complicate the interpretation of the reliable facial muscles. An innocent suspect may show the reliable fear display shown in figure 3B because he is afraid of being falsely accused. Worried that if he looks afraid people will think he is a liar, he may try to conceal his fear

Figure 4

so that the signs of fear remain only in his eyebrows, which are difficult to inhibit. The liar afraid of being caught, who attempts to conceal his fear, is likely to show the same expression. Chapter 6 explains ways for the lie catcher to deal with this problem.

The Brokaw hazard—failing to take account of individual differences that may cause a liar *not* to show a clue to deceit while a truthful person *does* show it—also has to be avoided in interpreting the reliable facial muscles. Some people—both psychopaths and natural liars—have an extraordinary ability to inhibit facial signs of their true feelings. For them, even the reliable facial muscles are not trustworthy. Many charismatic leaders are such extraordinary performers. Pope John Paul II reportedly showed his skill during his visit to Poland in 1983.*

Just a few years earlier, the shipyard strike in Gdansk sparked the hope that the communist rulers in Poland

*Our disapproval of lying is so strong that my use of the term *liar* for any who is respected seems wrong. As I explained in chapter 2, I do not use the term *liar* in a pejorative fashion, and as I will explain in the last chapter, I believe some lies are morally defensible.

might allow some political freedom. Many feared that if Lech Walesa, the labor union Solidarity's leader, pushed too far or too fast Soviet troops would march in, as they had years before in Hungary, Czechoslovakia, and East Germany. For months Soviets troops engaged in "military exercises" close to the border with Poland. Finally, the regime that had tolerated Solidarity resigned, and the Polish military, with Moscow's approval, took over. General Jaruzelski suspended the activity of labor unions, restricted the activity of Lech Walesa, and imposed martial law. Now, after eighteen months of martial law, the visit of the pope, himself a Pole, could have important consequences. Would the pope show support for Walesa, would his presence rekindle a strike, catalyze rebellion, or would he give his blessing to General Jaruzelski? Journalist William Safire described the filmed meeting between the general and the pope: ". . . the pontiff and puppet leader showed smiles and handshakes. The pope understands how public appearances can be used, and calibrates his facial expressions at such events. Here the sign was unmistakable: church and state have reached some secret agreement, and the political blessing sought by Moscow's chosen Polish leader [Jaruzelski] was given to be played and replayed on state television."[8]

Not every political leader can so skillfully manage his expressions. The late president of Egypt, Anwar Sadat, wrote about his attempts as a teen-ager to learn how to control his facial muscles: ". . . my hobby was politics. At that time Mussolini was in Italy. I saw his pictures and read about how he would change his facial expressions when he made public addresses, variously taking a pose of strength, or aggression, so that people might look at him and read power and strength in his very features. I was fascinated by this. I stood before the mirror at home and tried to imitate this commanding expression, but for me the results were very disappointing. All that happened was that the muscles of my face got very tired. It hurt."[9]

While not able to falsify his facial expressions, Sadat's success in secretly forging a joint Syrian-Egyptian surprise attack on Israel in 1973 shows that he was, nevertheless, skillful in deceit. There is no contradiction. Deceit does not require skill in falsifying or concealing facial expression, body movement, or voice. That is necessary only in intimate deceits, when the liar and victim are in face to face, direct contact, as in the meeting during which Hitler so ably misled Chamberlain. Reportedly Sadat never tried to conceal his true feelings when he met directly with his adversaries. According to Ezer Weizman, the Israeli minister of defense who negotiated directly with Sadat after the 1973 war: "He is not a man to keep his feelings to himself: they are immediately evident in his expression as well as in his voice and gestures."[10]

There is another, more limited way in which individual differences interfere with the interpretation of the reliable facial muscles. It involves the conversational facial signals I mentioned earlier. Some of the conversational signals are much like hand illustrators, providing emphasis to particular words as they are spoken. Most people either lower their brows or raise their brows (as shown in figures 3C and 3D). Very few people use either the sadness or fear (figures 3A and 3B) brow movement to emphasize speech. For those who do, these movements are not reliable. The actor-director Woody Allen is a person whose brow movements are not reliable. He uses the sadness brow movement as a speech emphasizer. While most people raise or lower their brows to emphasize a word, Woody Allen instead usually pulls the inner corner of his eyebrows up. This is part of what gives him such a wistful or empathic look. Others who, like Woody Allen, use the sadness brow as an emphasizer are easily able to make these actions deliberately.

Such people should be able to use these movements in a false expression and conceal them when they choose to. They have easy access to muscles most people can't reach. The lie catcher can tell that he can't rely on these muscles if the suspect frequently uses such actions as emphasizers.

A third problem can complicate the interpretation of reliable facial muscles and other clues to deceit: a theatrical technique can be used to bring these muscles into action in a false expression. The Stanislavski acting technique (also known as method acting) teaches the actor how to accurately show emotion by learning how to remember and re-experience an emotion. I mentioned near the end of the last chapter our use of this acting technique to study the autonomic nervous system. When an actor uses this technique, his facial expressions are not made deliberately but are the product of the re-experienced emotion, and as our study suggests, the physiology of emotion can be awakened. Sometimes when people cannot make the actions shown in figures 3A or 3B, I have asked them to use the Stanislavski technique, instructing them to re-experience sad feelings or fearful ones. The facial actions they could not make deliberately often then will appear. The liar could also use the Stanislavski technique, and if so there should be no signs that the performance is false, because, in a sense, it won't be. The reliable facial muscles would appear in such a liar's false expression because the liar feels the false emotion. The line between false and true becomes fuzzy when emotions are produced by the Stanislavski technique. Even worse is the liar who succeeds in deceiving herself, coming to believe her lie is true. Such liars are undetectable. It is only liars who know they are lying when they lie who are likely to be caught.

So far I have described three ways in which concealed feelings may leak: micro expressions; what can be seen before a squelch; and what remains on the face because it was not possible to inhibit the action of the reliable facial muscles. Most people believe in a fourth source for the betrayal of concealed feelings—the eyes. Thought to be the windows of the soul, the eyes are said to reveal the innermost true feelings. The anthropologist Margaret Mead quoted a Soviet professor who disagreed: "Before the revolution we used to say: 'The eyes are the mirror of the soul.' The eyes can lie—and how. You can express with your eyes a devoted attention which, in reality you are not feeling. You can express serenity or surprise."[11] This disagreement about the trustworthiness of the eyes can be resolved by considering separately each of five sources of information in the eyes. Only three of them provide leakage or deception clues.

First are the changes in the appearance of the eyes produced by the muscles surrounding the eyeballs. These muscles modify the shape of the eyelids, how much of the white and iris of the eye is revealed, and the overall impression gained from looking at the eye area. Some of the changes produced by these muscles are shown in figures 3A, 3B, 3C, and 3D, but, as already mentioned, the actions of these muscles do not provide reliable clues to deceit. It is relatively easy to move these muscles deliberately, and to inhibit their actions. Not much will leak except as part of a micro or squelched expression.

The second source of information from the eye area is the direction of gaze. The gaze is averted with a number of emotions: downward with sadness; down or away with shame or guilt; and away with disgust. Yet even the guilty liar probably won't avert his eyes much, since liars know that everyone expects to be able to detect deception in this way. The Soviet professor quoted by Mead noted how easy it is to control the direction of one's gaze. Amazingly, people continue to be misled by liars skillful enough to not avert their glance. "One of the things that attracted Patricia

Gardner to Giovanni Vigliotto, the man who may have married 100 women, was 'that honest trait' of looking directly into her eyes, she testified yesterday [at his trial for bigamy]."[12]

The third, fourth, and fifth sources of information from the eye area are more promising sources of leakage or deception clues. Blinking can be done voluntarily, but it is also an involuntary response, which increases when people are emotionally aroused. Pupils dilate when people are emotionally aroused, but there is no voluntary pathway that allows anyone the option to make this change by choice. Pupil dilation is produced by the autonomic nervous system, which also produces the changes in salivation, respiration, and sweating mentioned in chapter 4 and some other facial changes described below. While increased blinking and dilated pupils indicate a person is emotionally aroused, they do not reveal which emotion it is. These may be signs of excitement, anger, or fear. Blinking and pupil dilation could be valuable leakage only when evidence of any emotion would betray that someone was lying and the lie catcher can rule out the possibility that they are signs of an innocent person's fear of being wrongly judged.

Tears, the fifth and last source of information in the eye area, are also produced by autonomic nervous system activity, but tears are signs of only some, not all, emotions. Tears occur with distress, sadness, relief, certain forms of enjoyment, and uncontrolled laughter. They can leak distress or sadness when other signs are concealed, although I expect that the eyebrows would also show the emotion, and the person, if the tears began, would quickly acknowledge the concealed feeling. Tears of enjoyment should not leak if the laughter itself has been suppressed.

The autonomic nervous system produces other visible changes in the face: blushing, blanching, and sweating. Just as with the other facial and bodily changes produced by the autonomic nervous system, it is difficult to conceal blushing, blanching, or facial sweating. It is not certain whether sweating is, like increased eyeblinks and pupil dilation, a sign of the arousal of any emotion, or instead specific to just one or two emotions. Very little is known about blushing and blanching.

Blushing is presumed to be an embarrassment sign, occurring also with shame and perhaps with guilt. It is said to be more common in women than men, although why this might be so is not known. Blushing could leak that a liar is embarrassed or ashamed about what is being concealed, or it could be embarrassment itself that is being concealed. The face also turns red with anger, and no one knows how this reddening might differ from the blush. Presumably both involve dilation of the peripheral blood vessels in the skin, but the red of anger and the embarrassment or shame blush could differ in amount, areas of the face affected, or duration. I expect that the face reddens only when anger is not being controlled, or when a person tries to control anger that is verging on exploding. If that is so, then usually there would be other evidence of anger in face and voice, and the lie catcher would not have to rely just upon face coloration to pick up this emotion. In more controlled anger the face may whiten or blanch, as it also may with fear. Blanching might leak even when the expressions of anger or fear are concealed. Amazingly, there has been very little study of tears, blushing, reddening, or blanching in relation to the expression or concealment of specific emotions.

Let us turn from how the face may betray a concealed emotion to facial signs that an expression is false and that emotion is not really felt. One possibility, already mentioned, is that the reliable muscles may not be part of a false expression, as long as there is no Woody Allen or Stanislavski problem. There are three other clues that suggest an expression is false: asymmetry, timing, and location in the conversational stream.

In an *asymmetrical* facial expression, the same actions appear on both sides of the face, but the actions are stronger on one side than the other. They should not be confused with *unilateral* expressions, those that appear on only one side of the face. Such one-sided facial actions are not signs of emotion, with the exception of the contempt expressions in which the upper lip is raised or the lip corner is tightened on one side. Instead unilateral expressions are used in emblems such as the wink, or the skeptical raise of one eyebrow. Asymmetrical expressions are more subtle, much more common, and much more interesting than unilateral ones.

Scientists interested in the findings that the right hemisphere of the brain seems to specialize in dealing with emotion thought that one side of the face might be more emotional. Since the right hemisphere controls many of the muscles on the left side of the face, and the left hemisphere controls many of the muscles on the right side of the face, some scientists suggested that emotion would be shown more strongly on the left side of the face. In my attempt to figure out inconsistencies in one of their experiments, I discovered, by accident, how asymmetry can be a clue to deceit. Crooked expressions, in which the actions are slightly stronger on one side of the face than the other, are a clue that the feeling shown is not felt.

The accident happened because the first team of scientists who claimed to find that emotion is shown most strongly on the left side of the face didn't use their own materials but borrowed facial photographs from me. I examined their findings more closely than I otherwise would have and was able to learn things they didn't see because of what I knew as the photographer of the faces. Harold Sackeim and his colleagues cut each of our facial pictures in half to create a double-left photograph and a double-right photograph, each a full-face picture composed of a mirror image of one or the other side of the face. People rated emotion as more intense when they saw the double-left than the double-right pictures.[13] I noticed that there was one exception—there was no difference in the judgments of the happy pictures. Sackeim had not made much of this, but I did. As the photographer, I knew that the happy pictures were the only *real* emotional expressions. The rest I had made by asking my models to move particular facial muscles deliberately. I had shot the happy pictures by catching the models off-guard when they were enjoying themselves.

Putting this together with the studies on brain damage and facial expression I described early in this chapter suggested a very different interpretation of facial asymmetry. Those studies had shown that voluntary and involuntary expressions involve different neural pathways, for one may be impaired but not the other, depending upon where the brain is damaged. Since voluntary and involuntary expressions can be independent of each other, if one was asymmetrical the other might not be. The final bit of logic was based on the well-established fact that the cerebral hemispheres direct *voluntary*, not involuntary, facial movement; the latter are generated by lower, more primitive areas of the brain. Differences between the left and right hemispheres should influence voluntary expressions, not involuntary emotional expressions.

Sackeim had found, according to my reasoning, just the opposite of what he thought he had proven. It was not that the two sides of the face differ in emotional expression. Instead, asymmetry occurred just when the expression was a deliberate, voluntary, pose, one made on demand. When expression was involuntary, as in the spontaneous happy faces, there was little asymmetry. Asymmetry is a clue that the expression is not felt.[14] We conducted a number of experiments testing these ideas, comparing deliberate with spontaneous facial expressions.

Scientific argument about this matter has been intense, and only recently has partial agreement emerged—just about the actions involved in the positive emotional expressions. Most investigators now agree with our finding that when the expression is not felt, the principal muscle involved in smiling acts more strongly on one side of the face. When we asked people to smile deliberately or pose happiness we found asymmetry, as we did when we examined the smiles people sometimes show when watching one of our gory films. Typically, the action was slightly stronger on the left side of the face if the person was right-handed. In genuine, felt smiles we have found a much lower incidence of asymmetrical expressions, and no tendency for those that are asymmetrical to be mostly stronger on the left side of the face.[15]

We also have found asymmetry in some of the actions involved in the negative emotions, when the actions are produced deliberately, but not when they are part of a spontaneous display of emotion. Sometimes the actions are stronger on the left, sometimes they are stronger on the right, and sometimes there is no asymmetry. In addition to the smile, the brow-lowering action that is often part of the anger display usually is stronger on the left side of the face when the action is made deliberately. The nose-wrinkling action involved in disgust and the stretching of the lips back toward the ears found in fear are usually stronger on the right side of the face if the actions are made deliberately. These findings have just been published, and it is not yet certain whether they will convince those, like Sackeim, who proposed asymmetry in emotional expressions.[16]

I did not think it would matter much to the lie catcher. Asymmetry is usually so subtle that I thought no one could spot it without precise measurement. I was wrong. When we asked people to judge whether expressions were symmetrical or asymmetrical, they did far better than chance, even though they had to make this judgment without slow-motion or repeated viewing.[17] They did have the benefit of not having to do anything else. We don't know yet whether people will be able to do so well when they also have to contend with the distractions of seeing the body movements, hearing the speech, and making replies to the person they converse with. It is very difficult to devise an experiment to determine that.

If many facial expressions are asymmetrical it is likely they are not felt, but asymmetry is not certain proof that the expression is unfelt. Some felt expressions are asymmetrical; it is just that most are not. Similarly, the absence of asymmetry does not prove that the expression is felt; the lie catcher may have missed them, and apart from that problem, not *every* deliberate, unfelt expression is asymmetrical; only most are. *A lie catcher should never rely upon one clue to deceit; there must be many.* The facial clues should be confirmed by clues from voice, words, or body. Even within the face, any one clue shouldn't be interpreted unless it is repeated and, even better, confirmed by another type of facial clue. Earlier, three sources of leakage, or ways the face betrays concealed feelings, were explained—the reliable facial muscles, the eyes, and autonomic nervous system changes in facial appearance. Asymmetry is one of another set of three clues, not of leakage of what is being concealed but of deception clues that the expression shown is false. Timing is the second source of deception clues.

Timing includes the total duration of a facial expression, as well as how long it takes to appear (onset), and how long it takes to disappear (offset). All three can provide deception clues. Expressions of long duration—certainly ten seconds or more, and usually 5 seconds—are likely to be false.

Most felt expressions don't last that long. Unless someone is having a peak experience, at the height of ecstasy, in a roaring rage, or at the bottom of depression, genuine emotional expressions don't remain on the face for more than a few seconds. Even in those extreme states expressions rarely last so long; instead, there are many shorter expressions. The long expressions are usually emblems or mock expressions.

There is no hard and fast rule about deception clues in the onset and offset times except for surprise. Onset, offset, and duration all must be short, less than a second, if the surprise is genuine. If it is longer it is mock surprise (the person is playing at being surprised), a surprise emblem (the person is referring to being surprised), or false surprise, in which the person is trying to seem surprised when he isn't. Surprise is always a very brief emotion, lasting only until the surprised person has figured out the unexpected event. While most people know how to fake surprise, few could do so convincingly with the fast onset and offset that a natural surprise must have. A news story showed how valuable a genuine surprise expression can be. "A man wrongfully convicted of armed robbery was freed after a prosecutor—noticing the man's reaction to the guilty verdict—dug up new evidence that proved Wayne Milton innocent. Assistant State Attorney Tom Smith said he knew something was wrong after seeing Milton's face drop when a jury convicted him last month of the $200 holdup at the Lake Apopka Gas Co."[18]

All the rest of the emotional expressions can be very short, flashing on and off in a second, or they may last for a few seconds. The onset and the offset may be abrupt or gradual. It depends upon the context in which the expression occurs. Suppose a subordinate is faking enjoyment when hearing a dull joke told for the fourth time by an intrusive boss, who has no sense of humor and a poor memory. How long it should take for the smiling actions to appear depends upon the build-up to the punch line—whether it is gradual, with slightly humorous elements, or abrupt. How long it should take for the smiling actions to disappear depends upon the type of joke—how much recycling or redigesting of the story would be appropriate. Everyone is able to make some kind of smile to falsify enjoyment, but a liar is less likely to correctly adjust the onset and offset timing of that smile to the particulars demanded by the context.

The exact *location* of an expression in relation to the flow of speech, the voice changes, and the body movements is the third source of deception clues that an expression is false. Suppose someone is falsifying anger and says, "I'm fed up with your behavior." If the anger expression comes after the words it is more likely to be false than if the anger occurs at the start, or even a moment before, the words. There is probably less latitude about where to position facial expression in relation to body movement. Suppose during the "fed up" the liar banged a fist on the table. If the anger expression followed the fist bang it is more likely to be false. Facial expressions that are not synchronized with body movement are likely to be deception clues.

No discussion of facial signs of deceit would be complete without considering one of the most frequent of all the facial expressions—smiles. They are unique among the facial expressions. It takes but one muscle to show enjoyment, while most of the other emotions require the action of three to five muscles. This simple smile is the easiest expression to recognize. We found such smiles can be seen from further away (300 feet) and with a briefer exposure than other emotional expressions.[19] It is hard not to reciprocate a smile; people do so even if the smile they reciprocate is one shown in a photograph. People enjoy looking at most smiles, a fact well known to advertisers.

Smiles are probably the most underrated facial expressions, much more complicated than most people realize. There are dozens of smiles, each differing in appearance and in the message expressed. There are many positive emotions signaled by smiling—enjoyment, physical or sensory pleasure, contentment, and amusement, to name just a few. People also smile when they are miserable. These aren't the same as the false smiles used to convince another that positive feelings are felt when they aren't, often masking the expression of a negative emotion. We recently found that people are misled by these false smiles. We had people look only at the smiles shown by the student nurses in our experiment and judge whether or not each smile was genuine (shown while a nurse watched a pleasant film), or false (shown while a nurse concealed the negative emotions aroused by our gory film). People did no better than chance. I believe the problem was not just a failure to recognize deceptive smiles but stemmed from a more general lack of understanding of how many different kinds of smiles there are. The false can't be distinguished from the felt without knowing how each resembles and differs from all of the other principal members of the smile family. Following are descriptions of *eighteen* different kinds of smiles, none of them deceptive smiles.

The common element in most members of the smile family is the appearance change produced by the zygomatic major muscle. This muscle reaches from the cheekbones down and across the face, attaching to the corners of the lips. When contracted, the zygomatic major pulls the lip corners up at an angle toward the cheekbones. With a strong action this muscle also stretches the lips, pulls the cheeks upward, bags the skin below the eyes, and produces crow's-feet wrinkles beyond the eye corners. (In some individuals this muscle also pulls down slightly the tip of their nose; in still others there will be a slight tug at the skin near their ears). Other muscles merge with the zygomatic major to form different members of the smile family; and a few smiling appearances are produced not by the zygomatic but by other muscles. The simple action of the zygomatic major muscle produces the smile shown for genuine, uncontrolled, positive emotions. No other muscles in the lower part of the face enter into this *felt* smile. The only action that may also appear in the upper face is the tightening of the muscle that circles the eyes. This muscle produces most of changes in the upper face that also can be produced by a strong action of the zygomatic major—raised cheek, bagged skin below the eye, and crow's-feet wrinkles. Figure 5A (see next page) shows the felt smile. The felt smile lasts longer and is more intense when positive feelings are more extreme.[20] I believe that all of the positive emotional experiences—enjoyment of another person, the happiness of relief, pleasure from tactile, auditory, or visual stimulation, amusement, contentment—are shown by the felt smile and differ only in the timing and intensity of that action.

The fear smile in figure 5B (see next page) has nothing to do with positive emotions, but it is sometimes so mistaken. It is produced by the risorious muscle pulling the lip corners horizontally toward the ears so that the lips are stretched to form a rectangular shape. Risorious is from the Latin word for laughing, but this action occurs principally with fear, not laughter. The confusion probably arose because sometimes when risorius pulls the lips horizontally the corners will tilt upward, resembling a very widely stretched version of the felt smile. In a fear facial expression the rectangular shaped mouth (with or without an upward lip corner tilt) will be accompanied by the brows and eyes shown in figure 3B.

The *contempt* smile is another misnomer, for this expression too has not much to do with positive emotions,

Figure 5A   Felt smile

Figure 5B   Fear smile

Figure 5C   Contempt smile

although it is often so construed. The version of contempt shown in figure 5C involves a tightening of the muscle in the lip corners, producing a muscle bulge in and around the corners, often a dimple, and a slight angling up of the lip corners.* Again, it is the angling up of the lip corners, a shared characteristic with the felt smile, that causes the confusion. Another shared element is the dimple, which sometimes appears in the felt smile. The chief difference between the contempt smile and the felt smile is the tightened lip corners, which are present in contempt and absent in the felt smile.

In a *dampened* smile a person actually feels positive emotions but attempts to appear as if those feelings are less intense than they actually are. The aim is to dampen (but not suppress) the expression of positive emotions, keeping the expression, and perhaps the emotional experience, within bounds. The lips may be pressed, the lip corners tightened, the lower lip pushed up, the lip corners pulled down, or any combination of these actions may merge with the simple smile. Figure 5D (see next page) shows a dampened smile with all three dampening actions merged with the felt smile action.

The *miserable* smile acknowledges the experience of negative emotions. It is not an attempt to conceal but a facial comment on being miserable. The miserable smile usually also means that the person who shows it is not, at least for the moment, going to protest much about his misery. He is going to grin and bear it. We have seen this miserable smile on the faces of people when they were sitting alone in our laboratory watching one of our gory films, unaware of our hidden camera. Often it appeared early when they seemed to first become aware of just how

---

*Contempt can also be shown by a unilateral version of this expression in which one lip corner is tightened and slightly raised.

Figure 5D   Dampened smile   Figure 5E   Miserable smile

terrible our films are. We have also seen miserable smiles
on the faces of depressed patients, as a comment on their
unhappy plight. Miserable smiles are often asymmetrical.
They are often superimposed on a clear negative emotional
expression, not masking it but adding to it, or they may
quickly follow a negative emotional expression. If the miserable smile is acknowledging an attempt to control the
expression of fear, anger, or distress, the miserable smile
may appear much like the dampened smile. The lip pressing, lower lip pushed up by the chin muscle, and corners
tightened or down may be serving to control the outburst
of one of these negative feelings. The key difference between this version of the miserable smile (shown in figure
5E) and the dampened smile is the absence of any evidence
of the muscle around the eyes tightening. The action of
that muscle—pulling in the skin around the eye and crow's-
feet wrinkles—is part of the dampened smile because enjoyment is felt and absent from the miserable smile because

enjoyment is not felt. The miserable smile may also show in the eyebrows and forehead the felt negative emotions being acknowledged.

In a blend two or more emotions are experienced at once, registered within the same facial expression. Any emotion can blend with any other emotion. Here we are concerned just with the appearance of the emotions that often blend with the positive emotions. When people enjoy being angry, the *enjoyable-anger* blend will show a narrowing of the lips and sometimes also a raising of the upper lip, in addition to the felt smile, as well as the upper face appearance shown in figure 3C. (This could also be called a cruel smile, or a sadistic smile.) In the *enjoyable-contempt* expression the felt smile merges with the tightening of one or both lip corners. Sadness and fear can also be enjoyed, as those who make horror and tear-jerking films and books. In *enjoyable-sadness* the lip corners may be pulled down in addition to the upward pull of the felt smile, or the felt smile may just merge with the upper face shown in figure 3A. The *enjoyable-fear* blend shows the upper face in figure 3B together with the felt smile merged with the horizontal stretching of the lips. Some enjoyable experiences are calm and contented, but sometimes enjoyment is blended with excitement, in an exhilarating feeling. In *enjoyable-excitement* the upper eyelid is raised in addition to the felt smile. The film actor Harpo Marx often showed this excited, gleeful smile, and at times when pulling a prank, the enjoyable-anger smile. In *enjoyable-surprise* the brow is raised, the jaw dropped, the upper lid raised, and the felt smile shown.

Two other smiles involve merging the felt smile with a particular gaze. In the *flirtatious* smile the flirter shows a felt smile while facing and gazing away from the person of interest and then, for a moment, steals a glance at the person, long enough to be just noticed as the glance shifts away again. One of the elements that makes the painting of the

Mona Lisa so unusual is that Leonardo depicted her caught in the midst of such a flirtatious smile, facing one way but glancing sideways at the object of her interest. In life this is an action, with the gaze shift lasting but a moment. In the *embarrassment* smile the gaze is directed down or to the side, so that the embarrassed person does not meet the other's eyes. Sometimes there will be a momentary upward lift of the chin boss (the skin and muscle between the lower lip and the tip of the chin) during the felt smile. In still another version, embarrassment is shown by combining the dampened smile with a downward or sideways gaze.

The *Chaplin* smile is unusual, produced by a muscle that most people can't move deliberately. Charlie Chaplin could, for this smile, in which the lips angle upward much more sharply than they do in the felt smile, was his hallmark. (See figure 5F, next page.) It is a supercilious smile that smiles at smiling.

The next four smiles all share the same appearance, but they serve quite different social functions. In each the smile is deliberately made. Often these smiles will show some asymmetry.

The *qualifier* smile takes the harsh edge off an otherwise unpleasant or critical message, often trapping the distressed recipient of the criticism into smiling in return. The smile is set deliberately, with a quick, abrupt onset. The lip corners may be tightened and sometimes too the lower lip pushed up slightly for a moment. The qualifier smile is often marked with a head nod and a slightly down and sideways tilt to the head so that the smiler looks down a little at the person criticized.

The *compliance* smile acknowledges that a bitter pill will be swallowed without protest. No one thinks the person showing it is happy, but this smile shows that the person is accepting an unwanted fate. It looks like the qualifier smile, without that smile's head position. Instead, the

Figure 5F   Chaplin smile

brows may be raised for a moment, a sigh may be heard, or a shrug shown.

The *coordination* smile regulates the exchange between two or more people. It is a polite, cooperative smile that serves to smoothly show agreement, understanding, intention to perform, or acknowledgment of another's proper performance. It involves a slight smile, usually asymmetrical, without the action of the muscle orbiting the eyes.

The *listener response* smile is a particular coordination smile used when listening to let the person speaking know that everything is understood and that there is no need to repeat or rephrase. It is equivalent to the "mm-hmm," "good," and head nod it often accompanies. The speaker doesn't think the listener is happy but takes this smile as encouragement to continue.

Any of these four smiles—qualifier, compliance, coordination, or listener—may sometimes be replaced by a genuine felt smile. Someone who enjoys giving a qualifying message, who takes pleasure in complying, listening, or coordinating, may show the felt rather than one of the unfelt smiles I have described.

Now let's consider the *false* smile. It is intended to convince another person that positive emotion is felt when it isn't. Nothing much may be felt, or negative emotions may be felt that the liar tries to conceal by using the false smile as a mask. Unlike the miserable smile that acknowledges pleasure is not felt, the false smile tries to mislead the other person to think the smiler is having positive feelings. It is the only smile that lies.

There are a number of clues for distinguishing false smiles from the felt smiles they pretend to be:

False smiles are more asymmetrical than felt smiles.

The false smile will not be accompanied by the involvement of the muscles around the eyes, so that the slight to moderate false smile will not show raised cheeks, bagged skin below the eyes, crow's-feet wrinkles, or a slight lowering of the eyebrow that will appear in the slight to moderate felt smile. An example is shown in figure 6; compare it to figure 5A. If the smile is larger in size, the smiling action itself—the zygomatic major muscle—raises the cheeks, gathers the skin below the eyes, and produces crow's-feet wrinkles. But it will not lower the eyebrow. If you look in a mirror and slowly make a larger and larger smile, you will note that as the smile increases the cheeks rise and crow's-feet appear; but your eyebrow will not be pulled down unless the eye muscle also acts. The lack of eyebrow involvement is a subtle cue, but a crucial one for distinguishing felt from false smiles when the grin is broad.

The offset time of the false smile may appear noticeably inappropriate. The smile may drop off the face too abruptly, or there may be a stepped offset, in which the smile decreases, and then is held, before either disappearing or going through another stepped decrease as it leaves the face.

Figure 6   False smile

Figure 5A   Felt smile

When used as a mask the false smile will only cover the actions of the lower face and the lower eyelid. The reliable muscles that appear in the forehead to signal fear or distress may still appear. Even in the lower face, the false smile may not succeed in completely covering the signs of the emotion it is intended to conceal; instead, there may be a merging of elements so that some trace still appears, as if it is an emotion blend.

Our first test of these ideas was to measure the smiling expressions shown by the student nurses in our experiment. If my ideas about smiling are correct, they should have shown the felt smile in the honest interview, when they had watched a pleasant film and described their feelings frankly. They should have shown false smiles in the deceptive interview, when they had watched a very unpleasant film but tried to appear as if they were seeing another pleasant film. We measured only two of the signs that a smile is false—the absence of the muscle around the eyes and the presence of signs of disgust (nose wrinkling) or contempt (tightening of the lip corners). The results were exactly as predicted, and very strong: in the honest interview there were more felt than false smiles and no smiles that leaked either disgust or contempt; in the deceptive interview the leakage smiles appeared and also there were more false than felt smiles. I was amazed that these two clues to deceit worked so well, especially since I knew that people don't seem to make use of them when judging others. In earlier studies we have shown the very same videotapes of facial expression and asked people to judge when the nurses were lying. People do no better than chance. Are we measuring something too subtle to see, or is it that people don't know what to look for? Our next study will find out by telling people how to recognize when the eye muscle is acting, and the leakage smiles are occurring, and then checking on whether they can more accurately spot lying.

The face may contain many different clues to deceit: micros, squelched expressions, leakage in the reliable facial muscles, blinking, pupil dilation, tearing, blushing and blanching, asymmetry, mistakes in timing, mistakes in location, and false smiles. Some of these clues provide leakage, betraying concealed information; others provide deception clues indicating that something is being concealed but not what; and others mark an expression to be false.

These facial signs of deceit, like the clues to deceit in words, voice, and body described in the last chapter, vary in the precision of the information they convey. Some clues to deceit reveal exactly which emotion is actually felt, even though the liar tries to conceal that feeling. Other clues to deceit reveal only whether the emotion being concealed is positive or negative and don't reveal exactly which negative emotion or which positive emotion the liar feels. Still other clues are even more undifferentiated, betraying only that the liar feels some emotion but not revealing whether the concealed feeling is positive or negative. That may be enough. Knowing that some emotion is felt sometimes can suggest that a person is lying, if the situation is one in which except for lying the person would not be likely to feel any emotion at all. Other times a lie won't be betrayed without more precise information about which concealed emotion is felt. It depends upon the lie, the line taken by the person suspected of lying, the situation, and the alternative explanations available, apart from lying, to account for why an emotion might be felt but concealed.

It is important for the lie catcher to remember which clues convey specific and which convey only more general information. Tables 1 and 2, in the appendix, summarize the information for all clues to deceit described in this and the previous chapter. Table 3 deals with clues to falsification.

SIX

Dangers and Precautions

*M*OST LIARS can fool most people most of the time.* Even children, once they reach eight or nine years of age (some parents say it is much earlier), can successfully deceive their parents. Mistakes in spotting deceit not only involve believing a liar but also, what often is worse, disbelieving a truthful person. Such a mistaken judgment may scar the disbelieved truthful child despite later attempts to correct the mistake. The consequences can be disastrous for the disbelieved truthful adult as well. A friendship may be lost, or a job, or even a life. It makes the news when an innocent person, mistakenly judged to have been lying, is released after undeserved years in jail; but it isn't so rare as to make the front page. While it is not possible to avoid completely mistakes in detecting deceit, precautions can be taken to reduce them.

The first precaution involves *making the process of interpreting behavioral signs of deceit more explicit.* The information

---

*Our research, and the research of most others, has found that few people do better than chance in judging whether someone is lying or truthful. We also found that most people think they are making accurate judgments even though they are not. There are a few exceptional people who can quite accurately spot deceit. I don't yet know whether such people are naturally gifted or acquire this ability through special circumstances. My research has not focused on the question of who can best detect deceit, but what I have learned suggests that this ability is not produced by conventional training in the mental health professions.

provided in the last two chapters about how the face, body, voice, and speech may betray deceit won't prevent mistaken judgments about whether someone is lying, but it may make those mistakes more obvious and correctable. Lie catchers will no longer rely just upon hunches or intuitions. More knowledgeable about the bases of their judgments, lie catchers should better be able to learn with experience, discarding, correcting, or giving more weight to particular clues to deceit. The falsely accused may also benefit, better able to challenge a judgment when the basis of that judgment is specified.

Another precaution is to *understand better the nature of the mistakes that occur in detecting deceit*. There are two kinds of mistakes that are exactly opposite in cause and consequence. In *disbelieving-the-truth* the lie catcher mistakenly judges a truthful person to be lying. In *believing-a-lie* the lie catcher mistakenly judges a liar to be truthful.* It does not matter whether the lie catcher depends upon a polygraph test or his interpretation of behavioral clues to deceit; he is vulnerable to these same two mistakes. Recall the passage I quoted in chapter 2, from Updike's novel *Marry Me*, when Jerry overhears his wife, Ruth, talking on the telephone to her lover. Noticing that her voice sounds more womanly than it does when she talks to him, Jerry asks "Who was that?" Ruth makes up the cover story "Some woman from the Sunday school asking if we were going to enroll Joanna and Charlie." If Jerry were to believe Ruth's story he would be making a believing-a-lie mistake. Suppose a dif-

---

*In considering the mistakes than may occur with any kind of test procedure, the term *false positive* is often used to refer to what I call disbelieving-the-truth, and *false negative* to what I call believing-a-lie. I did not use those terms, because they can be confusing when considering a lie, where positive seems inappropriate to refer to someone detected as a liar. Also, I find it difficult to keep in mind which type of mistake false positive and negative refer to. Other terms that have been suggested are *false alarm* for a disbelieving-the-truth mistake, and *miss* for a believing-a-lie mistake. These have the advantage of brevity but are not as specific as the phrases I have adopted.

ferent plot: Ruth is a faithful wife actually talking to the Sunday school, and Jerry is her suspicious husband. If Jerry thought his faithful wife was lying when she was not, he would be making a disbelieving-the-truth mistake.

In World War II Hitler made a believing-a-lie mistake —and Stalin made an equally disastrous disbelieving-the-truth mistake. Through various means—simulating troop concentrations, starting rumors, feeding false military plans to known German agents—the Allies convinced the Germans that the Allied invasion of Europe, the opening of the "second front," would be at Calais, not at the Normandy beach. For six weeks after the Normandy invasion the Germans persisted in their error, keeping many of their troops in readiness at Calais rather than reinforcing their embattled army at Normandy, in the belief that the Normandy landing was but a diversionary prelude to a Calais invasion! This was believing-a-lie: the Germans judged the reports that the Allies planned to invade Calais to be truthful, when they were carefully fabricated deceits. The Germans judged a lie—the plan to invade at Calais—to be the truth.

Just the opposite mistake—judging the truth to be a lie —was Stalin's refusal to believe the many warnings he received, some from his own spies among the German troops, that Hitler was about to launch an attack against Russia. This was a disbelieving-the-truth: Stalin regarded the accurate reports of the German plans to be lies.

This distinction between believing-a-lie and disbelieving-the-truth is important because it forces attention to the twin dangers for the lie catcher. There is no way to avoid completely both mistakes; the choice only is between which one to risk more. The lie catcher must evaluate when it is preferable to risk being misled, and when it would be better to risk making a false accusation. What can be lost or gained by suspecting the innocent or crediting a liar depends upon the lie, the liar, and the lie catcher. The consequences may be much worse for one kind of mistake; or, the mistakes may be equally disastrous.

There is no general rule about which kind of mistake can be most easily avoided. Sometimes the chances of each are about the same, and sometimes one type of mistake is more likely than the other. Again it depends upon the lie, the liar, and the lie catcher. The issues the lie catcher might consider in deciding which mistake to risk are considered at the end of the next chapter after I discuss the polygraph and compare it with the use of behavioral clues to detect deceit. Now I will describe how each of the behavioral clues to deceit are vulnerable to these two types of mistake, and what precautions can be taken to avoid the mistakes.

Individual differences, what I earlier named the Brokaw hazard because of a failure to take into account how people differ in expressive behavior, are responsible for both types of mistake in detecting deceit. No clue to deceit, in face, body, voice, or words, is foolproof, not even the autonomic nervous system activity measured by the polygraph. Believing-a-lie mistakes occur because certain people just don't make mistakes when they lie. These are not just psychopaths but also natural liars, people who are using the Stanislavski technique, and those who by other means succeed in coming to believe their own lies. The lie catcher must remember that *the absence of a sign of deceit is not evidence of truth.*

The presence of a sign of deceit can also be misleading, causing the opposite mistake, disbelieving-the-truth, in which a truthful person is said to be lying. A clue to deceit may be set out deliberately by a con man to exploit his victim's mistaken belief that he has caught the con man lying. Poker players reportedly use this trick, establishing what in poker lingo is called a "false tell." "For example, a player might for many hours deliberately cough when bluffing. The opponent, hopefully astute enough, soon recognizes this pattern of coughing and bluffing. In a crucial hand of the game when the stakes are raised, the deceiver coughs again, but this time he is not bluffing and so wins a wallet-breaking pot from his confused opponent."[1]

The poker player in this example set up and exploited a disbelieving-the-truth mistake, profiting from being judged to be lying. More often when a lie catcher makes a disbelieving-the-truth mistake, the person who is mistakenly identified as lying suffers. It is not deviousness that causes some people to be judged lying when they are truthful but a quirk in their behavior, an idiosyncracy in their expressive style. What for most people might be a clue to deceit is not for such a person. Some people:

- are indirect and circumlocutious in their speech;
- speak with many short or long pauses between words;
- make many speech errors;
- use few illustrators;
- make many body manipulators;
- often show signs of fear, distress, or anger in their facial expressions, regardless of how they actually feel;
- show asymmetrical facial expressions.

There are enormous differences among individuals in all of these behaviors; and these differences produce not only disbelieving-the-truth but also believing-a-lie mistakes. Calling the truthful person who characteristically speaks indirectly a liar is a disbelieving-the-truth mistake; calling the lying smooth-talker truthful is a believing-a-lie mistake. Even though such a talker's speech when lying may become more indirect and have more errors, it may escape notice because it still is so much smoother than speech usually is for most people.

The only way to reduce mistakes due to the Brokaw

hazard is to *base judgments on a change in the suspect's behavior.*
The lie catcher must make a comparison between the suspect's usual behavior and the behavior shown when the
suspect is under suspicion. People are likely to be misled in
first meetings because there is no base for comparison, no
opportunity to note changes in behavior. Absolute judgments—she is doing so many manipulator actions that she
must be very uncomfortable about something she is not
saying—are likely to be wrong. Relative judgments—she is
doing so many more manipulators than is usual for her that
she must be very uncomfortable—are the only way to decrease disbelieving-the-truth mistakes due to individual
differences in expressive style. Skilled poker players follow
this practice, memorizing the idiosyncratic "tells" (clues to
deceit) of their regular opponents.[2] If a lie catcher must
make a judgment after a first meeting, the meeting should
be long enough for the lie catcher to have a chance to
observe the suspect's usual behavior. The lie catcher might
try, for example, to focus for a while on topics that are not
stress-producing. Sometimes that won't be possible. The
entire meeting might be stressful for a suspect who resents
or is fearful of being under suspicion. If that is so, the lie
catcher should realize that he is vulnerable to making mistaken judgments due to the Brokaw hazard, not knowing
any peculiarities in the suspect's usual behavior.

First meetings are especially vulnerable to errors in
judgment also because of individual differences in how people react to initial encounters. Some people are on their
very best behavior, following well-learned rules about how
to act, and for that reason provide an unrepresentative
sample of their usual behavior. Others find first meetings
anxiety-provoking, and their behavior too, for the opposite
reason, provides a poor basis for comparison. If possible the
lie catcher should base judgments on a series of meetings,
hoping to establish a better base-line as acquaintance

grows. While it might seem that detecting lies will be easier
when people are not only acquainted but know each other
intimately, that isn't always so. Lovers, family members,
friends, or close colleagues may develop blind spots or preconceptions that interfere with accurate judgments of behavioral clues to deceit.

The interpretation of four sources of leakage—slips of
the tongue, emotional tirades, emblematic slips, and micro
expressions—is not so vulnerable to the Brokaw hazard. A
comparison is not needed to evaluate them, for they have
meaning in and of themselves, in absolute terms. Recall the
example quoted from Freud, in which Dr. R. was supposedly describing someone else's divorce. "I know a nurse
who was named as co-respondent in a divorce case. The
wife sued the husband and named her as co-respondent,
and *he* got the divorce." It took knowledge of the divorce
laws at that time (that adultery was one of the only grounds
for divorce, only the betrayed spouse could sue, and the
person suing would be entitled to permanent and usually
considerable alimony) to deduce from the slip that Dr. R.
might have been the husband in the story who wished he
could have sued for divorce. Even without that knowledge,
the slip of saying "he" instead of "she" had a very specific
meaning, understandable in and of itself: Dr. R. wished the
husband not the wife had gotten the divorce. Slips are not
like pauses, which can be understood only if their number
changes. Slips can be understood without any reference to
whether the person is making more slips than usual.

Regardless of how often they occur, a slip, micro expression, or tirade reveals information. It breaks concealment. Recall the example from my experiment in which
the student who was being attacked by the professor
showed the "finger" emblematic slip. It is not like a decrease in illustrators that can be evaluated only by comparing how often someone is making them now with their

usual rate. The "finger" is unusual; its meaning is well known. Because it was an emblematic slip—only part of the emblematic movement, shown out of the usual presentation position—the "finger" message could be interpreted as leaking feelings the student was trying to conceal. When Mary, the patient concealing her suicide plans, showed a micro expression, the sadness message was interpretable in and of itself. The fact that sadness was shown in a micro, not a normal, longer expression, indicated that Mary was trying to conceal her sadness. Knowledge of the conversational context may help in interpreting the full extent of a lie, but the messages provided by slips, tirades, and micro expressions betray concealed information and are themselves meaningful.

These four sources of leakage—slips of the tongue, tirades, emblematic slips, and micro expressions—are unlike all other clues to deceit in this one respect. The lie catcher does not need a basis for comparison in order to avoid making disbelieving-the-truth mistakes. In first meetings, for example, the lie catcher does not need to worry about interpreting a slip, micro expression, or tirade because this may be a person who often shows those behaviors. Just the opposite. It is the lie catcher's good fortune if the suspect happens to be someone who is prone to slips, tirades, or micros. While the precaution requiring previous acquaintance to reduce disbelieving-the-truth mistakes can be waived for these four sources of leakage, the precaution for reducing believing-a-lie mistakes, mentioned earlier, still applies. The absence of these or any other clue to deceit cannot be interpreted as evidence that someone is truthful. Not every liar will make a slip, show a micro expression, or have a tirade.

So far we have considered just one source of errors in detecting deceit—the failure to take account of individual differences, the Brokaw hazard. Another equally important source of trouble, leading to disbelieving-the-truth mistakes, is the Othello error. This error occurs when the lie catcher fails to consider that a truthful person who is under stress may appear to be lying. Each of the feelings about lying (explained in chapter 3) that can produce leakage and deception clues may be felt for other reasons when truthful people know they are suspected of lying. Truthful people may be afraid of being disbelieved, and their fear might be confused with the liar's detection apprehension. Some people have such strong unresolved guilt about other matters that those feelings may be aroused whenever they realize they are suspected of any wrongdoing. Signs of those guilt feelings might be confused with a liar's deception guilt. Truthful people also may feel scorn toward those they know are falsely accusing them, excitement about the challenge of proving their accusers wrong, or pleasure anticipating their vindication, and the signs of those feelings may resemble a liar's duping delight. Other emotions also may be felt by either liars or truthful people who know they are under suspicion. Although the reasons would differ, either the liar or the truthful person might feel surprised, angry, disappointed, distressed, or disgusted by the lie catcher's suspicions or questions.

I have called this error after Othello because the death scene in Shakespeare's play is such an excellent and famous example of it. Othello has just accused Desdemona of loving Cassio and tells her to confess since he is going to kill her for her treachery. Desdemona asks that Cassio be called to testify to her innocence. Othello tells her that he has already had Cassio murdered. Desdemona realizes she will not be able to prove her innocence and that Othello will kill her.

DESDEMONA: Alas, he is betrayed, And I undone!
OTHELLO: Out, strumpet! Weep'st thou for him to my face?

DESDEMONA: O, banish me, my lord, but kill me not!
OTHELLO: Down, strumpet![3]

Othello interprets Desdemona's fear and distress as a reaction to the news of her alleged lover's death, confirming his belief in her infidelity. Othello fails to realize that if Desdemona is innocent she might still show these very same emotions: distress and despair that Othello disbelieves her and that her last hope to prove her innocence is gone now that Othello has had Cassio killed, and fear that he will now kill her. Desdemona wept for her life, for her predicament, for Othello's lack of trust, not for the death of a lover.

Othello's error is also an example of how *preconceptions* can bias a lie catcher's judgments. Othello is convinced before this scene that Desdemona is unfaithful. Othello ignores alternative explanations of Desdemona's behavior, not considering that her emotions are not proof one way or the other. Othello seeks to confirm, not to test his belief that Desdemona is unfaithful. Othello is an extreme example, but preconceptions often distort judgment, causing a lie catcher to disregard ideas, possibilities, or facts that don't fit what he already thinks. This happens even when the lie catcher suffers from his preconceived belief. Othello is tortured by his belief that Desdemona lies, but that does not cause him to lean over in the opposite direction, seeking to vindicate her. He interprets Desdemona's behavior in a way that will confirm what he least wants to be so, in a way that is most painful to him.

Such preconceptions that distort the lie catcher's judgment, leading to disbelieving-the-truth mistakes, can arise from many sources. Othello's belief that Desdemona was unfaithful was the work of Iago, his evil aide, who for his own gain brought about Othello's downfall by creating and then feeding Othello's suspicions. Iago might not have succeeded if Othello did not have a jealous nature. People who are sufficiently jealous may need no Iago to bring their jealousy into play. They seek to confirm their worst fears, discovering what they suspect—that everyone lies to them. Suspicious people should be terrible lie catchers, prone to disbelieving-the-truth mistakes. There are, of course, gullible people, who make the opposite, believing-a-lie mistakes, never suspecting those who deceive them.

When the stakes are high, when the costs to the lie catcher would be great if the suspect is lying, even non-jealous people may rush to the wrong judgment. When a lie catcher becomes angry, fears betrayal, already experiences the humiliation that would occur if his worst fears were founded, he may ignore anything that could reassure him and seek what will distress him more. He may accept the humiliation before his betrayal is proven rather than risk even worse humiliation if he were to be further duped. Better to suffer now than endure the torment of uncertainty about what one fears. He is more fearful of believing-a-lie—of being cuckolded, for example—than disbelieving-the-truth—being an unreasonably accusatory husband. These are not choices rationally made. The lie catcher has become the victim of what I call an *emotion wildfire*. Emotions can go out of control, acquiring a momentum of their own, not subsiding with time, as they usually do, but instead intensifying. Anything that will fuel the terrible feelings, magnifying their destructiveness, is seized upon. In such an emotional inferno one can not be reassured; that is not what one seeks. One acts to intensify whatever emotion is felt, turning fear into terror, anger into fury, disgust into revulsion, distress into anguish. An emotion wildfire consumes whatever it confronts—objects, strangers, loved ones, the self—until it is spent. No one knows what causes such wildfires to begin or to finally end. Clearly some people are much more susceptible to emotional wildfires than others. Obviously someone gripped by an emotion wildfire is a terrible judge of others, believing only what makes him feel worse.

Disbelieving-the-truth mistakes—seeing deceit when none is there—don't require an emotional wildfire, a jealous personality, or an Iago. Deceit may be suspected because it is a powerful and useful explanation of what otherwise would be a baffling world. An employee of the CIA for twenty-eight years wrote: "As a causal explanation, deception is intrinsically satisfying precisely because it is so orderly and rational. When other persuasive explanations are not available (perhaps because the phenomena we are seeking to explain were actually caused by mistakes, failures to follow orders, or other factors unknown to us), deception offers a convenient and easy explanation. It is convenient because intelligence officers are generally sensitive to the possibility of deception, and its detection is often taken as indicative of sophisticated, penetrating analysis. . . . It is easy because almost any evidence can be rationalized to fit the deception hypothesis; in fact, one might argue that once deception has been raised as a serious possibility, this hypothesis is almost immune to disconfirmation."[4]

These observations have much wider application than intelligence or police work. Even when it means accepting that one's child, parent, friend, or lover has betrayed trust, a lie catcher may make disbelieving-the-truth mistakes, wrongly suspecting deceit because it explains the inexplicable. Once begun, the preconception that the loved one is lying filters information to prevent disconfirmation.

Lie catchers should *strive to become aware of their own preconceptions about the suspect.* Whether it be due to the lie catcher's personality, emotion wildfires, input from others, past experience, pressures of the job, the need to reduce uncertainty—if preconceptions about the suspect are explicitly recognized, the lie catcher has a chance of guarding against the likelihood of interpreting matters only in a way to fit those preconceptions. At the least, a lie catcher may be able to realize that she is too much the victim of her preconceptions to be able to trust her judgments about whether or not a suspect is lying.

The lie catcher must make an effort to *consider the possibility that a sign of an emotion is not a clue to deceit but a clue to how a truthful person feels about being suspected of lying.* Is the sign of an emotion a feeling about lying or a feeling about being falsely accused or judged? The lie catcher must estimate which emotions a particular suspect is likely to feel not only if she is lying but, as importantly, if she is being truthful. Just as not all liars will have every possible feeling about lying, not all truthful people will have every feeling about being under suspicion. Chapter 3 explained how to estimate whether a liar is likely to feel detection apprehension, deception guilt, or duping delight. Now let us consider how the lie catcher can estimate which emotions a truthful person might feel about being suspected of lying.

The lie catcher may be able to make that estimate based on knowledge of the suspect's personality. Earlier in this chapter, I described the need for the lie catcher to be previously acquainted with the suspect in order to reduce errors based on first impressions, which can't take account of how individuals may differ in some of the behaviors that can be clues to deceit. Now, a different type of knowledge about the suspect is needed for a different purpose. The lie catcher needs to know the emotional characteristics of the suspect in order to discount the signs of certain emotions as clues to deceit. Not everybody is likely to feel afraid, guilty, angry, and so on when they know they are suspected of wrongdoing or lying. It depends in part upon the personality of the suspect.

A highly self-righteous person might feel angry if he knew he was suspected of lying but have little fear of being disbelieved and no free-floating guilt. A timorous individual, lacking confidence and often expecting failure, might fear being disbelieved but not be likely to feel anger or guilt. Already mention has been made of individuals who are so guilt-ridden that they feel guilty when they are suspected of a wrongdoing they didn't commit. Such guilt-ridden people may not, however, be particularly fearful, angry, surprised, distressed, or excited. The lie catcher must *discount the sign of an emotion as a clue to deceit if the suspect's personality would make the suspect likely to have such a feeling even if the suspect was being truthful.* Which emotions should be discounted depends upon the suspect—not every emotion will be easily aroused in every truthful person who knows she is under suspicion.

Which emotion, if any, innocent people may feel if they know they are suspected of wrongdoing depends also upon their relationship with the lie catcher, what their past history with that person would suggest. The *Winslow Boy*'s father knew that Ronnie considered him to be just. He had never falsely accused Ronnie nor punished him when he was in fact innocent. Because of their past relationship, the father did not have to discount signs of fear as being as likely whether Ronnie was truthful or lying. There was no reason for the boy to fear being disbelieved, only reason for him to fear being caught if he lied. People who often falsely accuse, who repeatedly disbelieve the truthful, establish a relationship that makes fear signs ambiguous, likely whether their suspect is truthful or lying. A wife who repeatedly has been accused of having affairs and who is subject to verbal or physical abuse despite her innocence has reason to be afraid whether she lies or tells the truth. Her husband has lost, among other things, the basis for utilizing signs of fear as evidence of lying. The lie catcher must *discount the sign of an emotion as a clue to deceit if the suspect's relationship with the lie catcher would make the suspect likely to have such a feeling even if the suspect was being truthful.*

In a first meeting, despite the fact that there is no past relationship, someone may be suspected of lying. It might be a first date, in which one suspects the other is concealing the fact of being married. An applicant may suspect an employer is lying about still having to interview others before making a decision. A criminal may suspect the police interrogator's claim that his buddy has confessed and is turning state's evidence against him. The buyer may wonder if the real estate agent is trying to jack up the price when he says that the owner would not even consider such a low offer. Without prior involvement with the suspect the lie catcher is doubly deprived. Neither knowledge of the suspect's personality nor knowledge of their past relationship can suggest whether there is any need to discount particular emotions as being a truthful person's feelings about being suspected. Even then, knowledge of the suspect's expectations about the lie catcher may provide a basis for estimating which emotions a truthful person might feel about being suspected of lying.

Not every suspect has a well-formed expectation about every lie catcher, and not everyone who does will share the same expectations. Suppose the suspect is someone with access to classified material who has been seen fraternizing with people that the FBI believes to be undercover Soviet agents. The suspect need never have had any contact with a particular FBI agent, or with any FBI agents, to have expectations about the FBI that should be taken into account. If she believes that the FBI never makes mistakes and is completely trustworthy, signs of fear need not be discounted but could be interpreted as a detection apprehension. However, if she believes the FBI is either inept or given to framing people, fear signs would have to be discounted. It could be fear of being disbelieved rather than detection apprehension. The lie catcher must *discount the sign of an emotion as a clue to deceit if the suspect's expectations would make the suspect likely to have such a feeling even if the suspect was being truthful.*

Until now I have dealt only with the confusion caused by the truthful person's feelings about being suspected of lying. The truthful person's emotional reactions can also clarify rather than confuse, helping to distinguish the truthful person from the liar. Confusion arises when the truthful person and the liar might both have the same emotional reactions to suspicion; clarity when their reactions are likely to differ. Someone might have entirely different feelings about being under suspicion if he is telling the truth than if he is lying.

The Winslow Boy is an example. The father had a great deal of information—knowledge of his son's personality and of their past relationship—which allowed him to make a very specific estimate of how his son would be likely to feel if Ronnie either told the truth or lied. He knew his son was neither a natural liar nor a psychopath, was not guilt-ridden, and held shared values. Therefore, deception guilt would be high if Ronnie was to lie. The lie, remember, would be to deny stealing if he had actually done so. The father knew his son's character was such that he would feel guilty about a crime, quite apart from whether he was to lie or be truthful about it. So, if Ronnie did steal and tries to conceal it, two sources of strong feelings of guilt could betray him—guilt about lying and guilt about the crime he was concealing. If Ronnie is telling the truth when he denies stealing he should feel no guilt.

The father also knew that his son trusted him. Their past relationship was such that Ronnie would accept his father's assertion that he would believe Ronnie if his son told the truth. Therefore, Ronnie should not fear being disbelieved. To heighten detection apprehension, the father, like the polygraph lie detector, claimed to be fool-proof—". . . if you tell me a lie, I shall know it, because a lie between you and me can't be hidden. I shall know it, Ronnie—so remember that before you speak." Ronnie, presumably on the basis of past experience, believed it. Therefore, Ronnie should be afraid of being caught if he lies. Finally, the father offered amnesty for confession: "If you did it, you must tell me. I shan't be angry with you, Ronnie —provided you tell me the truth." By this statement the father also raised the stakes; if Ronnie was to lie, he would be the object of his father's anger. Ronnie would probably feel quite ashamed if he had stolen, and this might still keep him from admitting it. His father should have said something about understanding how a boy may give in to temptation, but the important thing is not to conceal but admit a wrongdoing.

Having evaluated which emotions Ronnie will feel if he lies (fear and guilt), and having a basis for estimating that these emotions are not as likely if Ronnie tells the truth, one more step was still necessary before the father could diminish mistakes in interpreting clues to deceit. It must be certain that if Ronnie tells the truth he will not feel any other emotions that might resemble the signs of fear or guilt and thus confuse the judgment of whether or not he is lying. Ronnie might be angry at the schoolmaster for falsely judging him to be a thief; so, signs of anger, particularly if they appear when talking about the school authorities, must be discounted. Probably Ronnie would feel distressed about his circumstances, and these upset feelings might be general to his entire predicament, not specific to the mention of any particular aspect of it. His father, then, can interpret fear and guilt as evidence of lying, but anger or distress could be present even if Ronnie is truthful.

Even when matters are so clear-cut—when there is a basis for knowing which emotions the suspect would feel if lying or if telling the truth, and when they are not the same emotions—interpreting behavioral clues to deceit can still be hazardous. *Many behaviors are signs of more than one emotion, and those that are must be discounted when one of those emotions could be felt if the suspect is truthful while another could be felt when the suspect is lying.* Tables 1 and 2, in the appendix, provide ready access for checking which emotions can produce each behavioral clue.

Suppose the father noticed that Ronnie was sweating, and swallowing frequently. Those signs would be worthless, since they are signs of any emotion, positive or negative. If Ronnie was lying they would occur because of fear or guilt, and if Ronnie was telling the truth they might occur because he felt distressed and angry. If Ronnie showed many manipulators, that too would have to be discounted, since manipulators increase with any negative emotion. Even signs of only certain of the negative emotions, such as a lowering of the voice pitch, would have to be disregarded. If the voice pitch became lower because of guilt, that would be a sign of lying; but it could become lower due to sadness or distress, and Ronnie might well feel distressed whether he lies or tells the truth. Only those behaviors which mark fear or guilt but not anger, sadness or distress can be interpreted as clues to deceit. Behaviors which mark anger or distress but not fear or guilt can be interpreted as clues to honesty. Study of tables 1 and 2 shows that the following behaviors could show whether or not Ronnie is lying: slips of the tongue, emblematic slips, micro expressions, and actions of reliable facial muscles. These are the only behaviors that can signal information with sufficient precision to distinguish fear or guilt from anger or distress. Incidentally, giving Ronnie a polygraph test might not have worked. The polygraph only measures the arousal of emotion, not which emotion is felt. Ronnie would have been emotional, guilty or innocent. While studies evaluating the accuracy of the polygraph show it does better than chance, in quite a few of those studies there were many disbelieving-the-truth mistakes. I discuss these studies and what they mean in the next chapter.

Estimating which emotions the suspect would feel if he is telling the truth and whether these differ from the emotions the suspect feels if he is lying, as my analysis of *The Winslow Boy* has shown, is complicated. It requires a lot of knowledge about the suspect. Often there won't be enough knowledge to make these estimates. And when there is, the estimates may not help to spot the liar. The knowledge may suggest that the same emotion is likely to be felt whether the suspect lies or is truthful, as was so for Desdemona. Even when the estimate suggests that different emotions would be felt if the suspect is truthful or lies, the behavioral clues may be ambiguous. None may be specific to just the emotions that would differentiate the liar from the truthful person. In these instances—there is not enough knowledge to estimate the emotions felt by the suspect; the estimate is that the same emotions will be felt whether the suspect is lying or truthful; or different emotions would be felt by the liar or honest person, but the behavioral clues are ambiguous—the lie catcher cannot utilize the clues to deceit that involve emotion.*

It is only by realizing when he is in this predicament that the lie catcher can avoid making disbelieving-the-truth mistakes and can be properly wary of his vulnerability to being taken in by liars, making believing-a-lie mistakes. Of course, sometimes analyzing which emotions the liar would feel, and which emotions a truthful person might feel about being under suspicion, will help to catch a liar. As with the *Winslow Boy* example, such an analysis will isolate clues that are unambiguous signs of honesty or deceit and will make the lie catcher's task easier by alerting

---

*Remember that there are other clues to deceit that need not involve emotion, such as slips of the tongue, emblematic slips, and tirades.

him to just which behaviors he must search for.

My explanation of the dangers and precautions in detecting deceit has so far dealt only with situations in which the suspect knows he is suspected of lying. However, truthful people may never realize that every word they utter, every gesture and facial twitch is scrutinized at some point, by someone who suspects them of lying; and, some truthful people believe that they are subject to such scrutiny, when, in fact, they are not. Liars do not always know whether or not their victims suspect their deceits. An elaborate excuse designed to allay suspicion may raise a question in the mind of a previously trusting victim. Victims who suspect they are being deceived may themselves lie, concealing their suspicions, to lull the liar into a false move. There are other reasons why a victim may lull the liar. In counterintelligence, when a spy is uncovered the discovery may be concealed so as to feed false information through the spy to the enemy. Other victims may conceal their discovery of being misled in order to enjoy reversing the tables and, for a time, watch the liar continue to spin his fabrications unaware that the victim now knows all is false.

There are both gains and losses for the lie catcher if the suspect does not know that he is suspected of lying. A liar may not cover tracks, anticipate questions, prepare excuses, rehearse the line, and in other ways be cautious if he does not believe every move is being scrutinized by a suspicious victim. As time passes and the lie appears to be totally swallowed, a liar may become so relaxed that mistakes occur because of overconfidence. This gain for the lie catcher is offset by the likelihood that a liar who is so overconfident as to become sloppy is not likely to feel much detection apprehension. Careless mistakes are purchased at the cost of mistakes due to detection apprehension. Not only are the behavioral clues to deceit generated by detection apprehension sacrificed, but lost also are the disorganizing effects of such fear, which can, like overconfidence, produce poor planning. Perhaps the most important loss is the torment of fearing capture, which is not likely to become strong enough to motivate confession if the liar does not think anyone is on to him.

Ross Mullaney, an expert in training police interrogators, advocates what he calls the Trojan Horse strategy, in which the police officer pretends to believe the suspect, to get the subject to talk more and become entangled in his own fabrications. Even though the detection apprehension may decrease, the suspect is more likely to make a revealing mistake, according to Mullaney: "The officer should encourage the source [suspect] in his deceit by pulling him forward, seeking always more and more detail in the suspected fabrications being offered. In a real sense, the officer also deceives as he pretends to believe the source. . . . [I]t cannot harm the honest source. If the officer is in error in his initial suspicion that the . . . suspect may be deceiving . . . [this technique of interrogating] will not cause any injustice. Only the deceitful need fear [it]."[5] This strategy is reminiscent of Schopenhauer's advice: "If you have reason to suspect that a person is telling you a lie, look as though you believed every word he said. This will give him courage to go on; he will become more vehement in his assertions and in the end betray himself."[6]

While belief that the target is trusting seems certain to decrease a liar's detection apprehension, it is difficult to say how such knowledge will affect other feelings about lying. Some liars may feel more deception guilt in misleading a trusting target than a suspicious one. Others might feel less guilty, rationalizing that as long as the target does not know and is not tortured by suspicions, no harm is done. Such liars may believe their lies are motivated primarily by kindness, to spare their victim's sensibilities. Duping delight also could go either way, strengthened or diminished if the liar knows the target is trusting. Duping a totally trusting victim may be especially delicious, indulging enjoyable feelings of contempt; yet, deceiving a suspicious target may be exciting because of the challenge. There is no way, then, to predict whether a liar is more or less likely to make mistakes if his target makes his suspicions known. There is, of course, a chance that the suspicions are ungrounded; the suspect may be honest. Would it be easier to tell that a suspect is truthful if the suspect did not know he was under suspicion? If he does not know he is suspected of lying, he should not fear being disbelieved; nor would there be anger or distress about being suspected of lying, and the suspect, even if guilt-ridden, would have no special opportunity to act as if wrong had been done. This is all to the good, since the signs of any of these emotions can then be interpreted simply as clues to deceit without any need to worry that they might instead be a truthful person's feelings about being suspected. This gain is purchased, however, at the already-mentioned cost that some of the feelings about lying that produce clues to deceit, particularly detection apprehension, will be weaker if this person who does not know anyone suspects him of lying is indeed a liar. When the suspect doesn't know there is suspicion, the lie catcher is less likely to make disbelieving-the-truth errors because the signs of emotion, if they occur, are more likely to be clues to deceit; but there may be more believing-a-lie mistakes, because feelings about lying are less likely to be strong enough to betray the liar. The reverse probably happens if suspicion is known—more disbelieving-the-truth but less believing-a-lie.

Two other problems complicate the matter of whether the lie catcher would be better off if the suspect didn't know he was under suspicion. First, the lie catcher may have no choice. Not every situation will permit the target to conceal his suspicions. Even if possible, not everyone

who thinks he may be the target of a lie would want to
conceal his suspicions, lying to catch a liar. And not every
lie catcher has the talent as a liar to succeed undiscovered
in his deceit.

The second problem is worse. By trying to conceal his
suspicions, the lie catcher risks failing in this concealment
without realizing it. He certainly can't count on the liar to
be truthful about the matter! Some liars may boldly confront their target once they note that the target is suspicious, especially if they can expose their target's attempts
at concealment. The liar may pose self-righteousness, in-
dignant and hurt that the target was not forthright about
his suspicions, unfairly depriving the liar of a chance to
vindicate himself. Even if this ploy does not convince, it
may at least intimidate the target for a time. Not every liar
will be so brazen. Some might conceal their discovery that
the target has become suspicious so that they can gain time
to cover their tracks, prepare an escape, etc. Unfortunately,
it is not just the liar who may conceal such a discovery.
Truthful people may also conceal that they have discovered
they are under suspicion. Their reasons can be quite varied.
They may conceal knowing that they are under suspicion
in order to avoid a scene, or to buy time in which they hope
to gather evidence in their support, or to take actions that
those who suspect them will judge in their favor if it is
thought that they acted unaware of being suspect.

One advantage gained by revealing suspicions is that
this morass of uncertainties can be avoided. At least the
target knows that the suspect knows there is suspicion.
Even then the truthful person, like the liar, may attempt to
conceal any feelings about being under suspicion. Once
suspicion is acknowledged, the liar should want to conceal
any detection apprehension, but the truthful person may
also attempt to conceal fear of being disbelieved, and anger
or distress at being suspected, out of concern that these

feelings would be misconstrued as evidence of lying. If it were only the liars who tried to conceal feelings, it would be easier to detect deceit. But, if that were so, some liars would be smart enough to also show their feelings.

Another advantage gained if the victim is frank about being suspicious is that he may then be able to use what is called the Guilty Knowledge Technique. David Lykken, a physiological psychologist who is a critic of the use of the polygraph lie detector, believes that the guilty knowledge technique can improve the accuracy of the polygraph. The interrogator does not ask the suspect whether he committed the crime, but instead the suspect is asked about knowledge that only the guilty person would have. Suppose someone is suspected of murder; the suspect has a motive, was seen near the scene of the crime, and so on. With the guilty knowledge technique, the suspect would be asked a series of multiple-choice questions. In each question one of the choices would always describe what did happen, while the others, which sound equally plausible, would describe things that didn't happen. Only the guilty, not the innocent, suspect would know which was which. For example, the suspect might be asked, "Was the murdered person lying face down, face up, on his side, or sitting up?" The suspect is asked to say "No" or "I don't know" after each alternative is read. Only the person who committed the crime would know that the dead person was lying face up. In laboratory experiments on lying, Lykken has found that the person who has this guilty knowledge shows a change in autonomic nervous system activity, detected by the polygraph, when the true alternative is mentioned, while the innocent person responds about the same way on the polygraph to all the alternatives. Despite the guilty person's attempt to conceal that he has the knowledge only the guilty would have, when this technique is used the polygraph catches him.[7]

The virtue of the guilty knowledge test is that unusual reactions cannot be due to an innocent person's feelings about being suspected of lying. Even if the innocent suspect is afraid of being disbelieved, or angry about being suspected, or distressed about his predicament, only by chance would he show more emotional reaction to "lying face up" than to the other alternative descriptions. By using many such multiple-choice questions, any unusual reactions shown by an innocent suspect will be spread across the true and false alternatives. The guilty knowledge test, then, eliminates the greatest danger in spotting deceit —disbelieving-the-truth mistakes due to confusing the truthful person's feelings about being suspected with those of the liars.

Unfortunately, this promising technique for detecting lies has not been subject to much research to evaluate its accuracy, and studies that have been done do not show it to be always as accurate as Lykken's original work suggested. The recent Office of Technology Assessment report reviewing the polygraph noted that the guilty knowledge test ". . . detected a slightly lower average percentage of the guilty subjects than the [more usual polygraph test]." It was found to have a relatively higher proportion of believing-a-lie mistakes, but a lower rate of disbelieving-the-truth mistakes.[8]

In any case, the guilty knowledge test has very limited use outside of criminal interrogations. All too often the person who thinks he may be the victim of a lie does not have the information the liar has, and without it the guilty knowledge test can't be used. In Updike's novel *Marry Me* Ruth knew that she was having an affair and who she was having it with. Her husband, Jerry, only had his suspicions, and because he did not have information that only the guilty person would have he could not use the guilty knowledge technique. To use that technique the lie catcher must know what has happened, but only be uncertain about who did it.

Even if the lie catcher knows all of the alternatives, the guilty knowledge test can't be used to find out which one happened. The guilty knowledge test requires absolute certainty on the part of the lie catcher about a deed or event, the question being whether or not the suspect was the perpetrator. If the question is—what did this person do? how does this person feel?—if the lie catcher does not know what it is that the suspect did, the guilty knowledge test can't be used.

Precautions in Interpreting Behavioral Clues to Deceit

Evaluating behavioral clues to deceit is hazardous. The list below summarizes all the precautions for reducing those hazards that have been explained in this chapter. The lie catcher must always estimate the *likelihood* that a gesture or expression indicates lying or truthfulness; rarely is it absolutely certain. In those instances when it is—an emotion contradicting the lie leaking in a full, macro facial expression, or some part of the concealed information blurted out in words during a tirade—the suspect will realize that too and will confess.

1. Try to make explicit the basis of any hunches and intuitions about whether or not someone is lying. By becoming more aware of how *you* interpret behavioral clues to deceit, you will learn to spot your mistakes and recognize when you don't have much chance to make a correct judgment.

2. Remember that there are two dangers in detecting deceit: disbelieving-the-truth (judging a truthful person to

be lying) and believing-a-lie (judging a liar to be truthful). There is no way to completely avoid both mistakes. Consider the consequences of risking either mistake.

3. The absence of a sign of deceit is not evidence of truth; some people don't leak. The presence of a sign of deceit is not always evidence of lying; some people appear ill-at-ease or guilty even when they are truthful. You can decrease the Brokaw hazard, which is due to individual differences in expressive behavior, by basing your judgments on a *change* in the suspect's behavior.

4. Search your mind for any preconceptions you may have about the suspect. Consider whether your preconceptions will bias your chance of making a correct judgment. Don't try to judge whether or not someone is lying if you feel overcome by jealousy or in an emotional wildfire. Avoid the temptation to suspect lying because it explains otherwise inexplicable events.

5. Always consider the possibility that a sign of emotion is not a clue to deceit but a clue to how a truthful person feels about being suspected of lying. Discount the sign of an emotion as a clue to deceit if a truthful suspect might feel that emotion because of: the suspect's personality; the nature of your past relationship with the suspect; or the suspect's expectations.

6. Bear in mind that many clues to deceit are signs of more than one emotion, and that those that are must be discounted if one of those emotions could be felt if the suspect is truthful while another could be felt if the suspect is lying.

7. Consider whether or not the suspect knows he is under suspicion, and what the gains or losses in detecting deceit would be either way.

8. If you have knowledge that the suspect would also

have only if he is lying, and you can afford to interrogate the suspect, construct a Guilty Knowledge Test.

9. Never reach a final conclusion about whether a suspect is lying or not based solely on your interpretation of behavioral clues to deceit. Behavioral clues to deceit should only serve to alert you to the need for further information and investigation. Behavioral clues, like the polygraph, can never provide asbsolute evidence.

10. Use the checklist provided in the appendix (table 4) to evaluate the lie, the liar, and you, the lie catcher, to estimate the likelihood of making errors or correctly judging truthfulness.

Trying to spot lies by using the polygraph lie detector also is hazardous. Although my focus is upon behavioral clues to deceit, not the polygraph, and upon a wide range of situations in which people may lie or suspect lying, not the narrow confines of a polygraph exam, in the next chapter I discusses the polygraph. In a number of important situations—counterintelligence, crimes, and increasingly in business—the polygraph is used. My analysis of lying, in this and the previous chapters, can, I believe, help one understand better the strengths and weaknesses of polygraph lie detection. Also, consideration of the problems in establishing the accuracy of the polygraph will further help the lie catcher understand the hazards of detecting deceit from behavioral clues. And, there is an interesting— and practical—question to be addressed: Which is more accurate in detecting lies, the polygraph or behavioral clues to deceit?

SEVEN

The Polygraph as
Lie Catcher

A police officer from another California city made application to our department. He appeared to be the epitome of what a police officer should look like, he knew the codes, and since he had previous police experience he seemed to be the ideal candidate. He made no admissions during his polygraph pretest interview. Only after the polygraph indicated lying would he admit committing over 12 burglaries while on duty and using his police car to haul away the stolen goods, planting stolen narcotics on innocent suspects in order to make arrests, and that several times he had sexual intercourse in his police car with girls as young as 16 years.

—*Reply by Detective Sergeant W. C. Meek, Polygraphist, Salinas, California, Police Department to a survey on how police departments use the polygraph.*[1]

Fay was arrested in Toledo in 1978 and charged with the robbery-murder of an acquaintance who, before dying, had stated that the masked robber "looked like Buzz [Fay]." Fay was held without bond for two months while the police searched, in vain, for evidence tying him to the murder. Finally, the prosecutor offered to drop the charges if Fay passed a polygraph test, but required Fay to stipulate to the admissability of the results in court if the test indicated deception. Fay agreed, failed the test, failed a second test by a different examiner, was tried and convicted of aggravated murder and sentenced to life imprisonment. After more than two years, the real killers were caught; they confessed, exonerating Fay who who was then promptly released.

—*Case described by psychologist David Lykken in an article in which he calls the polygraph exam a "pseudo-scientific technique."*[2]

Examples like this, pro and con, feed the controversy about the polygraph, but there is very little scientific evidence about its accuracy. Of more than 4,000 published articles or books, less than 400 actually involve research, and of these no more than thirty to forty meet minimum scientific standards.[3] Not settled by the research studies, the argument about the polygraph is sharp and heated. Most advocates come from law enforcement, intelligence agencies, businesses concerned with pilferage and embezzlement, and some of the scientists who have done research. Critics include civil libertarians, some jurists and attorneys, and other scientists who have studied the polygraph.*

My goal in this chapter is to make the argument more understandable, not to settle it. I make no policy recommendations about whether or how the polygraph should be used. Instead I seek to clarify the nature of the argument for those who must make those judgments, making the choices clear, and the limits of the scientific evidence known. But I address not just government officials, policemen, judges, or attorneys. Everyone today should understand the argument about the polygraph, for when it is to be used and what is to be done with the results of the test are important public policy issues. It will not be wisely resolved without a better-informed public. There may also be personal reasons why everyone would want to be better informed. In many lines of work, in jobs unrelated to the government, requiring high and low levels of education and training, people who have never been suspected of

*Only a handful of scientists have done research on polygraph lie detection.

committing a crime are asked to take a polygraph test as part of a job application, to continue their employment, or to obtain advancement.

Many of my ideas about behavioral clues to deceit, explained in the first six chapters, apply with equal force to detecting deceit with a polygraph. Liars may be betrayed in a polygraph exam because of their detection apprehension, deception guilt, or duping delight. Lie catchers must be wary of the Othello error and the Brokaw hazard, errors due to individual differences in emotional behavior. Polygraph operators must contend with risking both believing-a-lie and disbelieving-the-truth mistakes. Most of the precautions and hazards in lie catching are the same no matter whether the lie is detected by polygraph or behavioral clues. But there are new, complicated concepts that need to be learned:

- the difference between *accuracy* and *utility*—how the polygraph might be useful even if it isn't accurate;
- the quest for *ground truth*—how hard it is to determine the accuracy of the polygraph without being absolutely certain who the liars are;
- *the base rate of lying*—how a very accurate test can produce many mistakes when the group of suspects includes very few liars;
- *deterring lying*—how the threat of being examined might inhibit some from lying, even if the examination procedure is faulty.

Who Uses the Polygraph Exam

Use of the polygraph to detect some form of lying is widespread and growing. It is hard to be certain just how many polygraph tests are given in the United States; the best guess is over one million a year.[4] The majority—about 300,000 a year—are given by private employers. These tests are given as part of preemployment screening, to control internal crime, and as part of procedures used in recommending promotions. Preemployment screening is "heavily relied upon by members of the National Association of Drug Stores and the National Association of Convenience Stores, by Brinks Inc. . . ." and Associated Grocers.[5] Although it is illegal in eighteen states, to ask employees to take the polygraph test, employers reportedly can find ways around those laws. "Employers may tell the employee that they suspect them of theft, but that if the employee can find a way to demonstrate innocence, the employer will not discharge the employee."[6] In 31 states, employees can be asked to take a polygraph test. The private employers who make most use of the polygraph are banks and retail operations. About half of the 4,700 McDonald's fast food outlets, for example, give a polygraph test for preemployment screening.[7]

After business, the next most frequent use of the polygraph test is as part of criminal investigations. It is not only used on criminal suspects but sometimes also with witnesses or victims whose reports are doubted. The Justice Department, FBI, and most police departments follow the policy of using the polygraph only after investigations have narrowed down the list of suspects. Most states do not allow the results of the polygraph to be reported in a trial. Twenty-two states do allow the polygraph test as evidence if it has been stipulated in advance of the test and agreed to by both prosecution and defense. Defense attorneys usually make such an agreement in return for the prosecutor's agreement to drop the case if the polygraph shows the suspect was truthful. That was what happened in the Buzz Fay case described at the opening of this chapter. Usually, as in his case, prosecutors don't make such an offer if they have strong evidence that they think would convince a jury of a suspect's guilt.

In New Mexico and Massachusetts, polygraph test results can be introduced over the objection of one of the parties. The results cannot be admitted unless stipulated in advance in most, but not all, Federal Judicial Circuit Courts of Appeal. No United States Circuit Court of Appeals has reversed a district court for denying the admission of polygraph evidence. According to Richard K. Willard, Deputy Assistant United States Attorney General, "There has never been a Supreme Court ruling on the admissibility of polygraph evidence in federal court."[8]

The federal government is the third largest user of the polygraph test to detect lying. In 1982 22,597 tests were reported by various federal agencies.* Most were given to investigate a crime, except for the polygraph tests given by the National Security Agency (NSA) and the Central Intelligence Agency (CIA). These agencies use the polygraph for intelligence and counterintelligence investigations. This includes testing people who have a security clearance but are suspected of engaging in activity that would jeopardize that clearance, testing people suspected of espionage, and testing people seeking a security clearance. The NSA reports giving 9,672 polygraph tests in 1982, the majority for preemployment screening. The CIA does not report how often it gives the polygraph but acknowledges using the polygraph in many of the same situations as NSA.

In 1982 the Department of Defense proposed several revisions to its regulations on polygraph testing. These revisions could have meant greater use of polygraph testing for preclearance screening and for aperiodic screening of employees with security clearances. Another major change

---

*The polygraph is currently used by: U.S. Army Criminal Investigation Command; U.S. Army Intelligence and Security Command; Naval Investigative Service; Air Force Office of Special Investigations; U.S. Marine Corps Criminal Investigation Division; National Security Agency; Secret Service; FBI; Postal Inspection Service; Alcohol, Tobacco and Firearms Administration; Drug Enforcement Administration; CIA; U. S. Marshalls; Customs Service; and the Department of Labor.

proposed by the Department of Defense would have meant that employees or applicants who refused to take a polygraph examination would possibly have been subject to "adverse consequences." In 1983 President Reagan proposed further broadening the use of the polygraph test. *All* executive departments were authorized to "require employees to take a polygraph examination in the course of investigations of unauthorized disclosures of classified information. . . . [As in the changes proposed by the Department of Defense, refusal] to take a polygraph test may result in . . . administrative sanctions and denial of security clearance. . . . [Another new government policy] would also permit government-wide polygraph use in personnel security screening of employees (and applicants for positions) with access to highly classified information. The new policy provides agency heads with the authority to give polygraph examinations on a periodic or aperiodic basis to randomly selected employees with highly sensitive access, and to deny such access to employees who refuse to take a polygraph examination."[9] Congress responded to the Department of Defense proposal by legislation postponing implementation of these policies until April 1984 and requested the Office of Technology Assessment (OTA) to prepare a report on the scientific evidence about the accuracy of the polygraph.[10] That report was published in November 1983, and as I write these words, the White House has revised its proposal about the use of the polygraph and Congress will begin hearings on it in a week.

The OTA report is an extraordinary document, providing a thorough, impartial review and critical analysis of the evidence on the scientific validity of polygraph testing.* It

*I have drawn very heavily from the OTA report in preparing this chapter. I am grateful to the four people who read a draft of this chapter and made many useful and critical suggestions: Leonard Saxe (assistant professor of psychology at Boston University) and Denise Dougherty (analyst, OTA), author and co-author,

was not an easy matter, for the issues are complex, and the passions about the legitimacy of the polygraph, even within the scientific community, are strongly felt. Importantly, the advisory panel that oversaw the report included the leading protagonists within the scientific community. Not everyone who knew them thought they would be able to agree that any report would be fair, but they did. The quibbles are minor, though of course there is some dissatisfaction.

Some professional polygraphers outside the scientific community believe that the OTA report is too negative about the accuracy of the polygraph test. So, too, would the Department of Defense polygraphers. A 1983 National Security Agency report, "The Accuracy and Utility of the Polygraph Testing," was authored by the Chiefs of the Polygraph Divisions from army, navy, air force, and NSA.[11] Their report, which they acknowledge was prepared in thirty days, did not utilize advice or review from the scientific community, with the exception of one polygraph advocate. The NSA and OTA reports agree about one use of polygraph testing—although OTA is more cautious than NSA, both agree there is some evidence that polygraph exams do better than chance in detecting lies when used in investigating specific criminal incidents. Later I will explain their disagreement about the strength of that evidence, and the conflict between OTA and NSA about the use of polygraph exams in security clearances and counterintelligence.

The OTA report does not provide a single, or simple, conclusion that can easily be translated into legislation. As we might expect, the accuracy of the polygraph (or any

---

respectively, of the OTA report; and David T. Lykken (University of Minnesota) and David C. Raskin (University of Utah). Denise Dougherty also generously and patiently answered my many questions as I weaved my way through the conflicting arguments and issues.

other technique of detecting lies) depends upon the nature of the lie, the liar, and the lie catcher (although the OTA report does not use these terms). With the polygraph lie detector, it depends also upon the particular questioning technique, the examiner's skill in designing the questions to be asked, and how the polygraph charts are scored.

How the Polygraph Works

Webster's Dictionary says the term *polygraph* means "an instrument for recording tracings of several different pulsations simultaneously; *broadly:* LIE DETECTOR." The pulsations are recorded by the deflections of pens on a moving paper chart. Usually the term polygraph refers to the measurement of changes in autonomic nervous system activity, although polygraph pens could measure any kind of activity. In chapter 4 I explained that autonomic nervous system activities—changes in heart rate, blood pressure, skin conductivity, skin temperature, and so on—are signs of emotional arousal. I mentioned that a few of these changes, such as increases in respiration, sweating, or facial flushing and blanching, can be observed without the polygraph. The polygraph records these changes more accurately, detecting smaller changes than can be seen, and recording autonomic nervous system activities, such as heart rate, which are never visible. It does so by amplifying signals picked up from sensors that are attached to different parts of the body. In the typical use of the polygraph to detect lies, four sensors are put on the subject. Pneumatic tubes or straps are stretched around the person's chest and stomach, measuring changes in the depth and rate of breathing. A blood pressure cuff placed around the bicep measures cardiac activity. The fourth sensor measures minute changes in perspiration picked up by metal electrodes attached to the fingers.

Webster's Dictionary is correct that the polygraph is sometimes called the lie detector, but that is misleading. The polygraph doesn't detect lies per se. It would be a lot simpler if there were some direct sign unique to lying that is never a sign of anything else. But there isn't. Although there is controversy about almost everything else about the polygraph, all those who use the polygraph agree that it does *not* directly measure lying. All that the polygraph measures is autonomic nervous system signs of arousal—physiological changes generated primarily because a person is emotionally aroused.* It is the same with the behavioral clues to deceit. Remember I earlier explained that no facial expression, gesture, or voice change is a sign of lying per se. These behaviors only signal emotional arousal or difficulty in thinking. Lying can be inferred from them because the emotion doesn't fit the line being taken or the person appears to be making up his line. The polygraph provides less precise information than behavioral clues about which emotion is aroused. A micro facial expression can reveal that someone is angry, afraid, guilty, and so on. The polygraph can only tell that *some* emotion has been aroused, not which one.

To detect lying, the polygraph examiner compares the activity recorded on the chart when the suspect is asked the crucial question, the one relevant to why the exam is being given—"Did you steal the $750?"—with the suspect's response to some other question not dealing with the matter at hand—"Is today Tuesday?" "Have you ever stolen anything in your life?" A suspect is identified as guilty if she shows more activity on the polygraph to the relevant question than to the other questions.

---

*Certain kinds of information processing—concentrating, seeking input, perhaps also perplexity—also can produce changes in autonomic nervous system activity. Although most accounts of why the polygraph detects lying have emphasized the role of emotional arousal, both Raskin and Lykken believe that information processing is at least as important in producing autonomic nervous system activity during a polygraph exam.

The polygraph exam, like behavioral clues to deceit, is vulnerable to what I termed the Othello error. Remember Othello failed to recognize that Desdemona's fear might not be a guilty adulterer's anguish about being caught but could be a faithful wife's fear of a husband who would not believe her. Innocents, not just liars, may become emotionally aroused when they know they are suspected of lying. Suspected of a crime, questioned about an activity that could jeopardize a security clearance necessary for employment, under suspicion for having leaked a classified document to the press, an innocent person may become emotionally aroused. Just being asked to take the polygraph test may be sufficient to arouse fear in some people. This might be especially strong if a suspect has reason to think that the polygraph operator and the police are prejudiced against him. Fear is not the only emotion a liar may feel about lying. As I explained in chapter 3, a liar may feel deception guilt or duping delight. Any of these emotions produces the autonomic nervous system activity measured by the polygraph. Any of these feelings might be felt not just by a liar but also by some innocent persons. Which emotions a suspect will feel depends upon the personality of the suspect, the past relationship between suspect and lie catcher, and the suspect's expectations, as I discussed earlier in chapter 6.

The Control Question Technique

All those using the polygraph, and those criticizing its use, recognize the need to reduce Othello errors. They disagree about how well the polygraph procedures for asking questions can reduce or eliminate it. There are four questioning procedures used with the polygraph, and more if some of the variations on these four are considered. We need consider only two now. The first of these, the Control Question Technique, is used most often when investigating criminal suspects. The suspect is not only asked questions *relevant* to the crime ("Did you steal the $750?") but also *control* questions. Much of the controversy about this technique stems from disagreements about just what this question *controls* for and how well it succeeds.

I will quote the psychologist David Raskin's explanation of it, for he is the leading scientist supporting the use of the Control Question Technique in criminal investigations. "The examiner might say to the subject, 'Because this is a matter of theft, I need to ask you some general questions about yourself with regard to stealing and your basic honesty. We need to do that in order to establish what type of a person you are with regard to stealing and determine whether or not you are the type of person who might have stolen that money and later lied about it. Therefore, if I ask you, "During the first 18 years of your life, did you ever take something that didn't belong to you", how would you answer that question?" The manner in which the question is posed to the subject and the behavior of the examiner are both designed to make the subject feel defensive and embarrass him into answering 'No'. . . . That procedure [Raskin writes] is designed to create the possibility that an innocent subject will experience greater concern with regard to the truthfulness of his answers to the control questions than to the relevant questions. However, a guilty subject would still be more concerned about his deceptive answers to the relevant questions because those questions represent the most immediate and serious threat to him. However, the innocent subject knows that he is answering truthfully to the relevant questions, and he becomes more concerned about deceptiveness or uncertainty of his truthfulness in regard to his answers to the control questions."[12]

David Lykken—the psychologist who favors the Guilty Knowledge Test, which I described at the end of the last chapter—is the principal critic of the Control Question Test. (Raskin criticizes the Guilty Knowledge Test.) In his recent book on the use of the polygraph, Lykken wrote: "For the Control Question Technique to work as advertised, each subject must be made to believe that the test is nearly infallible (not true) and that giving strong control responses will jeopardize him (the opposite is true). It is implausible to suppose that all polygraphers will be able to convince all subjects of these two false propositions."[13]

Lykken is correct that these propositions that the suspect must believe are both false. No one who uses the polygraph believes it is infallible, not even its most uncritical advocate. It does make mistakes. Yet Lykken is probably right to point out that the suspect must not know this.* If an innocent suspect knows the polygraph is fallible, he may be fearful throughout the exam, afraid of being misjudged by a faulty technique. Such a distrusting, fearful suspect might show no difference in response to the control and the relevant questions, and if he is emotionally aroused in response to every question the polygraph operator can not make a judgment about whether he is guilty or innocent. Even worse, an innocent suspect who believes the polygraph is fallible might show more fear when the crime-relevant questions are mentioned, and thereby score as guilty.†

The second proposition—that strong control responses will put him in jeopardy—is also false, and again all polygraph operators know this. Exactly the opposite is true— if the suspect shows more response to the control question

---

*Although Lykken's logic on this point seems plausible and is consistent with my own reasoning, Raskin points out that the evidence on this is not firm. In two studies, in which mistakes on a pretest were purposefully made so the suspect would know the polygraph exam was fallible, there was no noticeable decrease in the subsequent detection of lying. However, the adequacy of the studies cited by Raskin has been questioned. This is one of the many issues requiring more research.

†Raskin claims that a skilled polygrapher should be able to conceal from the suspect which question is more important to his fate—control or relevant. It does not seem plausible to me, and to others who criticize the Control Question Technique, that this will always succeed, particularly with bright suspects.

("Before you were eighteen, did you ever take anything that didn't belong to you?") than to the relevant one ("Did you steal the $750?"), he is *out* of jeopardy, judged to be not lying, innocent of the crime. It is the thief, not the innocent person, who is supposed to be more aroused by the $750, crime-relevant question.

For the polygraph exam to work, the control question must emotionally arouse the innocent person—arouse him at least as much as, if not more than, the crime-relevant question. The hope is to make the innocent suspect more concerned about the control question than the crime-relevant question, and to accomplish this by making him believe that his answer to the control question does matter, will influence how he is judged. For example, the polygraph examiner assumes that nearly everyone has, before the age of eighteen, taken something that didn't belong to him. Ordinarily, some people might admit such an early misdeed. But during the polygraph exam the innocent suspect doesn't because the examiner led him to think that admitting such a wrongdoing would show that he is the kind of person who would steal the $750. The polygraph examiner *wants* the innocent person to lie on the control question, denying that he has ever taken anything that didn't belong to him. The examiner expects the innocent suspect will be emotionally upset about lying, and that that will register on the polygraph chart. When the innocent suspect is asked the crime-relevant question—"Did you steal the $750?"—he truthfully will say no. Because he is not lying, he won't be emotionally upset, or at least not as upset as he was when he lied to the control question, and there won't be much activity on the polygraph chart. The thief will also say no when asked if he stole the $750, but he will be much more emotionally aroused by this crime-relevant lie than by his lie to the control question. The logic then is that the innocent's polygraph chart will show more emotional arousal for the "Did you ever take anything" than for the "Did you steal the $750" question. Only the guilty will show more emotional arousal to the $750 question.

The Control Question Technique eliminates the Othello error *only* if the innocent suspect is thus more emotionally aroused by the control question than the question relevant to the crime. Otherwise a disbelieving-the-truth mistake occurs. Let's consider what may produce such a mistake. What might lead an innocent suspect to be more emotionally aroused with the relevant question ("Did you steal the $750?") than the control question ("Before you were eighteen, did you take anything that didn't belong to you?")* Two requirements must be met, one intellectual and the other emotional. Intellectually, the suspect must have recognized that the two questions differ, despite the polygrapher's attempts to obscure that fact. The innocent suspect might note only that the question about the $750 is about a more recent and *specific* event. Or, the innocent suspect might figure out that the relevant question is more *threatening* to him. It is about something that could bring about a punishment, while the control questions deal with matters in the past no longer subject to punishment.†

The polygraph might still work *if* the innocent suspect shows no greater emotional responses when asked the more specific, threatening, crime-relevant question. Let us consider a few of the reasons why *some* innocent suspects may do the reverse and be judged guilty because they are more emotional in response to the relevant than to the control questions:

1. *The police are fallible:* Not everyone who could have

*In practice, many relevant and control questions are asked; but that would not change the substance of my analysis.
†A defender of the Control Question Technique would say that the skilled polygrapher can make the suspect feel so badly about the past, so convinced that his past error will affect the evaluation of him, and so worried that he will be caught in his lie of not admitting it that his response to the control question will be more pronounced than his response to the relevant question.

committed a specific crime is given a polygraph test. The innocent suspect asked to take the polygraph test knows the police have made a mistake, a serious one, one that may have already damaged her reputation, in suspecting her. She has already given her explanation of why she did not commit the crime, why she could not or would not do so. Obviously they don't trust her even though they should. While she could view the test as a welcome opportunity to prove her innocence, she also could fear that those who made the mistake of suspecting her will make more mistakes. If police methods are fallible enough to make them suspect her, their polygraph test may also be fallible.

2. *The police are unfair:* A person may dislike and distrust law enforcement personnel, prior to becoming a suspect in a crime. If the innocent suspect is a member of a minority group, or a subculture that scorns or distrusts the police, then the suspect is likely to expect and fear that the polygraph examiner will misjudge them.

3. *Machines are fallible:* Someone may, of course, think it perfectly reasonable that the police are investigating her for a crime she did not commit. Even such a person may distrust the polygraph. It may be based on a distrust of technology in general, or the person may have seen one of the many articles, magazines, or TV accounts criticizing the polygraph.

4. *The suspect is a fearful, guilty, or hostile person:* Someone who is generally fearful or guilty might respond more to the more specific, recent, and threatening questions, and so might someone who is generally hostile, especially if the person tends to be angry toward authority. Any of these emotions will register on the polygraph.

5. *The suspect, even though innocent, has an emotional reaction to the events involved in the crime:* It is not just the guilty who may have more emotional reaction to the crime-relevant question than to the control question. Suppose an innocent

person, suspected of murdering his co-worker, had been envious of the co-worker's greater advancement. Now that his competitor is dead, the suspect might feel remorse about having been envious, some delight in having "won" the competition, guilt about feeling the delight, and so forth. Or, suppose the innocent suspect was very upset when he found his co-worker's bloody, mutilated body. When asked about the murder, the memory of that scene reawakens those feelings, but he is too macho to admit it. The suspect might not be aware of all of these feelings. The suspect would be found to be lying on the polygraph test, and indeed he would be, but it was uncivilized feelings, or being macho, that he concealed, not murder. In the next chapter I will discuss such a case, in which an innocent suspect failed the polygraph test and was convicted of murder.

Supporters of the use of the Control Question Technique in investigating criminal incidents acknowledge some of these sources of error but claim they rarely happen. Critics have argued that a large percentage of innocent suspects—the harshest critics claim 50 percent of the innocent—show more emotional response to the relevant question than to the control question. When that happens the polygraph fails; it is an Othello error, and a truthful person is not believed.

The Guilty Knowledge Test

The Guilty Knowledge Test, described in the last chapter, purportedly reduces the chances of making such disbelieving-the-truth mistakes. To use this questioning technique, the lie catcher must have information about the crime that only the guilty person has. Suppose no one but the employer, the thief, and the polygraph examiner know exactly how much money was stolen, and that it was all in

$50 bills. A guilty knowledge test would ask the suspect: "If you stole the money from the cash register, you will know how much was taken. Was it: $150? $350? $550? $750? $950?" And: "The money stolen was all in bills of the same denomination. If you took the money, you will know what size the bills were. Were they: $5 bills? $10 bills? $20 bills? $50 bills? $100 bills?"

"An innocent person would have only one chance in five of reacting most strongly to the correct item on one question, only one chance in twenty-five of reacting most strongly to the correct item on two questions, and only one chance in ten million of reacting most strongly to the correct question if ten such questions about the crime were constructed."[14] "[T]he important psychological difference between the guilty suspect and one who is innocent is that one was present at the scene of the crime; he knows what happened there; his mind contains images that are not available to an innocent person. . . . Because of this knowledge, the guilty suspect will recognize people, objects, and events associated with the crime. . . . his recognition will stimulate and arouse him. . . ."[15]

One limitation of the Guilty Knowledge Test is that it can't always be used, even in criminal investigations. Information about the crime may have been so widely publicized that the innocent as well as the guilty know all the facts. Even if the newspapers do not disclose the information, the police often do in the process of interrogating suspects. Some crimes do not lend themselves as readily to using the Guilty Knowledge Test. It would be difficult, for example, in evaluating whether a person who admitted a murder was lying in his claim that it was in self-defense. And, sometimes an innocent suspect may be present at the scene of the crime and know as much as the police do about all of the particulars.

Raskin, the defender of the Control Question Technique, claims that the Guilty Knowledge Test produces more believing-a-lie mistakes. ". . . the perpetrator of the crime must be assumed to have knowledge of the details which are covered by the questions asked. If the perpetrator did not pay adequate attention to those details, did not have an adequate opportunity to observe the details, or was intoxicated at the time of the event, a concealed information test would not be appropriate on that subject."[16]

The Guilty Knowledge Test also will not be useful if the suspect happens to be one of those people who does not show much of a response on those autonomic nervous system activities measured by the polygraph. As I discussed in the last chapter in regard to behavioral clues to deceit, there are large individual differences in emotional behavior. There are *no* signs of emotional arousal that are completely reliable, no clues that are shown by everybody. No matter what is examined—facial expression, gesture, voice, heart rate, respiration—it won't be sensitive for some people. Earlier I emphasized that the absence of a slip of a tongue, or an emblematic slip, does not prove a suspect is truthful. Similarly, the absence of autonomic nervous system activity as typically measured by the polygraph does not—for everybody—prove that the person is unaroused. With the Guilty Knowledge Test people who do not show much autonomic nervous system activity when emotional will test out as inconclusive. Lykken says that that happens very rarely; but there has been too little research to know how often it might occur among people suspected of crimes, of being spies, and so on. People who do not show much autonomic nervous system activity also will yield inconclusive results on the Control Question Test, since there won't be any difference in their responses to the control and the relevant questions.

Drugs may suppress autonomic nervous system activity and thereby yield inconclusive results on the polygraph, whether Guilty Knowledge or Control Question tests are given. I will discuss this and the question of whether psychopaths can evade either type of polygraph exam later when summarizing the evidence to date.

The OTA report, which critically reviewed all of the evidence, found that both questioning techniques are vulnerable to the errors their critics claim. The Guilty Knowledge Test usually produces more believing-a-lie mistakes, while the Control Question Test produces more disbelieving-the-truth mistakes. Even that conclusion, however, is disputed by some polygraph operators and researchers. Ambiguities continue to exist in part because there have been few studies,* in part because it is so difficult to do research evaluating the accuracy of the polygraph. Faults can be found with almost any study done so far. A crucial problem is establishing what is called *ground truth,* some way of knowing, independently of the polygraph, whether someone was truthful or lying. Unless the investigator knows ground truth—who lied and who was truthful— there is no way to evaluate the polygraph's accuracy.

Studying the Polygraph's Accuracy

The research approaches to studying the accuracy of the polygraph differ in how certain they can be about ground truth. *Field* studies examine actual, real-life incidents. In *analog* studies, some situation, usually an experiment, arranged by the investigator is examined. Field and analog studies mirror each others' strengths and weaknesses. In field studies the suspects really do care about the

---

*While there have been thousands of articles written about the polygraph, few involved any research. OTA screened 3,200 articles or books, of which only about 320 involved research. Most of those did not meet minimal scientific standards. In OTA's judgment there have been only about 30 bona fide scientific studies of the polygraph's accuracy in detecting lies.

polygraph test outcome, and therefore strong emotions are likely. Another strength is that the right kinds of people are studied—real suspects, not college freshmen. The weakness of field studies is the ambiguity about ground truth. Certainty about ground truth is the chief strength of analog studies; it is easy to know, since the researcher arranges who will lie and who will be truthful. Their weakness is that because the "suspects" usually have little or nothing at stake, the same emotions are not likely to be aroused. Also, the people tested may not resemble the kinds of people who most often actually take the polygraph test.

Field Studies

Let's consider first why it is so difficult to establish a criterion of ground truth in field studies. People actually suspected of crimes are given a polygraph test not for research purposes but as part of the investigation of a crime. Information subsequently becomes available about whether they confessed or were found guilty or innocent, or charges were dismissed. It would seem that with all of that information it would be easy to establish ground truth, but it isn't. I quote from the OTA report:

Cases may be dismissed for lack of sufficient evidence rather than innocence. If a jury acquits a defendant, it is not possible to determine the extent to which the jury felt that the defendant was actually innocent or whether they felt that there was not enough evidence to meet the standard of 'guilty beyond a reasonable doubt.' Many guilty pleas are actually confessions of guilty to (lesser) crimes; as Raskin notes, it is difficult to interpret the meaning of such pleadings in regard to guilt on the original charge. The result is that, using the criminal justice system outcomes, polygraph examinations may appear to have a high number of [disbelieving-the-truth mistakes] in the case of acquittals, or [believing-a-lie mistakes] in the case of dismissals.[17]

Although it might seem that these problems could be solved by having a panel of experts review all the evidence and come to a decision about guilt or innocence, that has two fundamental difficulties. The experts don't always agree, and when they do there is no way to be certain when they are wrong. Even confessions are not always problem-free. Some innocent people confess, and even when valid, confessions provide ground truth only about a small, and perhaps highly unusual, proportion of those who take the polygraph. Almost all field studies suffer from the problem that the population of cases from which the cases were selected is not identified.

Analog Studies

The problems are no easier with analog studies, just different. There is certainty about ground truth—the researcher tells some people to commit a "crime" and others not to. The uncertainty is whether a mock crime will ever be taken as seriously as a real one. Researchers have developed mock crimes that will involve the subjects, trying to motivate them by a reward if they are not caught when they then take a polygraph test. Occasionally, subjects are threatened with punishment if their lie is detected, but for ethical reasons these punishments are minor (e.g., loss of course credit for participating in the experiment). Almost all of those using the Control Question Technique have used a version of the mock crime used by Raskin:

Half of the subjects received a recording which simply told them that a ring had been stolen from an office somewhere in the building and that they would be given a lie detector test to establish whether or not they were being truthful when they denied participation in that theft. They were told that if they appeared truthful on the test, they would receive a substantial monetary bonus. The other half of the subjects were given instructions on the crime which they were to commit. . . . They went to a room on a different floor, lured the secretary out of the office, entered her office after she left, searched her desk for a cashbox which contained a ring, concealed the ring on their person, and then returned to the laboratory for the polygraph test. They were warned not to disclose to anyone the fact that they were participating in an experiment and to have an alibi ready in case someone surprised them in the secretary's office. They were also warned not to disclose any details of the crime to the polygraph examiner because he would then know they were guilty of the crime and they would not earn the money which they would normally be paid, nor would they be eligible for the bonus ($10).[18]

While this is an impressive attempt to resemble a real crime, the question is whether emotions about lying are aroused. Since the polygraph measures emotional arousal, a mock crime can tell us how accurate the polygraph is only if the same emotions, at the same strength, are aroused as they would be for real crimes. In chapter 3 I explained three emotions that can become aroused when someone lies, and for each of these emotions I explained what will determine how strongly the emotion is felt. Let us consider whether those emotions are likely to be felt in a mock crime committed to study the accuracy of the polygraph.

Detection apprehension: What is at stake is the most important determinant of how much a suspect fears being caught. I suggested in chapter 3 that the larger the reward for success and the greater the punishment for failure the more deception apprehension will be felt; and, that the severity of punishment is probably most important. The severity of the punishment will influence the truthful person's fear of being misjudged just as much as the lying person's fear of being spotted—both suffer the same consequence. In mock crimes the rewards are small, and there is no punishment; neither the truthful person nor the liar should feel detection apprehension. Perhaps the subjects may feel some worry about whether they are doing what they are being paid to do, but that almost certainly is a much weaker feeling than the fear that either an innocent or guilty person has when a real crime is investigated.

Deception guilt: Guilt is strongest when liar and target share values, which should be so in the mock crimes, but guilt is reduced if lying is authorized, required, and approved to perform one's job. In mock crimes the liar is told to do so, and by lying he is helping science. Liars should feel little deception guilt in mock crimes.

Duping delight: The excitement of the challenge, the pleasure in putting one over is felt more strongly if the liar has a reputation for being tough to fool. Fooling the polygraph should represent such a challenge, and that feeling should be particularly strong if there are no other emotions —fear or guilt—to dilute it.* Only the liar, not the truthful person, will feel duping delight.

The above analysis suggests that mock crimes will generate only one of the three emotions that may be felt when someone is suspected of a real crime—duping delight. Furthermore, that emotion will only be felt by the liar, not the truthful person. Since the liar is the only one likely to be aroused emotionally, detection should be easy, easier, I suggest, than it typically will be with real crimes when the truthful person is more vulnerable to having some of the same feelings as the liar. Research using mock crimes will,

---

*Before he knew of my analysis of the polygraph exam, Raskin told me that he believes it is the response to a challenge, more than detection apprehension or duping delight, that betrays the liar. While this does not prove my point, it strengthens my argument that the mock crimes may not be a good analog to the range of emotions felt when real crimes are committed and the stakes for both the innocent and guilty parties are high.

by this reasoning, overestimate the accuracy of the polygraph.

Hybrid Studies

There is one more research approach that tries to avoid the weaknesses of both the field and analog study by combining the best features of each. In such a *hybrid* study the researcher arranges matters so that a real crime can occur. There is no doubt about ground truth, just as in an analog study, and quite a lot is at stake for both the truthful and lying suspects, as it is in field studies. In a master's thesis by Netzer Daie, a member of the Scientific Interrogation Unit of the Israeli Police in Jerusalem, just such a hybrid study was done. The lie was ". . . authentic, and freely undertaken rather than simulated; . . . the subjects believe that the interrogator does not know who committed the act; the subjects . . . [were] genuinely concerned about the outcome of the polygraph test; . . . and the polygrapher [did] not know the proportion of guilty and innocent subjects in the sample."[19] The research subjects were twenty-one Israeli policemen who took paper and pencil tests "that were presented as required aptitude tests. Subjects were asked to score their own tests, which provided an opportunity to cheat, i.e., to revise their initial answers. The test answer sheets, however, were chemically treated so that cheating could be detected. Seven of the twenty-one subjects actually changed their initial answers. Later, subjects were told they were suspected of cheating, were offered an opportunity to take a polygraph examination, and were told their careers might depend on the outcome."[20]

It is realistic to allow the policemen to refuse to take the polygraph—in criminal investigations polygraph exams are an option, not absolutely required of a suspect. Three of the seven cheaters confessed, another cheater and two innocent suspects refused to take the polygraph, and a third cheater did not show up for the test.* In total, then, only fifteen of the original twenty-one policemen took the polygraph exam, two cheaters and thirteen noncheaters. The Control Question Technique was used, and both cheaters were accurately detected. Two of the thirteen truthful noncheaters were also judged, mistakenly, to be lying.

No conclusions can be reached from this study, because so few people were examined. But such hybrid studies might be very useful, although there are ethical problems in leading someone to cheat and lie. The Israeli investigators believe it is justifiable because a correct evaluation of the polygraph is so important: "Thousands of people are interrogated yearly by the polygraph . . . and important decisions are based on the results of such testing. Yet the validity of this tool is not known. . . ."[21] Perhaps it is more justifiable to impose in this fashion on the police, since they take on special risks as part of their job, and they are more specifically involved in the use or misuse of the polygraph. The strength of this hybrid experiment is that it is real. Some policemen do cheat on tests. "A hush-hush internal investigation by high-level FBI officials has determined that several hundred bureau employees were involved in widespread cheating on examinations for coveted special agent appointments".[22] The Israeli hybrid experiment wasn't a game. It was not simply a challenge to succeed in fooling the experimenter. Fear of being caught would be high, and for some at least, there would also be guilt about lying, for a reputation (if not a career) was at stake.

---

*These figures suggest what polygraph examiners claim, that the threat of taking a polygraph exam does produce confessions among the guilty. And, refusal to take the polygraph exam is no certain guarantee of guilt.

Research Findings

There have been ten field studies and fourteen analog studies using the Control Question Technique and six analog studies using the Guilty Knowledge Test that meet minimum scientific standards.* The chart below, based on these studies, shows that the polygraph does work. It catches liars more often than not, but it makes mistakes. How many mistakes—and what kind—depends upon whether the studies were field or analog, whether the Control or Guilty Knowledge test was used, and the particulars of each study. There are a few findings overall:

1. Accuracy is greater in the field than in the analog studies. A number of factors might be involved. In the field studies there is more emotional arousal, the suspects are less educated, there is less certainty about ground truth and often about the representativeness of the cases selected for the study.

2. Disbelieving-the-truth mistakes are high except in the Guilty Knowledge Analog Test. There is a great need for more research, especially field or hybrid studies, using the Guilty Knowledge Test.

3. Believing-a-lie mistakes are high, highest when the Guilty Knowledge Test is used.

---

*I have used OTA's judgment about which of the field and which of the Control Question Analog studies meet scientific standards. Lykken has told me that he believes OTA credited field studies that selectively sampled the records examined, and thus the estimates of the field study are inflated. OTA did not include any of the Guilty Knowledge Test results in its final summary. I included them so that the reader can compare them with the Control Question Test results. I included all of the studies in OTA's table 7, except for Timm's experiment, which had no innocent subjects. I utilized the first test data from the Balloun and Holmes study, and the EDR data from the Bradley and Janisse study. (H.W. Timm, "Analyzing Deception from Respiration Patterns," *Journal of Political Science and Administration* 10 (1982): 47–51; K. D. Balloun and D. S. Holmes, "Effects of Repeated Examinations on the Ability to Detect Guilt with a Polygraphic Examination: A Laboratory Experiment with a Real Crime," *Journal of Applied Psychology* 64 (1979): 316–22; and M. T. Bradley and M. P. Janisse, "Accuracy Demonstrations, Threat, and the Detection of Deception: Cardiovascular, Electrodermal, and Pupillary Measures," *Psychophysiology* 18 (1981): 307–14).

POLYGRAPH ACCURACY

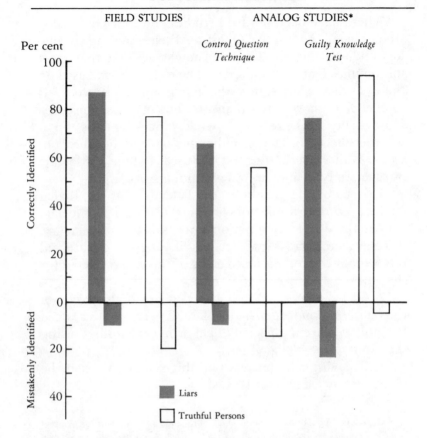

FIELD STUDIES   ANALOG STUDIES*

Per cent

Control Question Technique

Guilty Knowledge Test

Correctly Identified

Mistakenly Identified

Liars

Truthful Persons

*The graph gives the averages, which are not always an accurate reflection of the range of research results. The ranges are as follows: For liars correctly identified in field studies, 71–99%; in analog studies using the control question technique, 35–100%; in analog studies using the guilty knowledge tests, 61–95%. For truthful persons correctly identified: in field studies, 13–94%; in analog studies using the control question technique, 32–91%; in analog studies using the guilty knowledge test, 80–100%. For truthful persons incorrectly identified: in field studies, 0–75%; in analog studies using the control question technique, 2–51%; in analog studies using the guilty knowledge test, 0–12%. For liars incorrectly identified: in field studies, 0–29%; in analog studies using the control question technique, 0–29%; in analog studies using the guilty knowledge test, 5–39%.

Although Raskin believes that the figures in the chart underestimate polygraph accuracy, and Lykken believes that they overestimate it, neither disagrees with these three overall findings. Disagreements remain about a number of issues vital to how much confidence should be placed in polygraph test results. Are psychopaths better able to escape detection by the polygraph? The evidence is contradictory with the Control Question Technique. Lykken believes that psychopaths would be detected with the Guilty Knowledge Test. Lykken reasons that even if they show no fear of being caught or (what I call) duping delight, simply recognizing the correct response in the test items will produce autonomic changes. But no research has yet been done to evaluate whether Guilty Knowledge Test polygraph exams work with psychopaths. More research is needed, studying psychopaths, and also attempting to identify other kinds of people who are minimally responsive on polygraph exams.

Can countermeasures—deliberate attempts used by liars to avoid detection—succeed? Again, more research could resolve the contradictory findings. I believe it would be judicious to allow for the possibility that an unknown number of liars will succeed in avoiding detection through the use of countermeasures. I think this would be likely if there were opportunity to spend months training the liar in the use of countermeasures, making use of sophisticated technology. While no one knows whether spies are currently being so trained, it would be unwise, in my judgment, to presume they are not. There are rumors of a such a special training school in an Eastern bloc country that teaches agents how to beat the polygraph. This was supposedly revealed in the confession of a KGB agent who didn't learn his lessons well enough.

The concluding paragraph of the OTA report states that the research on the polygraph provides ". . . some evidence for the validity of polygraph testing as an adjunct to typical criminal investigations of specific incidents. . . ."[23] I believe it is possible to go a bit beyond that cautious conclusion and still preserve some semblance of a consensus among the chief protagonists.

More weight should be given to a test outcome that suggests the suspect is truthful than to one that suggests the suspect is lying. If the evidence is not otherwise compelling, investigators might well decide to dismiss charges against a suspect who tests truthful. Raskin and others make this suggestion specifically when the Control Question Test is used, since it yields few believing-a-lie mistakes. Lykken believes that the Control Question Test is of *no* use and that only the Guilty Knowledge Technique has promise for use in criminal investigation.

When a suspect's polygraph test suggests lying, this should not be regarded as an "adequate basis for conviction or even for proceeding with a prosecution. . . . a deceptive polygraph examination would simply be the cause for pursuing the investigation. . . ."[24] Lykken agrees with this quote from Raskin, but only when applied to the Guilty Knowledge (not the Control Question) Test.

In chapter 8 I will explain what I call *lie checking,* and in the appendix (table 4) I list thirty-eight questions that can be asked about any lie in order to estimate the chances that it can be detected from either the polygraph or behavioral clues. One of my illustrations of lie checking is a detailed account of a murder suspect's polygraph exam. That example provides another opportunity to reconsider the question of how the polygraph exam should be used in criminal investigation. Now let us consider other uses of the polygraph, about which much of the current controversy centers.

Polygraph Testing Job Applicants

The OTA report, Raskin, and Lykken all agree on this one—they are all against using the polygraph in pre-employment screening of job applicants. On the other side, favoring its use are many employers, professional polygraphers, and some government officials, particularly those in intelligence agencies. Although giving polygraph tests to job applicants is the most frequent use of the polygraph, there have been no scientific studies to determine how accurately the polygraph detects which job applicants are lying about matters that, if known, would cause them not to be hired. It is not hard to see why. Determining ground truth in field studies would not be easy. One measure of ground truth would come from a study in which all applicants were hired regardless of their polygraph test results, with on-the-job surveillance subsequently determining which ones stole or engaged in other injurious actions. Another approach to determining ground truth would be to investigate carefully the past job history of all job applicants to determine which had lied about their past. To do this thoroughly, so that there would be few errors, would be very costly. There have been only two analog studies done—one found high accuracy and the other did not; but there are too many discrepancies between the studies and difficulties within each study to draw any conclusions.*

The accuracy of the polygraph in preemployment screening can't be estimated by assuming that it would be the same as it was found to be in the studies of criminal incidents (see chart above). The people tested may be quite

---

*I have used OTA's judgment of these two studies.[25] Those who favor preemployment polygraph testing regard these as creditable and important studies. Even if the studies were accepted, I believe it is reasonable to say that there is still no scientific basis for drawing any conclusions about the accuracy of the polygraph in preemployment screening—more than two studies are needed on such an important and controversial matter.

different, and the examiners and the examination testing
techniques are also different. In preemployment screening
an applicant has to take the test in order to get the job,
while criminal suspects have the option to not take a test
without that refusal being used as evidence against them.
Raskin says that the preemployment polygraph examination ". . . is coercive and is likely to produce feelings of
resentment which could strongly interfere with the accuracy of a polygraph examination."[26] What is at stake is also
quite different. The punishment for being caught by the
polygraph should be much less in preemployment screening than in criminal applications. Because the stakes are
lower, liars should feel less detection apprehension and be
harder to catch. Innocents, however, who most want the
job, may fear being misjudged and because of that fear be
misjudged.

The counterargument made by those advocating this
use of the polygraph is that it works. Many applicants make
damaging admissions after taking the polygraph test, admitting to things they had not acknowledged before taking
the polygraph test. This is a *utility* argument. It does not
matter whether the polygraph accurately catches liars if
those who shouldn't be hired are identified by taking the
test. That makes it useful. Lykken argues that such utility
claims may not themselves be valid.[27] The reports of damaging admissions may overstate the number that actually
occur, and some of the damaging admissions may be false
confessions made under pressure. Furthermore, those who
have done things that would cause them not to be employed
may not be sufficiently intimidated by the polygraph test
to confess. Without accuracy studies there is no way to
know how many people who fail the polygraph test would
actually be faithful employees nor how many who pass it
are going to steal from their employers.

Gordon Barland, a psychologist trained by Raskin, who

does preemployment polygraph screening, makes another, quite different argument for its use. Barland studied 400 applicants for jobs such as truck driver, cashier, warehouseman, and so on who were sent by the employers to a private polygraph testing firm. Half of the 155 applicants who scored as lying admitted it when they were told the polygraph results. Barland found that employers went ahead and hired 58 percent of these people who admitted lying. "Many employers use polygraph examinations not so much to decide whether to hire an applicant, as much as in deciding what position to put him in. For example, if an applicant is found to be an alcoholic, he may be hired as a dock worker rather than a driver."[28]

Barland rightly points out we should be especially interested in the fate of the 78 people who tested as liars but denied it, for these may be the victims of disbelieving-the-truth mistakes. Barland says we should be reassured that 66 percent of them were hired anyhow. But there is no way to know if they were hired into jobs as desirable as they would have obtained if not for the polygraph results. Most of those not hired who had denied lying despite the polygraph results that suggested they had were rejected because of information they admitted in the prepolygraph interview. "Only a very small proportion (less than 10%) of those applicants judged deceptive, but who did not admit it, were rejected by the potential employer for that reason."[29]

How one regards that *less than 10 percent* figure, how much damage could be done by it, depends upon the *base rate* of lying. The phrase base rate refers to how many people do something. The guilty base rate among criminal suspects who take the polygraph test is probably pretty high, perhaps as high as 50 percent. The polygraph isn't typically given to everyone but only to a small group suspected because of prior criminal investigation. Barland's study suggests that the base rate of lying among job applicants is about 20 percent. About one out of five applicants will lie about something that could, if known, prevent them from being hired.

Even if the polygraph test is assumed to be more accurate than it probably is, with a 20 percent base rate there are some unfortunate outcomes. Raskin in arguing against preemployment polygraph testing assumes for argument's sake that the accuracy of the polygraph exam is 90 percent, higher than he thinks it actually is.

Given those assumptions, preemployment polygraph tests on 1,000 subjects would yield the following results: of the 200 deceptive subjects, 180 would be correctly diagnosed as deceptive and 20 would be incorrectly diagnosed as truthful; of the 800 truthful subjects, 720 would be correctly diagnosed as truthful and 80 would be incorrectly diagnosed as deceptive. Of the 260 subjects diagnosed as deceptive, 80 of those were actually truthful. Thus, of those found to be deceptive, 31% were actually being truthful. That is a very high rate of [disbelieving-the-truth mistakes] leading to denials of employment if the polygraph examinations were used as the basis for decision. Similar results would not occur in the criminal investigation context, since the base rate for deception in that situation is probably 50% or higher, and the accuracy of the technique would not lead to such a high rate of false positives.[30]

The counterargument might be:

Twenty percent may be too low an estimate of the base rate of lying among job applicants. It is based on only one study, of applicants in Utah. Maybe in states with a lower proportion of Mormons, there would be a higher number of liars. Even if it is as high as 50 percent, the opponent of preemployment screening would reply that it should not be done without evidence about how accurate the polygraph is in this use. It is probably much less than 90 percent.

The accuracy of the polygraph test doesn't really matter. Taking the test, or the threat of taking it, causes people to admit damaging information that they otherwise wouldn't admit. The reply again would be that without accuracy studies there is no way to know how many people who are not admitting things did something that could injure their employer.

A related use of the polygraph is to periodically test people already employed. This use is subject to all of the criticisms described for preemployment screening.

Polygraph Testing Police Applicants

This is another, widely used application of polygraph testing. All of the arguments just discussed regarding the use of the polygraph in preemployment screening for other jobs apply here as well. I am treating the police applicant separately, however, because some data about utility are available, and the nature of the job allows for a new argument for using the polygraph in preemployment screening.

The title of an article by Richard Arther, a professional polygrapher, gives the gist of the argument: "How Many Robbers, Burglars, Sex Criminals Is Your Department Hiring This Year?? (Hopefully, Just 10% of Those Employed!)."[31] Arther's findings are based on survey responses from thirty-two different law enforcement agencies. (He provides no information about what percentage this represents of those he sought to obtain information from.) Arther reports that in 1970, 6,524 preemployment polygraph exams were administered by the law enforcement people who responded to his survey. "Significant derogatory information was learned for the very first time from 2,119 of the applicants! This is a disqualification rate of 32%! The most important thing to know is that the great majority of these 6,524 examinations were given after the applicants had already passed their background examinations." Arther buttresses his argument by quoting numerous examples of how important it was to use the polygraph. Here is one sent in by Norman Luckay, polygraphist with the Cleveland, Ohio, police department: "[The] [p]erson was among the top 10 on our certified appointment list when he was given his pre-employment [polygraph] examination. He confessed being involved in an unsolved armed robbery."[32]

Despite such impressive stories, and the astounding figures about how many applicants for police jobs are liars, we must not forget that there is still no scientifically acceptable evidence about the accuracy of the polygraph in screening police applicants. If that seems hard to believe it is because it is so easy to confuse utility with accuracy. Arther's data are about utility. Consider what he doesn't tell us:

How many of those applicants tested as lying did not *admit to lying, did* not *confess to any wrongdoings?* What happened to them? These are utility data also, but most of those who advocate using the polygraph for preemployment screening leave out those figures.

Of those tested as lying who denied it, how many were actually telling the truth and should have been hired? To answer this question—how many disbelieving-the-truth mistakes were made—requires an accuracy study.

How many of those found not to be lying actually were? How many burglars, robbers, rapists, and so forth fooled the polygraph test? To answer this question—how many believing-a-lie mistakes there were—requires an accuracy study.

I am amazed that there is no definitive evidence on this. It would not be easy, it would not be inexpensive; but utility data are not sufficient. The stakes are too high to not know how many believing-a-lie mistakes occur, let alone disbelieving-the-truth mistakes.

Until that evidence is obtained an argument can be made to justify polygraph testing police applicants no matter how many mistakes are made, because it does ferret out a substantial number of undesirables. Even if it does not get all of them, even if some people who would have been perfectly good policemen are not hired (victims of disbelieving-the-truth mistakes), that may not be too high a price to pay.

This is a social, political judgment. It should be made knowing that there is no scientific evidence about how accurate the polygraph may be in screening applicants to be hired as policemen. I do believe that those who argue for polygraph testing because it screens out at least some undesirables, should feel obligated to see that while this practice is followed, accuracy studies are undertaken, if only to find out how often people are wrongly rejected.

Polygraph Testing to Catch Spies

An Army Sergeant who had access to cryptologic information applied for a civilian position [with an intelligence agency]. During the polygraph examination, he reacted to various relevant questions. In the post-test interview, he admitted to various petty crimes and miscellaneous wrongdoing. The polygraph examiner noted continued specific reactions to relevant questions and when the Sergeant was reexamined several weeks later, the same situation continued. His access was withdrawn and an investigation opened. While that investigation was still in progress, he was found dead in his automobile. It was subsequently determined that he had been engaged in espionage on behalf of the Soviet Union.[33]

The National Security Agency's report on its use of the polygraph gives this and numerous other examples of spies caught through routine preemployment polygraph testing. Presumably, some nonspies—truthful, perfectly employable people—also fail the test. NSA does not provide information about how many spies it catches or how many it later learns the polygraph missed. But it does report figures on how many people were rejected because of a variety of admissions, such as drug use, subversive activity, past criminal convictions, and so forth. One set of data reported is about 2,902 applicants for jobs requiring a security clearance who took a preemployment polygraph exam. Forty-three percent tested as truthful; but subsequent information showed that 17 of the 2,902 were concealing derogatory information. Thus the *known* percentage of believing-a-lie mistakes was less than 1 percent (17 out of the 2,902 people tested). Twenty-one percent failed the polygraph test and then made major admissions that caused them not to be hired. Twenty-four percent failed the polygraph test and then made minor admissions that did not prevent them from being hired. Eight percent failed the polygraph test and then did *not* make any admissions.

The 8 percent might be instances of disbelieving-the-truth mistakes. NSA does not mention them in their report, but I deduced how many there must have been from the figures they did report. NSA emphasizes that the polygraph is only one tool used in determining who should be hired, not the final arbiter. People who fail the test are interviewed afterward and an attempt is made to uncover the reasons why the person showed an emotional response on the polygraph to a particular question. Gordon Barland told me that NSA does not hire people if their failure on the polygraph cannot be explained.

Again, we must remember that these are only utility figures, not accuracy figures. Without accuracy data it is not possible to answer the following questions: How many more successful liars might there be who are still in place in NSA? NSA believes in their figure of less than 1 percent, but they do not have an accuracy study to back it up. While they may think the polygraph does not miss any liars, they cannot be certain. The OTA report notes that "those individuals who the Federal Government would most want to detect (e.g., for national security violations) may well be the most motivated and perhaps the best trained to avoid detection."[34] Without an accuracy study there is no way to be certain how many believing-a-lie mistakes are made. An accuracy study would no doubt be hard to do, but not impossible. Hybrid studies, such as the Israeli policemen study I described earlier, might be a feasible approach.

Can countermeasures fool the polygraph? This would include physical activities like biting one's tongue, the use of drugs, hypnosis, and biofeedback. There have been studies that suggest countermeasures do work to some extent, but given the costs in national security applications of missing someone who is a spy—a believing-a-lie mistake—much more research should be done. It should focus on instances in which the "agent" using the countermeasures who tries to fool the polygraph has the help of experts, technical equipment, and months to practice, which is what one would expect a real agent might have. Dr. John Beary III, formerly acting assistant secretary of defense for health affairs, ". . . warned the Pentagon that its reliance on the polygraph was endangering rather than protecting national security. I am told the Soviets have a training school in an Eastern Bloc country where they teach their agents how to beat the polygraph. Because many of our DOD managers think it works, they get a false sense of security, thus making it easier for a Soviet mole who passes the polygraph to penetrate the Pentagon.' "[35] Given that possibility, it is surprising that NSA is only doing a small-scale pilot project on countermeasures, according to OTA.

How many of the 8 percent who tested as lying but denied it—245 people, by my count—are actually liars, and how many are truthful people misjudged by the polygraph? Again, only an accuracy study could produce an answer.

There has been only *one* accuracy study, according to the response of both NSA and the CIA, to the OTA's inquiry—an analog study using students, in which there is doubt about the criteria for establishing ground truth and the questions asked had nothing to do with national security! Again, it is amazing that in matters of such importance so little relevant research has been done. Even if there is no concern about disbelieving-the-truth mistakes, when the stakes are so high there should be the utmost concern about believing-a-liar mistakes.

Undoubtedly, even without accuracy data, a strong case can be made for using the polygraph to screen people applying for jobs where they have access to secret information that could, if given to an adversary, endanger national security. Deputy Assistant Attorney General Richard K. Willard put it succinctly: "Even if use of the polygraph may unfairly screen out some candidates who are actually qualified, we view it as more important to avoid hiring candidates who may pose a risk to national security."[36] Lykken provides the counterargument in his comment on Britain's recent decision to use the polygraph test in their agencies dealing with secret matters: "Apart from the damage done to the careers and reputations of innocent persons, this decision is likely to result in the loss to the government of some of its most conscientious civil servants. . . . [And,] because of the tendency to slight more expensive but more effective security procedures, once polygraph testing has been introduced, this decision may well open the door to easy penetration of the security services by foreign agents trained to beat the polygraph."[37]

On-the-Job Polygraph Check-ups

If it is worth trying to keep undesirables from becoming employees of intelligence agencies, diamond merchants, or supermarket clerks, it would seem obvious that it would be useful to have them take polygraph tests periodically once they are employed to see whether any have slipped. This is done in many businesses. Again, there are no data on whether the polygraph test would be accurate when used this way. Probably the base rates of lying are lower: many of the bad apples should already have been screened out by the preemployment test; and, fewer employees than job applicants might have something to hide. The lower the base rates of lying, the more mistaken judgments there will be. If we take the earlier example of 1,000 employees in which we assumed that the polygraph would be 90 percent accurate, but this time instead of assuming a lying base rate of 20 percent we assume 5 percent, here is what would happen: 45 liars would be correctly identified, but 95 truthful people would be mistakenly identified as lying; and, 855 truthful people would be correctly identified, but 5 liars would slip by, mistakenly identified as truthful.

Figures 7 and 8 graphically illustrate the effects of having such a low base rate of lying. To highlight what the change in base rates does to the numbers of people mistakenly judged to be lying, I have kept the estimated accuracy figure of 90 percent constant.* When the base of lying is 20 percent, two liars, on average, are caught for every truthful person misjudged. When the base rate of lying is 5 percent, it reverses, and two truthful persons are misjudged for every liar caught.

The argument that resentment about having to take the test may make it harder to obtain accurate results should apply here also. Employees may feel even more resentment about having to take the test once they have been on the job than before, when they were job seekers.

---

*There is no way to know what the accuracy might be in either case, since there has been no adequate study. But it is unlikely that it is as high as 90 percent.

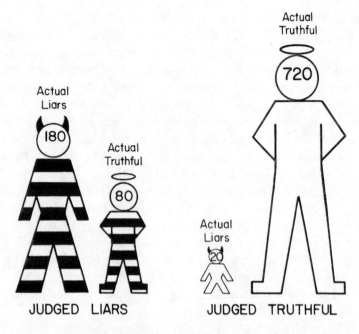

POLYGRAPH TEST RESULTS
1000 People Tested 20% (200) Are Liars
Figure 7

The same justification for polygraph testing prior to employment can be made for giving the test during employment with either policemen or employees of an agency such as NSA. The police rarely do this, although with the temptations of the job, and the incidence of corruption, a case could be made to justify it. NSA does do some on-the-job polygraph testing. If an employee fails the test, and a subsequent interview does not resolve the reason why, a security investigation is made. To my question about what would happen if the matter cannot be resolved—if someone fails the polygraph test repeatedly but nothing adverse is uncovered;—I was told: it has never happened; there is

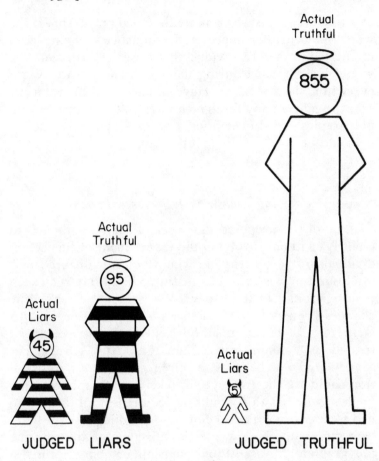

POLYGRAPH TEST RESULTS
1000 People Tested 5% (50) Are Liars

Figure 8

no policy other than to decide such a matter case by case; and a decision never has had to be made. It would be a delicate matter. To fire someone who has been employed for many years would be very hard if there was no evidence of wrongdoing, just the repeatedly failed polygraph. If she were innocent, her anger at the injustice of being fired might tempt her to divulge the secret information she would have learned during her employment. And yet if every time she was asked "Have you divulged any information to agents of any foreign country in the last year?" the polygraph showed an emotional response when she said no, it would be hard not to do anything.

Catching Leaks and Deterrence Theory

One of the proposed new uses of the polygraph is to identify, without involving the Department of Justice, individuals in the government who have made unauthorized disclosures of classified information. Up until now all such investigations had to be treated as criminal cases. If the changes proposed by the Reagan administration in 1983 were to take effect, unauthorized disclosures could be treated as "administrative" matters. Any government agency head who believes an employee has leaked information could ask the employee to take a polygraph test. It is unclear whether this would be required of all those who had access to the leaked document—in which case the lying base rate would be low and the mistake rate in using the polygraph high—or just to those people whom prior investigation suggested as likely suspects.

The OTA report points out that there have not been any studies to determine the polygraph's accuracy in detecting a lie about unauthorized disclosures. The FBI did, however, provide data that indicated it had successfully used the polygraph in twenty-six such cases over four years —successful in that most of those who failed the polygraph confessed.[38] But the FBI's use of the polygraph differs from what might be allowed by the new regulations. The FBI did not test all those who might have made an unauthorized disclosure. (Such a procedure has been termed a *dragnet* use of the polygraph). Instead, only a narrower group of suspects suggested by prior investigation were tested, so the base rate of lying was higher and the mistakes lower than in a dragnet. FBI regulations prohibit the use of polygraph tests for "dragnet type screening of large numbers of subjects or as a substitute for logical investigation by conventional means."[39] The new regulations proposed in 1983 could allow dragnet polygraph testing.

The kind of people examined, the content of the exam, and the examination procedures in administrative polygraph testing would all be likely to differ from when people suspected of criminal acts take a polygraph test. Resentment would presumably be high, since an employee could lose access to classified information unless he took the test. NSA's survey of its own employees found that NSA employees feel polygraph testing is justified. That may be true; but unless the survey was done in a way to insure anonymity, those who resent polygraph testing might not admit it. It is much less likely, I believe, that government employees in other agencies will feel polygraph testing is justified to catch leaks, particularly if it seems that the purpose is to suppress information more damaging to the administration than to the nation's security.

Deputy Assistant Attorney General Willard testified before Congress about quite another rationale for using the polygraph: "An additional benefit of polygraph use is its deterrent effect upon certain kinds of misconduct that can be difficult to detect through other means. Employees who know they are subject to polygraph examinations may be more likely to refrain from such misconduct."[40] This may not work as well as it seems. Polygraph testing is probably going to make many more mistakes trying to catch those people lying about unauthorized disclosures when the suspects are not employees of an intelligence agency. Even if that is not so—and no one knows whether it is so—if the people who are tested think that, or at least know that no one knows, deterrence may fail. The polygraph works if most people who take the test think it will. Using the polygraph with unauthorized disclosures may cause the innocent, rightly or not, to be just as fearful, and certainly just as angry about being tested, as the guilty.

It might be argued that it doesn't matter if the test works or not, it can still have a deterrent effect on some, and no punishment need be given to those who fail the test, avoiding the ethical dilemma of punishing any innocents misjudged. But if the consequences of being judged a liar on the polygraph are negligible, the test is unlikely to work at all, and it certainly won't have much deterrent value if it is known that those who fail are not punished.

Comparing the Polygraph and Behavioral Clues to Deceit

Polygraph examiners do not make their judgments about whether a suspect is lying from the polygraph chart alone. The polygraph examiner not only knows what the prior investigation has revealed, but in a pretest interview the examiner obtains more information as he explains the examination procedure and develops the questions that will be used in the exam. The examiner also gains impressions from the subject's facial expressions, voice, gestures, and manner of speaking during the pretest interview, in the examination itself, and in the post-test interview. There are two schools of thought about whether the examiner should consider behavioral clues in addition to the polygraph chart in making his evaluation about whether a suspect is lying. The training materials I have seen, used by those who do consider behavioral clues to deceit, are woefully out of date, not based on the latest published research findings. They include a number of wrong ideas and some right ones about how to interpret behavioral clues to deceit.

Only four studies compared judgments based on polygraph tests *and* behavioral clues with judgments made by polygraphers who had not examined the subjects but just inspected the charts. Two studies suggested that accuracy based on just the behavioral clues was equal to accuracy from the polygraph charts, and one study found the behavioral clues yielded judgments that were accurate but not as accurate as those made from the polygraph record. All three studies suffered from major flaws: uncertainty about ground truth, too few suspects examined, or too few examiners making judgments.[41] These problems were remedied in the fourth study, by Raskin and Kircher, which has not yet been published.[42] They found that judgments based on behavioral clues were not much better than chance, while judgments based just on the polygraph charts, without contact with the suspects, were much better than chance.

People are often so misled, misinterpreting or missing the behavioral clues to deceit. Remember my report (in the beginning of chapter 4) of our study that found that people could not tell from our videotapes whether the nursing students were lying or truthfully describing their emotions. Yet, we know there were unrecognized clues to deceit. When these nursing students lied, concealing the negative emotions they felt when watching the surgical films, the pitch of their voice became higher, they used fewer hand movements to illustrate their speech, and they made more shrug emblematic slips. We have just finished our facial measurements on these subjects and not yet had time to publish the results, but they appear to be the most prom-

ising of all in identifying lies. The most powerful of the
facial measurements was one that spotted subtle signs of
muscle movements showing disgust or contempt embed-
ded within seemingly happy smiles.

We must be measuring information that people either
don't know about *or* can't see. In the next year we will find
out which it is. We will train a group of people, telling
them what to look for, and then show them the videotapes.
If their judgments are still wrong, we will know that accuracy in spotting these behavioral clues to deceit requires
slowed and repeated viewing and precise measurement.
My bet is that accuracy will be good as a result of training,
but not as high as it is with precise measurement.

It would be important in a study such as Raskin and
Kircher's to compare the accuracy of judgments made from
polygraph charts with measurements of behavioral clues to
deceit, and with the judgments of trained, not naïve, observers. I expect we would find that for at least some suspects, behavioral measurements added to judgments made
from the polygraph charts alone will increase the accuracy
of lie detection. The behavioral clues to deceit can give
information about which emotion is felt. Is it fear, anger,
surprise, distress, or excitement that is producing the signs
of arousal on the polygraph chart?

It may be possible also to extract such specific information about which emotion is felt from the polygraph records themselves. Recall our findings (described at the end
of chapter 4) suggesting a different pattern of autonomic
nervous system activity for each emotion. No one has yet
tried this approach to the interpretation of polygraph
charts in detecting lies. Information about specific emotions—derived from both behavioral clues and the polygraph chart—could help to decrease the incidence of both
disbelieving-the-truth mistakes and believing-a-lie mistakes. Another important matter that needs to be investi-

gated is how well sophisticated countermeasures to evade detection of lying can be spotted by combining behavioral clues and emotion-specific interpretations of polygraph charts.

The polygraph can only be used with a cooperative, consenting suspect. Behavioral clues can always be read, without permission, without advance notice, without the suspected liar knowing that he is under suspicion. While it might be possible to outlaw polygraph testing in certain applications, one could never outlaw the use of behavioral clues to detect deceit. Even if polygraph testing is not made legal to catch government employees who leak information, lie catchers can and will still scrutinize the behavior of those they suspect.

In many instances in which deceit is suspected— whether it be spousal, diplomatic, or bargaining—a polygraph test is out of the question. It does not matter that trust is not expected; not even an interrogatory set of questions is allowed. When trust is expected, as between spouses, friends, or parent and child, asking questions in a directed sequence, even without a polygraph, jeopardizes the relationship. Even a parent who may have more authority over her child than most lie catchers have over those they suspect may not be able to afford the costs of interrogation. The failure to accept the child's initial claim of innocence could permanently undermine their relationship, even if the child submitted, and not all would.

Some people may feel it is best, or moral, not to try to spot lies, to accept people at their word, take life at face value, and do nothing to diminish the chances of being misled. The choice is made not to risk wrongfully accusing someone of lying, even though it means increasing the risk of being deceived. Sometimes that may be the best choice. It depends upon what is at stake, who might be under suspicion, what the likelihood is of being misled, and the lie catcher's attitude toward others. In Updike's novel *Marry Me*, what would Jerry lose by believing that his wife, Ruth, is truthful when she is lying about an affair, and how would that compare to what he would lose or gain by believing she is lying if she has instead been truthfully faithful? In some marriages the damage done by a false accusation might be greater than the damage done by allowing a deceit to proceed unchallenged, until the evidence is overwhelming. That will not always be the case. It depends upon the particulars of each situation. Some people may not have much choice; they may be too suspicious to risk believing-a-lie, better able to risk making false accusations then to risk being taken.

The only suggestion about what should always be considered in trying to decide which risks to take is *never reach a final conclusion about whether a suspect is lying or truthful based solely on either the polygraph or behavioral clues to deceit.* Chapter 6 explained the hazards, and precautions that can be taken to reduce those hazards, in interpreting behavioral clues. This chapter should have made clear the hazards involved in interpreting a polygraph chart as evidence of lying. The lie catcher must always estimate the *likelihood* that a gesture, expression, or polygraph sign of emotional arousal indicates lying or truthfulness; rarely is it ever absolutely *certain.* In those rare instances when an emotion contradicting the lie leaks in a full facial expression, or some part of the concealed information is blurted out in words during a tirade, the suspect will realize that too and will confess. More often, recognizing the presence of behavioral clues to deceit or clues to honesty, as with the polygraph, can only provide a basis for deciding whether or not to pursue further inquiry.

The lie catcher should also evaluate the particular lie in terms of the likelihood that there will be any mistakes at all. Some deceits are so easy to accomplish that there is little chance any behavioral clues will surface. Other lies are so difficult to accomplish that many errors should occur, and there will be many behavioral clues to consider. The next chapter describes what to consider in estimating whether a lie will be easy or hard to spot.

EIGHT

Lie Checking

*M*OST LIES succeed because no one goes through the work to figure out how to catch them. Usually it doesn't much matter. But when the stakes are high—when the victim would be severely harmed if misled or the liar severely harmed if caught and benefited if wrongly judged to be truthful—there is reason to do that work. Lie checking isn't a simple task, quickly done. Many questions have to be considered to estimate whether or not mistakes are likely and, if they are, what kind of mistakes to expect and how to spot those mistakes in particular behavioral clues. Questions have to be asked about the nature of the lie itself; about the characteristics of the specific liar and of the specific lie catcher. No one can be *absolutely certain* whether or not a liar will fail or a truthful person will be exonerated. Lie checking provides only an informed guess. But making such an *estimate* should reduce both believing-a-lie and disbelieving-the-truth mistakes. At the least, it makes both liar and lie catcher aware of how complicated it is to forecast whether a liar can be caught.

Lie checking will allow a suspicious person to estimate his chances of confirming or disproving his suspicions. Sometimes all he will learn is that he can't find out; would that Othello had known that. Or, he may learn which mistakes are likely, and what to look and listen for. Lie checking could be useful also to a liar. Some may decide the odds are against them and not embark on a lie or not continue their lie. Others may be encouraged by how easy it appears to get away with a lie or may learn what to focus their efforts upon to avoid the mistakes they are most likely to make. In the next chapter, I will explain why the information in this and other chapters usually will help the lie catcher more than the liar.

Thirty-eight questions have to be answered to check a lie. Most of them have already been mentioned in the course of explaining other matters in earlier chapters. Now I have gathered them into a single checklist, adding a few questions that I haven't yet had reason to describe. I will analyze a number of different lies, using the checklist to show why some lies are easy and some hard. (The entire list of thirty-eight questions appears as table 4 in the appendix.)

An *easy* lie for the liar should produce few mistakes and therefore be *hard* for the lie catcher to detect, while a *hard* lie for the liar should be *easy* for the lie catcher to detect. An easy lie would not require concealing or falsifying emotions, there would have been ample opportunity to practice the specific lie, the liar would be experienced in lying, and the target, the potential lie catcher, would not be suspicious. A newspaper article entitled "How Head-Hunters Stalk Executives in the Corporate Jungle"[1] described a number of such very easy lies.

Head-hunters find executives who can be lured from one company to fill a job with another competing company. Since no company wants to lose talented employees to competitors, head-hunters can't be direct in their attempts to learn about prospects. Sara Jones, a head-hunter with a New York firm, told how she gets the information she needs from a "mark" by posing as an industrial researcher: " 'We're doing a study correlating education and career paths. Could I ask you a couple of questions? I'm not interested in your name, just the statistics about your career path and education.' And I ask the fellow everything about himself: how much money he makes, is he married, how old is he, number of children. . . . Head-hunting is manipulating other people into giving you information. Flat out, that's what it is."[2] Another head-hunter described his job this way: "When people ask me at a party what I do I tell them I lie, cheat, and steal for a living."[3]

The interview with the psychiatric patient Mary, whom I described in the first chapter, provides an example of a very hard lie:

DOCTOR: Well Mary, uh, how are you feeling today?

MARY: Fine doctor. I'm looking forward to spending the weekend, uh, with my family, you know. It's, uh, been five weeks now since I came into the hospital.

DOCTOR: No more depressed feelings, Mary? No thoughts of suicide, you're sure now?

MARY: I'm really embarrassed about that. I don't, I sure don't feel that way now. I just want to go, be home with my husband.

Both Mary and Sara succeeded in their lies. Neither was caught, but Mary could have been. On all counts the odds were against Mary and favored Sara. Mary's is a more difficult *lie* to pull off. Mary is also a less skilled *liar,* and the doctor had a number of advantages as a *lie catcher.* Let's consider first the ways in which the lies themselves differed, quite apart from the characteristics of the liars and the lie catchers.

Mary has to lie about feelings, and Sara does not. Mary is concealing the anguish that is motivating her suicidal plans. Those feelings might leak, or the burden of concealing them might give away her pretended positive feelings. Mary not only has to lie about feelings, but, unlike Sara, she has strong feelings about lying itself, feelings she also has to conceal. Because Sara's lie is authorized—part of the job

—she doesn't feel guilty about lying. Mary's unauthorized lie generates guilt. A patient is supposed to be honest with the doctor who is trying to help her, and, besides, Mary liked her doctor. Mary also feels ashamed about lying and about planning to take her life. *The hardest lies are those about emotion felt at the time of the lie; the stronger the emotions and the greater the number of different emotions that have to be concealed, the harder the lie will be.* So far I have explained why in addition to feeling anguish Mary would also feel guilt and shame. When we turn now from considering the lie to analyzing the liars, we shall see why Mary would feel a fourth emotion that she also has to conceal.

Mary is less practiced and skilled in lying than Sara. She has not before attempted to conceal anguish and suicide plans and has no experience lying about anything to a psychiatrist. Her lack of practice makes her afraid of being caught, and that fear, of course, may itself leak, adding to the burden of emotions she must conceal. Her psychiatric illness makes her especially vulnerable to fear, guilt, and shame. And further, she is not likely to be able to conceal these feelings.

Mary has not anticipated all the questions the doctor is likely to ask, and she has to make up her line as she goes along. Sara is just the opposite. She is practiced at this type of lie, has done it many times, is confident about her ability based on past successes, and has a well-worked-out, rehearsed line. Sara also has the advantage of a background in acting, enabling her to play roles skillfully, often convincing even herself.

The doctor has three advantages over the executive as a lie catcher. This is not a first meeting, and his previous knowledge of Mary gives him a better chance of avoiding the Brokaw hazard due to a failure to take account of individual differences. While not all psychiatrists are trained in how to spot signs of concealed emotion, he has such skill.

And, unlike the executive, the doctor is wary. He is alert to the possibility of deceit, having been taught that suicidal patients after a few weeks in the hospital may conceal their true feelings in order to get out of the hospital and kill themselves.

Mary's mistakes were evident in her speech, voice, body, and expressions. She is unpracticed as a liar, not a smooth talker, and she provides clues to deceit in her choice of words and in her voice: speech errors, circumlocutiousness, inconsistencies in her line, and speech pauses. The strong negative emotions she feels also acted to produce those errors in her speech and higher pitch. Clues to these concealed emotions—anguish, fear, guilt, and shame—also were evident in the leakage emblems such as the shrug, self-manipulator movements, decreased illustrator movements, and micro facial expressions showing these four emotions. All four emotions leaked in the reliable facial muscles despite Mary's attempts to conceal them. Because the doctor is already acquainted with Mary, he should have been better able to interpret her illustrator and manipulator body movements that otherwise he might misinterpret because of individual differences in a first encounter. In fact, her doctor did not pick up on the clues to her deceit, although I presume that if he had been alerted to what I have explained, he and most others would have detected her lie.

Sara has nearly the ideal situation for a liar: no emotions to conceal; practice in exactly this lie; time to rehearse; confidence due to past successes; natural and developed skills to draw upon in her performance; authorization to lie; an unsuspecting victim who is liable to errors in judgment because of a first encounter; and a victim who is not especially talented as a judge of people. Of course, with Sara, unlike Mary, I had no opportunity to examine a film or videotape to search for any clues to deceit, since I am relying just upon a newspaper account. I can only predict that neither I nor anyone else would find any clues to her deceit. It was a very easy deceit; there were no reasons for her to make mistakes.

The only other advantage Sara could have had would have been a victim who actively collaborated in the deceit, who needed to be misled for his own reasons. Neither Sara nor Mary had that. Ruth, the philandering wife in the incident I have quoted in earlier chapters (taken from John Updike's novel *Marry Me*), had that advantage. Hers was a very hard lie that should have been full of mistakes, but her willing victim did not detect them. Recall that Ruth's husband, Jerry, overhears her speaking on the telephone to her lover. Noticing something different in the sound of her voice, Jerry asks Ruth to whom she has been talking. Caught unprepared, Ruth makes up the line that the Sunday school was calling, which Jerry challenges as not fitting what he had heard her say. Jerry does not push further, and Updike implies that Jerry fails to detect Ruth's deceit because he has a reason to avoid a confrontation about infidelity: Jerry is also concealing an affair, and, as it turns out, it is with the wife of Ruth's lover!

Let us compare Ruth's very hard, but undetected, lie with a very easy lie, which also goes undetected but for very different reasons. This easy lie comes from a recent analysis of the lying techniques used by con artists:

In "mirror play" . . . the con artist confronts the victim with a hidden thought, disarming him by anticipating the actual confrontation sensed from the victim. John Hamrak, one of the most inventive con men of the first years of this century in Hungary, and an accomplice dressed as a technician, walked into the office of an alderman in City Hall. Hamrak announced that they had come for the clock which was to be repaired. The alderman, probably because of the great value of the clock, was reluctant to hand it over. Instead of further substantiating his role, Hamrak responded by calling the alderman's attention to the extraordinary value of the clock, declaring that it was for this reason that he had come for it in person. Thus con artists are eager to direct their victim's attention to the most sensitive issue, thus authenticating their role by seeming to injure their own cause.[4]

The first issue to consider in estimating whether or not there will be any clues to deceit is whether or not the lie involves emotions felt at the moment of the lie. As I explained in chapter 3 and illustrated in my analysis of the psychiatric patient Mary's lie, the hardest lies involve emotions felt at the moment of the lie. Emotions are not the whole story; other questions must be asked even to make an estimate about whether emotions will be successfully concealed. But asking about emotions is a good place to begin.

Concealing emotions might be the principal aim of the lie—as it is with Mary, but not with Ruth. Even when that is not so, when the lie is not about feelings, feelings about lying can become involved. There are many reasons why Ruth may feel detection apprehension and deception guilt. Clearly, she would fear the consequences if her attempt to conceal her affair is discovered. It is not just that Ruth won't be able to continue to obtain the rewards provided by her affair if her lie fails; she might be punished. Her husband, Jerry, might leave her if he discovers her infidelity; and, if there is a divorce, testimony about her adultery could cause her to receive less favorable financial terms (Updike's novel was written before the era of no-fault divorce). Even in no-fault states, adultery can adversely affect child custody. If the marriage continues, it may be damaged, at least for a time.

Not every liar is punished if caught; neither the headhunter Sara nor the psychiatric patient Mary would suffer any punishment if their lies failed. While the con man Hamrak would, like Ruth, be punished, other matters make him feel less detection apprehension. Hamrak is practiced in just this kind of lie, and he knows that he has the personal assets that aid him as a liar. Although Ruth has been successfully deceiving her husband, she is not highly practiced in exactly what this lie requires—covering an overheard phone call. Nor does she feel confident about her talents as a liar.

Her knowledge that she will be punished if her lie fails is only one source of Ruth's fear of being caught. She also fears punishment for the very act of lying. If Jerry discovers that Ruth has been willing and able to deceive him, his distrust of her could be a source of trouble quite apart from her infidelity. Some who are cuckolded claim it is the loss of trust, not the infidelity, that is beyond their capacity to forgive. Again, note that not every liar is punished for the act of lying itself; that is only so when the liar and victim have an intended future that could be jeopardized by distrust. If caught lying, the head-hunter Sara would only lose her ability to get information from this particular "mark." Hamrak would be punished not for impersonation but for theft or attempted theft. Even the psychiatric patient Mary would not be punished for lying itself. The discovery that she lied would, however, make her doctor more wary. Trust that the other person will be truthful is not assumed or required in every enduring relationship, not even in every marriage.

Ruth's detection apprehension should be magnified by her realization that Jerry is suspicious. Hamrak's victim, the alderman, is also suspicious of anyone who wants to remove his valuable clock. The beauty of the "mirror play" is that directly addressing and making public a privately held suspicion reduces it. The victim thinks that a thief would never be so audacious as to acknowledge just what his victim fears. That logic can also cause a lie catcher to discount leakage because he can't believe that a liar would

make such a mistake. In their analysis of military deceptions, Donald Daniel and Katherine Herbig note that "
... the bigger the leak, the less likely the target will believe
it since it seems too good to be true. [In a number of cases
military planners discounted leakage] ... as too blatant to
be anything but plants."[5]

Ruth, like the patient Mary, shares values with her victim and might feel guilt about lying. But it is less clear
whether Ruth feels that concealing her affair is authorized.
Even people who condemn adultery do not necessarily
agree that unfaithful spouses should reveal their infidelity.
With Hamrak it is more certain. Like the head-hunter Sara,
he feels no guilt—lying is part of what they do to make
their living. Probably Hamrak also is a natural liar or psychopath, which would also diminish the chance he would
feel guilty about lying. Among Hamrak's peers, lying to
"marks" is authorized.

Ruth's and Hamrak's lies illustrate two more points.
She doesn't anticipate when she will need to lie, and so she
did not work out and practice her line. This should magnify Ruth's fear of being caught, once the lie begins, since
she knows she cannot fall back upon a prepared set of
answers. Even if Hamrak was to be caught in such a predicament—and a professional liar won't often be—he has the
talents to improvise that she doesn't. But Ruth has one
great advantage over Hamrak, the one mentioned in introducing this example—she has a willing victim, who for his
own reasons does not want to catch her. Sometimes such
a victim may not even be aware that he is colluding in
maintaining the deceit. Updike leaves the reader uncertain
whether or not Jerry is aware of his collusion and if Ruth
realizes this is happening. There are two ways in which
willing victims make the liar's task easier. Liars are less
afraid of being caught if they know that their victims are
blind to their mistakes. And, liars feel less guilty about

deceiving such victims, for they can believe that they are only doing what their victims want them to do.

So far we have analyzed four lies, identifying why in Mary's and Ruth's cases there would be clues to deceit and why there should be no clues to deceit in the lies of either Sara or Hamrak. Now let us consider a case in which a truthful person was judged to be lying to see how lie checking might have helped to prevent such a mistaken judgment.

Gerald Anderson was accused of raping and murdering Nancy Johnson, the wife of his next-door neighbor. Nancy's husband had come home in the middle of the night from work, found her body, run over to the Andersons' house, told them that his wife was dead and that he couldn't find his son, and asked Mr. Anderson to get the police.

A number of incidents made Anderson a suspect. The day following the murder he had stayed home from work, drank too much at a local bar, talked about the murders and, when brought home, had been overheard sobbing while saying to his wife, "I didn't want to do it, but I had to." His later claim that he was talking about getting drunk, not murder, was not believed. When the police asked him about a spot in the upholstery of his car, Anderson claimed it had been there before he bought it. Later, during the interrogation, he admitted that he had lied, having felt ashamed about admitting that he had slapped his wife during an argument, causing a nosebleed. His interrogators repeatedly told Anderson that this incident proved that he was a violent person who could kill and a liar who would deny it. During the interrogation Anderson admitted that when he was twelve he had been involved in a minor sex offense that had not harmed the girl and had never been repeated. It later came out that he was not twelve but fifteen at the time. This, his interrogators insisted, was further proof that he was a liar, as well as evidence that he had a sex problem and therefore could be the person who raped and then murdered his neighbor Nancy.

Joe Townsend, a professional polygraph operator, was brought in and identified by the interrogators as someone who had never been wrong in catching a liar.

Townsend initially ran two long series of tests on Anderson, and got some baffling and contradictory readings. When questioned on the murder itself, Anderson showed "blips" on his tapes that were indicative of deception in denying guilt. But when questioned about the murder weapon and how and where he had disposed of it, the polygraph tape showed that he came out "clean." In simplistic terms, Anderson indicated "guilt" about Nancy's murder and "innocence" on the weapon with which she had been hideously stabbed and slashed. When asked where he had obtained the knife, what kind of knife it was, and where he had got rid of it Anderson said "I don't know" and the tape didn't blip. . . . Townsend reran Anderson three times on the murder weapon and got the same results. When he was through, Joe Townsend told Anderson that he had failed the lie-detector test.[6]

The polygraph operator's judgment fit with the interrogators' beliefs that they had their man. They questioned Anderson for a total of six days. Audiotapes of the interrogation revealed how Anderson was worn down and had finally confessed to a crime he did not commit. Almost until the end, he claimed innocence, protesting that he couldn't have done it since he had no memory of killing or raping Nancy. The interrogators countered by telling him that a killer might have a blackout. Failure to remember the act, they said, did not prove that he had not done it. Anderson signed a confession after the interrogators told him his wife said she knew that he had killed Nancy, a statement his wife later denied ever having made. A few days later Anderson repudiated his confession, and seven months later the true killer, charged with another rape-murder, confessed to killing Nancy Johnson.

My analysis suggests that Anderson's emotional reactions to the murder questions during the polygraph test could have been due to other factors apart from the possibility that he was lying when he said he did not commit the murder. Remember that the polygraph test is *not* a lie detector. It only detects emotional arousal. The question is whether Anderson could have been emotionally aroused when questioned about the crime *only* if he had murdered Nancy. Are there other reasons why Anderson might have been emotionally aroused about the crime even if he did not commit it? If there were, the polygraph test would prove inaccurate.

The stakes are so great—the punishment so severe—that *most** suspects who were guilty of such a crime would be fearful; but so would some innocents. Polygraph operators try to reduce the innocent's fear of being disbelieved and magnify the guilty person's fear of being caught by telling the suspect that the machine never fails. One reason why Anderson would fear being disbelieved is the nature of the interrogation that preceded the polygraph test. Police experts[7] distinguish between interviews, which are conducted to obtain information, and interrogations, which presume guilt and are conducted in an accusatory way, attempting to coerce a confession. Interrogators often, as they did with Anderson, use the force of their own conviction about the suspect's guilt, openly acknowledged, to force the suspect to give up his claim to innocence. While this may intimidate the guilty into confessing, it does so at the cost of scaring the innocent suspect, who realizes that his interrogators do not have an open mind about his guilt. After twenty-four hours, nonstop, of such interrogation, Anderson took the polygraph test.

Anderson's emotional reactions to the murder ques-

---

*I say *most* guilty suspects would be afraid, because not everyone who murders is afraid of being caught. Neither the professional nor the psychopath would be.

tions registered by the polygraph could have been generated not only by his fear of being disbelieved but also by
feelings of shame and guilt. Even though innocent of the
murder, Anderson was ashamed of two other crimes. His
interrogators knew that he was ashamed about hitting his
wife and about having, as an adolescent, committed a sex
offense. He also felt deception guilt about his attempts to
conceal or misrepresent these incidents. The interrogators
repeatedly played on these incidents to persuade Anderson
that he was the type of person who could kill and rape, but
this could also have magnified his feelings of shame and
guilt and linked those feelings with the crime he was accused of committing.

Lie checking explains why any signs of fear, shame, or
guilt—whether they be in Anderson's expressions, gestures, voice, speech, or autonomic nervous system activity
as measured by the polygraph—would be ambiguous as
clues to deceit. These emotions were just as likely to surface
if Anderson was innocent as if he was indeed the murderer.
One more incident that the interrogators did not know
about made it impossible for them to tell from Anderson's
emotional reactions whether or not he was lying. After
Anderson was out of jail, James Phelan, the journalist
whose story had helped win Anderson's freedom, asked
Anderson about what might have made him "fail" the polygraph test. Anderson revealed still another source of his
emotional reactions to the crime he did not commit. The
night of Nancy's murder, when Anderson went with the
police to his neighbor's home, he had looked at Nancy's
naked body a couple of times. He felt that this was a terrible
thing for him to have done. In his mind he had committed
a crime, a different one than murder but one that nevertheless made him feel and register guilt and shame. He lied,
concealing this terrible act from the interrogators and the
polygraph operator, and, of course, he felt guilty about
lying to these men.

Anderson's interrogators made the Othello error. Like Othello, they correctly recognized that their suspect was emotionally aroused. Their error was in misidentifying the cause of the emotion, in not realizing that the correctly identified emotions might be felt whether their suspect was guilty or innocent. Just as Desdemona's distress was not at the loss of her lover, Anderson's shame, guilt, and fear were not related to the murder but to his other crimes. Like Othello, the interrogators became victims of their own preconceptions about their suspect. They too could not tolerate uncertainty about knowing whether their suspect was lying or not. Incidentally, the interrogators did have information, details about the murder weapon, that only the guilty person would also have and would not be known to an innocent person. The fact that Anderson did not respond on the polygraph to the questions about the knife should have suggested to the polygraph operator that Anderson might be innocent. Instead of repeating the test three times, the polygrapher should have constructed a Guilty Knowledge Test, using information about the crime that only the perpetrator would have known.

Hamrak, the con man, and Anderson, the accused murder, exemplify the two types of mistakes that plague attempts to catch criminal liars. In an interrogation or during a polygraph test Hamrak would probably be unaroused emotionally, appearing quite innocent of any wrongdoing. Lie checking made clear why such an experienced, professional, natural liar or psychopath rarely makes mistakes when lying. Hamrak is an example of the person whose lie will be believed. Anderson represents just the opposite problem. He was an innocent who was, for all the reasons explained, judged to be guilty—a disbelieving-the-truthful mistake.

My purpose in examining these two cases is not to argue that polygraph lie detection or the use of expressive clues to deceit should be banned when criminal suspects are examined. Even if one wished to there is no way to stop people from making use of behavioral clues to deceit. Everyone's impressions of others is based, in part, upon the other person's expressive behavior. Such behavior conveys impressions about much more than truthfulness. Expressive behavior is a major source for impressions about whether someone is friendly, outgoing, dominating, attractive and attracted, intelligent, interested in or understanding of what one is saying, and so on. Usually such impressions are formed unwittingly, without the person being aware of the particular behavioral clue he considered. I explained in chapter 6 why I believe that errors are less likely if such judgments are made more explicitly. If one is aware of the source of one's impressions, if one knows the rules that one follows in interpreting specific behaviors, corrections are more likely. One's judgments are more available to challenge, by one's colleagues, by the person whom one is judging, and through learning by experience which judgments turn out to be correct and which mistaken. Most police training does not emphasize behavioral clues to deceit. I presume that a detective usually does not know the explicit basis for his hunch that this suspect is guilty and that one innocent. While the current training of some polygraph lie detectors does emphasize the importance of nonverbal clues to deceit, their information about what are the behavioral clues to deceit is out of date or unsubstantiated, and too little attention is given about when such clues will be useless or misleading.

It is not possible to abolish the use of behavioral clues to deceit in criminal interrogations, and I am not certain that justice would be served if it were. In deadly deceits, when a truthful person could be falsely imprisoned or executed for a crime or a lying murderer could escape conviction, every legal attempt should be made to discover the truth. Instead, my argument is to make the process of interpreting such clues more explicit, more deliberate, and more cautious. I have emphasized the potential for making errors, and how the lie catcher, by considering each of the questions on my lie-checking list (table 4 in the appendix), can estimate the chances of either detecting a lie or recognizing the truth. I believe that training in how to spot the clues to deceit, learning the hazards and precautions, and engaging in lie checking could make detectives more accurate, decreasing both disbelieving-the-truth and believing-a-lie mistakes. But it would take field research, studying police interrogators and criminal suspects, to find out whether I am right. Such work was begun, and the results appeared promising, but unfortunately it was not completed.[8]

When opposing national leaders meet during an international crisis, deceit may be much more deadly than it is in police work, and detecting it more dangerous and difficult. The stakes for a mistaken judgment—disbelieving-the-truth or believing-a-lie—are greater than even in the most dastardly of criminal deceits. Only a few political scientists have written about the importance of lying and detecting deceit in personal meetings among heads of state or high-ranking officials. Alexander Groth says, "The tasks of divining the attitude, intentions and sincerity of the other side are crucial to any estimate of policy."[9] While a national leader may not wish to gain the reputation of being a bald-faced liar, that cost may be offset, says Robert Jervis, ". . . when successful deception can change the basic power relationships in the international system. For if the use of a lie can help a state gain a dominant position in the world it may not matter a great deal that it has a reputation for lying."[10]

Henry Kissinger seems to disagree, emphasizing that lying and trickery are unwise practices: "Only romantics think they can prevail in negotiations by trickery. . . .

trickery is not the path of wisdom but of disaster for a diplomat. Since one has to deal with the same person over and over again, one can get away with it only once at best, and then only at the cost of [permanent] stifling of the relationship."[11] Perhaps a diplomat can acknowledge the importance of deceit only after his career is over, and it is not by any means certain that is yet so for Kissinger. In any case, his account of his own diplomatic efforts is replete with examples of how he engaged in what I term concealment and half-concealment lies, as well as many instances in which he wondered whether his counterparts were engaging in concealment or falsification lies.

Stalin put it most bluntly: "[A] diplomat's words must have no relations to actions—otherwise what kind of diplomacy is it? . . . Good words are a concealment of bad deeds. Sincere diplomacy is no more possible than dry water or iron wood."[12] This is obviously too extreme a statement. Sometimes diplomats do speak truthfully, but certainly not always, and rarely when being truthful would seriously harm their nations' interests. When there is no doubt that only one policy can advance a nation's interests, other nations know what to expect, lying won't be an issue, and it probably won't be tried, because it would be so obviously false. Often matters are more ambiguous. One nation believes that another nation thinks it could gain by secret acts, cheating, or misleading proclamations, even if their dishonest acts are discovered later. Then assessments of national interests are not sufficient, and nor are the distrusted nation's words or public actions. A nation suspected of deceit would claim to be trustworthy just as would a truly trustworthy nation. Jervis notes: "Whether the Russians were going to cheat [in regard to the nuclear test ban] or not they would try to create the impression of honesty. Both an honest man and a liar will answer affirmatively if asked whether they will tell the truth."[13]

It is no wonder then that governments seek ways to detect lying by their adversaries. International deceits can occur in a number of different contexts, to serve quite different national objectives. One context, already mentioned, is when leaders, or high-ranking officials who represent a leader, meet in an attempt to resolve an international crisis. Each side may wish to bluff, to have offers that are not final perceived to be, and to have true intentions not recognized. Each side will also wish at times to make certain that the adversary accurately perceives those threats that are not bluffs, those offers that are final, those intentions that will be realized.

Skill in lying or lie catching is also important to conceal or uncover a surprise attack. The political scientist Michael Handel described a recent example: "By 2 June [1967] it became clear to the Israeli Government that war was unavoidable. The problem was how to launch a successful surprise attack while *both* sides were fully mobilized and alert. As part of a deception plan to conceal Israel's intention to go to war, Dayan [the Israeli defense minister] told a British journalist on 2 June that it was both too early and too late for Israel to go to war. He repeated this statement during a news conference on 3 June."[14] While this was not the only means Israel used to fool its opponents, Dayan's skill in lying was relevant to their success in achieving a total surprise in their attack on June 5.

Still another use of deception is to mislead an opponent about the deceiver's military capability. Barton Whaley's analysis of Germany's covert rearmament from 1919 to 1939 provides numerous examples of how skillfully the Germans did this.

. . . [I]n August 1938, as the Czechoslovak crisis was heating up under Hitler's pressure, [German Air Marshal] Hermann Göring invited the chiefs of the French Armée de l'Air to an inspec-

tion tour of the *Lüftwaffe*. General Joseph Vuillemin, Chief of the
Air General Staff, promptly accepted. . . . [German General
Ernst Udet] took Vuillemin up in his personal courier plane.
. . . As Udet brought the slow plane in at near stalling speed, the
moment he had carefully planned . . . for his visitor's benefit
arrived. Suddenly a Heinkel He-100 streaked past at full throttle,
a mere blur and a hiss. Both planes landed and the Germans took
their startled French visitors over to inspect. . . . "Tell me, Udet,"
[German General] Milch asked with feigned casualness, "how far
along are we with mass production?" Udet, on cue, replied, "Oh,
the second production line is ready and third will be within two
weeks." Vuillemin looked crestfallen and blurted out to Milch
that he was "shattered." . . . The French air delegation returned
to Paris with the defeatist word that the *Lüftwaffe* was unbeatable.[15]

The He-100 aircraft, whose speed was magnified by this
trick, was one of only three ever built. This kind of
bluffing, pretending unbeatable air power, ". . . became an
important ingredient in Hitler's diplomatic negotiations
which led to his brilliant series of triumphs; the policy of
appeasement was founded partially on the fear of the *Lüftwaffe*."[16]

   While international deceits do not always require direct
personal contact between liar and target (they can be accomplished by camouflage, false communiqués, and so on),
these examples illustrate that there are occasions when the
lie is face-to-face. A polygraph or any other intrusive device
that requires the opponent to cooperate in having his truthfulness measured can't be used. So interest in the last ten
years has turned to whether it would be possible to use
scientific studies of behavioral clues to deceit. I explained
in the Introduction that when I met with officials from our
own government, and officials from other governments,
my cautions about the dangers did not seem to impress
them. One of my motives in writing this book is to make

my case for caution again, with more care and complete-
ness, and to make it available to more than just the few
officials with whom I have consulted. As with criminal
deceits, the choices are not simple. Sometimes behavioral
clues to deceit might help to identify whether a leader or
other national spokesman is lying. The problem is to figure
out when that will be possible and when it won't, and when
leaders may be misled by their own or their experts' assessments of clues to deceit.

Let's go back to the example I used in the first page of
this book, when Chamberlain met Hitler for the first time,
at Berchtesgaden, on September 15, 1938, fifteen days before the Munich Conference.* Hitler sought to convince
Chamberlain that he did not plan war against Europe, that
he only wished to solve the problem of the Sudeten Germans in Czechoslovakia. If Britain would agree to his plan
—a plebiscite should be held in those areas of Czechoslovakia in which the majority of the population were Sudeten Germans, and if the people voted for it, those areas
would be annexed to Germany—then Hitler would not go
to war. Secretly Hitler was already committed to war. He
had already mobilized his army to attack Czechoslovakia on
October 1, and his plans for military conquest did not stop
there. Recall my earlier quote from Chamberlain's letter to
his sister after this first meeting with Hitler: ". . . [Hitler
is] a man who could be relied upon when he had given his
word."[17] In response to criticisms from the leaders of the
opposition Labor Party, Chamberlain described Hitler as a
"most extraordinary creature," a "man who would be
rather better than his word."[18]

A week later Chamberlain met with Hitler for the second time at Godesberg. Hitler now made new demands—

---

*I am indebted to Telford Taylor's book *Munich* (see notes) for the information
about Chamberlain and Hitler. I am grateful also to Mr. Taylor for checking the
accuracy of my interpretation and use of his material.

German troops must immediately occupy the areas in which the Sudeten Germans lived, a plebiscite could come later, not before, German military occupation, and the territories he claimed were larger than before. Afterward, in persuading his cabinet to accept those demands, Chamberlain said: "In order to understand people's actions it was necessary to appreciate their motives and to see how their minds worked. . . . Herr Hitler had a narrow mind and was violently prejudiced on certain subjects, but he would not deliberately deceive a man whom he respected and with whom he had been in negotiation, and he was sure that Herr Hitler now felt some respect for him. When Herr Hitler announced that he meant to do something it was certain that he would do it."[19] After this quote from Chamberlain, the historian Telford Taylor asks, "Had Hitler indeed deceived Chamberlain so completely, or was Chamberlain deceiving his colleagues in order to win acceptance of Hitler's demands?"[20] Let us presume, as Taylor did, that Chamberlain did believe Hitler, at least in their first meeting at Berchtesgaden.*

These very high stakes could have made Hitler feel detection apprehension, but he probably didn't. He had a willing victim. He knew that if Chamberlain were to discover that he was lying, Chamberlain would realize that his entire policy of appeasing Hitler had failed. At the time *appeasement* was not a shameful policy but an admired one; the meaning changed a few weeks later when Hitler's surprise attack made clear that Chamberlain had been fooled. Hitler was determined to take Europe by force. If Hitler could have been trusted, if he had kept to his agreements,

---

*While all the accounts by people involved at the time make this judgment, there is one exception. Joseph Kennedy's report to Washington of his meeting with Chamberlain states that "Chamberlain came away with an intense dislike [of Hitler]. . . . he is cruel, overbearing, has a hard look and . . . would be completely ruthless in any of his aims and methods" (Taylor, *Munich*, p. 752).

Chamberlain would have enjoyed the world's praise for having saved Europe from war. Chamberlain wanted to believe Hitler, and Hitler knew it. Another factor decreasing his fear of being caught was that Hitler knew exactly when he would need to lie and what he would need to say, so he could prepare and rehearse his line. There was no reason for Hitler to feel guilty or ashamed about his deceit —he considered deceiving the British an honorable act, required by his role, and demanded by his perception of history. It is not just a despised leader such as Hitler who would feel no shame or guilt about lying to his adversaries. In the view of many political analysts, lies are to be expected in international diplomacy, only questionable when they don't serve national interests. The one emotion that Hitler might have felt that could have leaked is duping delight. Reportedly, Hitler took pleasure in his ability to mislead the English, and the presence of other Germans who watched this successful deceit may well have magnified Hitler's excitement and delight in fooling Chamberlain. But Hitler was a very skilled liar, and apparently he prevented any leakage of these feelings.

When liar and target come from different cultures and do not share a language, detecting deceit is, for a number of reasons, much more difficult.* Even if Hitler made mistakes and Chamberlain had not been a willing victim, Chamberlain would have had difficulty spotting those mistakes. One reason is that their conversation was through translators. This offers the liar two advantages over direct conversation. If he makes any verbal mistakes—slips, pauses that are too long, or speech errors—the translator can cover them. And, the process of simultaneous transla-

---

*Groth noted this problem, although he did not explain how or why it would operate: ". . . personal impressions [by leaders] are likely to be most misleading in proportion as the gap, political, ideological, social and cultural, between the participants increases" (Groth, "Intelligence Aspects," p. 848; see notes).

tion allows the speaker time, as each phrase is translated, to think about exactly how he will word the next part of his lie. Even if the listener understands the liar's language, if it is not his native language, he is likely to miss subtleties in delivery and wording that could be clues to deceit.

Differences in national and cultural background can also obscure the interpretation of vocal, facial, and bodily clues to deceit, but in more complicated and intricate ways. Each culture has its own prescribed styles that govern, to some extent, the rate, tone, and loudness of speech, as well as the use of hands and face to illustrate speech. Facial and vocal signs of emotion are also governed by what I described in chapter 5 as *display rules,* which dictate the management of emotional expression, and these too vary with culture. If the lie catcher does not know about these differences and does not explicitly take account of them, he is more vulnerable to misinterpreting all of these behaviors and making disbelieving-the-truth or believing-a-lie mistakes.

An intelligence official might ask, at this point, how much of my analysis of the Hitler-Chamberlain meetings could have been done at the time. If it is possible only many years later when facts not available at the time emerge, lie checking would not be of practical use to the principal actors or their advisors when they want such help. My reading of accounts of that time suggests that many of my judgments were obvious, at least to some, in 1938. Chamberlain had so much at stake in wishing to believe Hitler that others, if not he, should have realized the need for him to be cautious in trusting his judgments of Hitler's truthfulness. Reportedly, Chamberlain felt superior to his political colleagues, was condescending toward them,[21] and might not have accepted any such caution.

Hitler's willingness to lie to England was also well established by the time of the Berchtesgaden meeting. Chamberlain would not even have to have read or believe what Hitler said in *Mein Kampf*. There were many examples, such as his concealed violations of the Anglo-German naval pact, or his lies about his intentions toward Austria. Before he met Hitler, Chamberlain had voiced his suspicion that Hitler was lying about Czechoslovakia, concealing his plan to conquer Europe.[22] Hitler was also known to have been an able liar, not just through diplomatic and military maneuvers but when face-to-face with his victim. He could turn on charm or fury and could with great mastery impress or intimidate, inhibit, or falsify feelings and plans.

Experts in political science and history who specialize in English-German relations in 1938 should be able to judge whether I am correct in suggesting that enough was known then to answer the questions in the checklist of lies (see appendix). I don't believe that lie checking at that time could have predicted with certainty that Hitler was going to lie. But it might have predicted that Chamberlain would not be likely to catch Hitler if he did. There are some other lessons about lying to be learned from the Hitler-Chamberlain meeting, but they are best considered after examining another example when a leader's lie might have been detected from behavioral clues to deceit.

During the Cuban missile crisis, two days before a meeting between President John F. Kennedy and Soviet Foreign Minister Andrei Gromyko,* on Tuesday, October 14, 1962, President Kennedy was informed by McGeorge Bundy that a U-2 flight over Cuba had yielded incontrovertible evidence that the Soviet Union was placing missiles in Cuba. There had been repeated rumors to that effect, and with an election coming up in November,

---

*I am indebted to Graham Allison for checking the accuracy of my interpretation of the meeting between Kennedy and Gromyko. My account was also checked by a person who was a member of Kennedy's administration and, at the time, in intimate contact with all of the principals involved in this incident.

Khrushchev (in the words of political scientist Graham Allison) "had assured the President, through the most direct and personal channels that he understood Kennedy's domestic problem and would do nothing to complicate it. Specifically, Khrushchev had given the President solemn assurances that the Soviet Union would not put offensive missiles in Cuba."[23] Kennedy was "furious" (according to Arthur Schlesinger);[24] although ". . . angry at Khrushchev's efforts to deceive him . . . [he] . . . took the news calmly but with an expression of surprise" (Theodore Sorenson's account).[25] In the words of Robert Kennedy, ". . . as the representatives of the CIA explained the U-2 photographs that morning . . . we realized that it had all been lies, one gigantic fabric of lies."[26] The president's chief advisors began to meet that day to consider what actions the government should take. The president decided that ". . . there should be no public disclosure of the fact that we knew of the Soviet missiles in Cuba until a course of action had been decided upon and readied. . . . Security was essential, and the President made it clear that he was determined that for once in the history of Washington there should be no leaks whatsoever" (Roger Hilsman, then in the State Department).[27]

Two days later, on Thursday, October 16, as his advisors still debated what course the country should take, President Kennedy saw Gromyko. "Gromyko had been in the United States for over a week, but no American official knew exactly why. . . . [H]e had asked for an audience at the White House. The request had come in about the same time as the . . . [U-2 photographic evidence]. Had the Russians spotted the U-2 plane? Did they wish to talk to Kennedy to feel out his reactions? Would they use this talk to inform Washington that Khrushchev was at this moment going public about the missiles, revealing his coup before the United States could spring its reaction?"[28]

Kennedy ". . . was anxious as the meeting approached, but managed to smile as he welcomed Gromyko and [Anatoly] Dobrynin [the Soviet ambassador] to his office" (Sorenson).[29] Not yet ready to act, Kennedy believed it important to conceal his discovery of the missiles from Gromyko, to avoid the Soviets having a further advantage.*

The meeting began at 5 P.M. and lasted until 7:15. Secretary of State Dean Rusk, Llewellyn Thompson (former United States Ambassador to the Soviet Union), and Martin Hildebrand (director of the Office of German Affairs) watched and listened from one side, while Dobrynin, Vladimir Semenor (Soviet deputy minister of foreign affairs), and a third Soviet official watched from the other side. Translators from each side were also present. "Kennedy sat in his rocker facing the fireplace, Gromyko to his right on one of the beige sofas. Cameramen came in, took pictures for posterity [see photo], then left. The Russian leaned back against a striped cushion and began speaking. . . ."[30]

After talking at some length about Berlin, Gromyko finally spoke of Cuba. According to Robert Kennedy's account, "Gromyko said he wished to appeal to the United States and to President Kennedy on behalf of Premier Khrushchev and the Soviet Union to lessen the tensions that existed with regard to Cuba. President Kennedy listened, astonished, but also with some admiration for the boldness of Gromyko's position. . . . [the president spoke] . . . firmly, but with great restraint considering the provocation. . . ."[31] Journalist Elie Abel relates: "The President gave Gromyko a clear opportunity to set the record straight by referring back to the repeated assurances of Khrushchev

---

*On this point different accounts disagree. While Sorensen reports Kennedy to have had no doubts about the need to deceive Gromyko, Elie Abel (*The Missile Crisis*, p. 63; see notes) reports that immediately afterward, Kennedy asked Rusk and Thompson whether he had made a mistake in not telling Gromyko the truth.

Seated, left to right: Anatoly Dobrynin, Andrei Gromyko, John F. Kennedy.

and Dobrynin that the missiles in Cuba were nothing but anti-aircraft weapons. . . . Gromyko stubbornly repeated the old assurances, which the President now knew to be lies. Kennedy did not confront him with the facts."[32] Kennedy "remained impassive. . . . he gave no sign of tension or anger" (Sorenson).[33]

Gromyko was in a mood of "unwonted joviality"

(Abel)[34] when he left the White House. Reporters asked him what was said in the meeting. "Gromyko smiled at them, obviously in a good mood, and said that the talks had been "useful, very useful."[35] Robert Kennedy reports, "I came by shortly after Gromyko left the White House. The President of the United States, it can be said, was displeased with the spokesman of the Soviet Union."[36] "I was dying to confront him with our evidence," Kennedy said, according to political scientist David Detzer.[37] In his office Kennedy commented to Robert Lovett and McBundy, who had come in: "Gromyko . . . in this very room not over ten minutes ago, told more bare-faced lies than I have ever heard in so short a time. All during his denial . . . I had the low-level pictures in the center drawer of my desk and it was an enormous temptation to show them to him."[38]

Let us consider Ambassador Dobrynin first. He was probably the only one at the meeting who was not lying. Robert Kennedy thought that the Soviets had lied to Dobrynin, not trusting Dobrynin's skill as a liar, and that Dobrynin had been truthful, as he knew it, in denying there were any missiles in Cuba in his earlier meetings with Robert Kennedy.* It would not be unusual for an ambassador to be so misled by his own government for such a purpose. John F. Kennedy had done just that with Adlai Stevenson, not informing him about the Bay of Pigs,

---

*The debate about Dobrynin continues: "From this meeting dates one of the enduring questions about Dobrynin. Did he know about the missiles when he, in effect, joined his Foreign Minister in an attempt to deceive the President? "He must have known" says George W. Ball, then under Secretary of State. "He had to lie for his country." "The President and his brother were taken in by Dobrynin to some extent," says former Supreme Court Justice Arthur J. Goldberg. "It's inconceivable that he didn't know." Others are less certain. Kennedy's national security adviser, McGeorge Bundy, says it is his guess that Dobrynin did not know. Many American specialists agree, explaining that, under the Soviet system, information on military matters is so closely held that Dobrynin may not have been fully aware of the nature of the Soviet weapons in Cuba" (Madeline G. Kalb, "The Dobrynin Factor," *New York Times Magazine*, May 13, 1984, p. 63).

and, as Allison points out, "similarly the Japanese Ambassador was not informed of Pearl Harbor; the German Ambassador in Moscow was not informed of Barbarossa [the German plan to invade Russia]."[39] In the period between June 1962, when the Soviets are presumed to have decided to put missiles in Cuba, and this meeting in mid-October, the Soviets used Dobrynin and Georgi Bolshakov, a public information official at the Soviet Embassy, to repeatedly assure members of the Kennedy administration (Robert Kennedy, Chester Bowles, and Sorenson) that no offensive missiles were being put into Cuba. Bolshakov and Dobrynin did not need to know the truth and probably, in fact, did not. Neither Khrushchev, Gromyko, nor anyone else who did know the truth ever directly met with their opponents until October 14, two days before the meeting between Gromyko and Kennedy. Khrushchev met in Moscow with the American Ambassador, Foy Kohler, and denied there were any missiles in Cuba. It was only then that the Soviets for the first time took the risk that their lies could have been discovered if Khrushchev or, two days later, Gromyko, made a mistake.

At the meeting in the White House, there were two lies, one by Kennedy and the other by Gromyko. Some readers may find it strange that I use the word *lie* to describe Kennedy, and not just Gromyko. Most people do not like to use that word about someone who is admired, because they, but not I, consider lying inherently evil. Kennedy's actions at that meeting fit my definition of a concealment lie. Both men, Kennedy and Gromyko, concealed from each other what each knew to be true—that there were missiles in Cuba. My analysis suggests why Kennedy was more likely than Gromyko to have provided a clue to his deceit.

As long as each had worked out his line in advance— and each would have had opportunity to do so—there should have been no problem in concealing from each other the knowledge they shared. Both men might have felt detection apprehension because the stakes involved were so great. Presumably the anxiety Kennedy is reported to have felt when he greeted Gromyko was detection apprehension. The stakes (and therefore the detection apprehension) may have been greater for Kennedy than for Gromyko. The United States still had not decided what to do. Not even the intelligence information about just how many missiles were in Cuba, in what stage of readiness, was complete. Kennedy's advisors thought that he must keep the discovery secret, for if Khrushchev were to learn before the United States acted, they feared Khrushchev would, through evasions and threats, complicate American action and gain a tactical advantage. According to McGeorge Bundy, "It made all the difference—I felt then and have felt since—that the Russians were caught pretending, in a clumsy way, that they had not done what it was clear to the whole world they had in fact done."[40] The Soviets, too, wanted time, to complete the construction of their missile bases, but it did not matter much if the Americans were to learn about the missiles now. The Soviets knew that American U-2 planes would soon discover the missiles if they had not done so already.

Even if one does not grant any difference in the stakes, Kennedy might have felt more detection apprehension than Gromyko, because he probably felt less confident about his ability to lie. Certainly he was less practiced than Gromyko. Also, Gromyko probably would feel more confident if he shared Khrushchev's opinion of Kennedy, formed at the Vienna summit meeting a year earlier, that Kennedy was not very tough.

Quite apart from the possibility that Kennedy felt more detection apprehension than Gromyko, he also reportedly had the burden of other emotions to conceal. The accounts

I quoted report that during their meeting Kennedy felt astonished, admiring, and displeased. Leakage of any of those emotions could have betrayed him, for those feelings would, in that context, suggest that Kennedy knew about the Soviet deceit. On the other side, Gromyko may have felt duping delight. That would be consistent with the reports that he looked so jovial when he left.

The chances for leakage or clues to deception would not be great, since both men were skilled and each had personal characteristics that made him able to conceal whatever emotions he felt. Yet Kennedy had more of a burden than Gromyko, more emotions he reportedly felt, and he was less skilled and less confident about his skill as a deceiver. The cultural and language differences might have covered any of his clues to deceit, but Ambassador Dobrynin should have been in a position to spot them. Highly knowledgeable, after many years in this country, about American behavior, very comfortable with the language, Dobrynin also had the advantage of being an observer rather than a direct participant, able to devote himself to scrutinizing the suspect. Ambassador Thompson was in a similar position, most able to spot any behavioral clues to deceit in Gromyko's performance.

While I have been able to draw on many accounts of this meeting from the American side, there is no information from the Soviet side and thus no way to guess whether or not Dobrynin did indeed sense the truth. Reports that Dobrynin appeared dumbfounded and visibly shaken when, four days later, Secretary of State Rusk informed him of the discovery of the missiles and the beginning of the American naval blockade have been interpreted as evidence that the Soviets did not know until then about the American discovery.[41] If his own government had kept him ignorant about the installation of missiles, this would have been the first he learned of it. Even if Dobrynin knew about the missiles, and even if he knew that the United States had discovered the missiles, he still might have been dumbfounded and shaken by the American decision to respond militarily. Most analysts agree that the Soviets did not expect Kennedy to respond to the discovery with military action.

The point is not to determine whether Kennedy's concealment was uncovered but to explain why there was a chance it might have been and to demonstrate that, even then, recognizing clues to deceit would not have been an easy, uncomplicated matter. Reportedly, Kennedy sensed no mistakes in Gromyko's lies. Since Kennedy already knew the truth he had no need to spot clues to deceit. Armed with that knowledge Kennedy could admire Gromyko's skill.

In analyzing these two international deceits I said that Hitler, Kennedy, and Gromyko were all natural liars, inventive and clever in fabricating, smooth talkers, with a convincing manner. I believe that any politician who comes to power, in part, through his skill in debate and public speeches, who is agile in handling questions at news conferences, with a glistening TV or radio image, has the conversational talents to be a natural liar. (While Gromyko did not reach power by such means, he survived when few did, over a very long period, and by 1963 was already highly experienced in both diplomacy and the politics of internal struggles within the Soviet Union.) Such people are convincing; it is part of their stock in trade. Whether or not they choose to lie, they have the requisite abilities to do so well. Of course there are other routes to political power. The skills relevant to interpersonal deceit are not necessary to stage a coup d'etat. Nor would a leader who achieves power through bureaucratic skills, by inheritance, or by

outwitting domestic rivals through private maneuvers necessarily have to be a natural liar, talented as a conversational performer.

Conversational skill—the ability to conceal and falsify
words as they are spoken, with appropriate expressions and
gestures—is not needed as long as the liar doesn't have to
face or converse with his target. Targets can be deceived in
writing, through intermediaries, press releases, by military
actions, and so forth. Any form of lying, however, fails if
the liar does not have strategic skills, is unable to think out
his moves and those of his target. I presume that all political
leaders must be shrewd, strategic thinkers but that only
some have the conversational skills that allow them to lie
when face-to-face with their quarries, in the kinds of deceits we have considered in this book.

Not everyone is able to lie or is willing to do so. I
presume that most political leaders are willing to lie, at
least to certain targets, under certain circumstances. Even
Jimmy Carter, who campaigned on the pledge that he
would never lie to the American people, and who demon-
strated that by acknowledging his lustful fantasies in a
Playboy magazine interview, later lied, concealing his plans
to rescue by force the hostages held in Iran. Analysts specializing in military deceit have attempted to identify leaders more ready or able to lie. One possibility is that they
come from cultures that condone deceit,[42] but the evidence
that there are such cultures is weak.* Another untested

---

*Soviets have been said to be both more secretive and more truthful than other
nationals. Soviet expert Walter Hahn argues that secrecy has a long history and
is a Russian, not a Soviet, characteristic ("The Mainsprings of Soviet Secrecy,"
Orbis 1964 : 719–47). Ronald Hingley says that Russians are quicker to volunteer
information on private aspects of their lives, and more prone to utter emotionally
charged statements in the presence of strangers. This does not mean that they are
any more or less truthful than other nationals. "They can be dry, austere, and
reserved as the most tight-lipped or strait-laced Anglo-Saxon of legend, since
there is much scope for variety in Russian as in any other national psychology"
(Hingley, *The Russian Mind*, [New York: Scribners, 1977], p. 74). Sweetser believes

idea is that leaders more willing to lie are found in countries (especially where there is a dictatorship) in which
leaders take a strong role in military decisions.[43] An attempt to discover from historical material a deceptive personality type characterizing leaders known to have lied was
not successful, but information about that work is not
available to evaluate why it did not succeed.[44]

There is no hard evidence, one way or the other, about
whether or not political leaders actually are unusually able
as liars, more skilled and willing to lie than, let us say,
business executives. If they are, it would make international deceits all the harder, and it would also suggest the
importance, for the lie catcher, of identifying the exceptions, those heads of state who are notable for not having
the usual skill as liars.

Now let's consider the other side of the coin, whether
or not heads of state are more able than others as lie catchers. Research has found that some people are unusually
skilled as lie catchers, and that ability as a lie catcher is not
related to ability as a liar.[45] Unfortunately that research has
mostly examined college students. No work has examined
people who are in leadership positions in organizations of
any kind. If testing such people did suggest that some of
them are skilled as lie catchers, then the question would
arise whether it is possible to identify skilled lie catchers
from a distance, without giving them a test to find out. If
unusually skilled lie catchers could be identified from the
kind of information that is generally available about public
figures, a political leader who is considering lying might be

---

that cultures differ only in what types of information are subject do deceit, not
in one culture being more deceitful than another ("The Definition of a Lie," in
Cultural Models in Language and Thought, ed. Naomi Quinn and Dorothy Holland [in press]). While I have no reason to argue, any conclusion now would be
premature, since there has been so little study of national or cultural differences
in lying or lie catching.

able to more accurately gauge how able his adversary may be to detect any leakage or clues to deception.

The political scientist Groth has argued, to me convincingly, that heads of state are unusually *poor* lie catchers, less cautious than their professional diplomats about their ability to evaluate the character and trustworthiness of their adversaries. "Heads of states and foreign ministers frequently lack the elementary skills of negotiation and communication or the background information, for instance, which would enable them to make competent appraisals of their adversaries."[46] Jervis agrees, noting that heads of state may overestimate their ability as lie catchers if "their rise to power was partly dependent on a keen ability to judge others."[47] Even if a leader is correct in believing that he is unusually skilled as a lie catcher, he may fail to take account of how much harder it is to detect lying when the suspect is from another culture and speaks another language.

I judged Chamberlain to be a willing victim of deceit, so committed to avoiding war if that was at all possible that he desperately wanted to believe Hitler and overestimated his ability to read Hitler's character. Yet Chamberlain was not a foolish man; nor was he unaware of the possibility that Hitler could be lying. But Chamberlain had a very strong motive to want to believe Hitler, for if he couldn't, then war was immediately at hand. Such errors in judgment by heads of state and mistaken belief in their own own abilities as lie catchers are, according to Groth, not that unusual. In my terms, it is especially likely whenever the stakes are very high. It is then, when the most damage might be done, that a head of state may be quite vulnerable to becoming a willing victim of his adversary's deceit.

Consider another example of a willing victim. To even the score, I selected this time, from the many examples furnished by Groth, Chamberlain's opponent Winston Churchill. Churchill reports that the fact that Stalin "spoke as often of 'Russia' as of the 'Soviet Union', and made references to the Deity"[48] led him to wonder whether Stalin did not retain some religious beliefs.* In another incident, after returning from Yalta, in 1945, Churchill defended his faith in Stalin's pledges as follows: "I feel that their word is their bond. I know of no government which stands to its obligations even in its own despite, more solidly than the Russian government."[49] One of his biographers said of Churchill, ". . . for all his knowledge of the Soviet past, Winston was prepared to give Stalin the benefit of the doubt and to trust to his intentions. It was difficult for him to do other than believe in the essential probity of those in high station with whom he did business."[50] Stalin did not reciprocate that respect. Milovan Djilas quotes Stalin as saying in 1944: "Perhaps you think that just because we are the allies of the English . . . we have forgotten who they are and who Churchill is. They find nothing sweeter than to trick their allies. Churchill is the kind who, if you don't watch him, will slip a Kopeck out of your pocket. . . ."[51] Churchill's focus on destroying Hitler and his need for Stalin's help may have made him a willing victim for Stalin's deceits.

I have given more space to deceits between statesmen than to any of the other forms of deceit I considered in this chapter. I did so not because this is the most promising arena for detecting behavioral clues to deceit but because it is the most hazardous, where mistaken judgments can be

---

*Jimmy Carter was similarly impressed. In describing his first meeting with Soviet President Leonid Brezhnev Carter quoted from his opening response given the following day to Brezhnev: "There has been an excessive delay in this meeting, but now that we are finally together, we must make maximum progress. I was really impressed yesterday when President Brezhnev told me, 'If we do not succeed, God will not forgive us!'" Carter's comment that "Brezhnev seemed somewhat embarrassed" by his remark implies that Carter, like Churchill, took this reference to the deity seriously (Carter, *Keeping the Faith* [New York: Bantam Books, 1982], p. 248).

most costly because the deceits may be deadly. Yet, as with detecting deceits among criminal suspects, there is no point in arguing that detecting deceit from behavioral clues should be abolished. It can't be stopped, in any nation. It is human nature to gather such information, at least informally, from behavioral clues. And, as I argued in discussing the hazards of detecting deceit during interrogations, it is probably safer if the participants and those who advise them are aware of their judgments of expressive clues to deceit than if such impressions were to remain in the realm of intuitions and hunches.

As I noted in regard to detecting deceit among criminal suspects, even if it were possible to abolish the interpretation of behavioral clues to deceit in international meetings, I don't believe that would be desirable. Clearly the historical record shows infamous international deceits in very recent history. Who would not want their own country to be better able to spot such lies? The problem is how to do so without increasing the chances of mistaken judgments. I fear that the overconfidence of Chamberlain and Churchill in their ability to read deceit and gauge the character of their counterparts might pale next to the arrogance of a behavioral science expert who makes his living claiming to be able to detect signs of deceit in foreign leaders.

I have tried to challenge, albeit indirectly, any behavioral experts working for any nation as deceit detectors, making them more cognizant of the complexity of their task, and making their clients—those they advise—more skeptical. My challenge must be indirect, since such experts, if they do exist, are working secretly,* as are those

---

*Although no one will admit to working on this problem, I have had some correspondence with people employed by the Department of Defense and some phone conversations with the CIA that imply that there are people studying clues to deceit in counterintelligence and diplomacy. The one such unclassified study I have seen, funded by the Department of Defense, was quite dreadful and did not meet the usual scientific standards.

who are doing classified research on how to detect deceit among negotiators or heads of state. I hope to make such anonymous researchers more cautious, and to make those who pay for their work more demanding and more critical of any claims about the utility of their product.

I should not be misunderstood. I want to see such research done, I think it is urgent, and I understand why any nation would conduct at least some of that research secretly. I expect that research that tries to identify the good and bad liars and lie catchers among the kinds of people who become national decision makers will prove it is nearly impossible to do so, but that should be found out. Similarly, I believe that research on situations that closely resemble summit meetings or negotiations during crises—in which the participants are highly skilled and from different nations, and the studies are arranged so that the stakes are very high (not the usual lab experiment on college freshmen)—will find that the yield is very meager. But that too should be found out, and if it is so, the results should be unclassified and shared.

This chapter has shown that whether or not deceit succeeds does not depend upon the arena. It is not that all spousal deceits fail or that all business, criminal, or international deceits succeed. Failure or success depends upon the particulars of the lie, the liar, and the lie catcher. It does get more complicated at the international level than between parent and child, but every parent knows that it isn't always easy to avoid error even then.

Table 4 in the appendix lists all thirty-eight items in the lying checklist. Almost half of those questions—eighteen of them—help in determining whether the liar will have to conceal or falsify emotions, lying about feelings or feelings about lying.

Using the checklist may not always provide an estimate. Not enough may be known to answer many of the questions, or the answers may be mixed, some suggesting that it would be an easy, and others that it would be a hard, lie to detect. But that should be useful to know. Even when an estimate can be made, it may not correctly predict, for liars may be betrayed not by their behavior but by third parties, and the most blatant clues to deceit may, by accident, be missed. But both liar and lie catcher should want to know that estimate. Who is helped more by that knowledge—liar or lie catcher? That is the first point I will discuss in the next chapter.

NINE

Lie Catching in the 1990s

I BEGAN THIS BOOK by describing the first meeting in
1938 between Adolf Hitler, the chancellor of Nazi
Germany, and Neville Chamberlain, the British
prime minister. I chose this event because it was one of the
most deadly deceits in history, containing an important
lesson about why lies succeed. Recall that Hitler had already secretly ordered the German Army to attack Czechoslovakia. It would take some weeks, however, for his army
to fully mobilize for the attack. Wanting the advantage of
a surprise attack, Hitler concealed his decision to go to war.
Instead he told Chamberlain that he was willing to live in
peace if the Czechs would consider his demands about re-
drawing the borders between their countries. Chamberlain
believed Hitler's lie and tried to persuade the Czechs not
to mobilize their army while there was still a chance for
peace.

In a sense Chamberlain was a willing victim who
wanted to be misled. Otherwise he would have had to confront the failure of his entire policy towards Germany and
how he had jeopardized his country's safety. The lesson
about lying is that some victims unwittingly cooperate in
being misled. Critical judgment is suspended, contradictory information ignored, because knowing the truth is
more painful, at least in the short run, than believing the
lie.

While I still believe this is an important lesson that applies to many other lies, not just ones between heads of nations, now, seven years after having written this book, I worry that the meeting between Hitler and Chamberlain may imply two other incorrect lessons about lying. It might appear that if Chamberlain had not wanted to be misled Hitler's lie would have failed. Our research since the original 1985 publication of *Telling Lies* suggests that even Winston Churchill, Chamberlain's rival who had warned against Hitler, might well have been unable to spot Hitler's lie. If Chamberlain had brought experts on spotting lies—from Scotland Yard or from British Intelligence—they too probably would not have done much better.

This chapter explains our new research findings which led me to these new conclusions. I describe what we have learned about who can catch liars, and some new evidence on how to catch lies. I will add also some tips I have learned about how to apply our experimental research to real-life lies, based on my experience over the last five years teaching those who daily deal with people suspected of lying.

Because Hitler was so evil, this example may also imply that it is always wrong for a national leader to lie. Such a conclusion is too simple. The next chapter explores the arguments about when lying is justified in public life, considering a number of famous incidents in recent American political history. Considering former president Lyndon Johnson's false claims about American military successes during the Viet Nam war, and also the decisions by the National Aeronautics and Space Administration (NASA) to launch the space shuttle *Challenger* when there was a considerable risk it might explode, I will raise the question of whether these were cases of self-deceit. And, if they were, should those who lied to themselves still be held responsible for their actions?

Who Can Catch Liars?

When I wrote *Telling Lies* I thought that the type of lie I had been studying—deceptions undertaken to conceal strong emotions felt at the very moment of the lie—had little relevance to the lies told by diplomats, politicians, criminals, or spies. I feared that professional lie catchers—police, Central Intelligence Agency (CIA) agents, judges, and psychological or psychiatric experts who worked for the government—might be overly optimistic about their ability to tell when someone is lying from behavioral clues. I wanted to warn those whose job requires that they make judgments about lying and truthfulness to distrust anyone who claims to be able to detect deceit from behavioral clues, what the criminal justice system calls *demeanor.* I wanted to caution them to be less confident themselves about their own ability to spot a liar.

There is now strong evidence that I was right in warning professional lie catchers that most of them should be more cautious about their ability. But I also found that I may have overstated the case. To my surprise I found some professional lie catchers are very good in spotting lies from behavioral clues. I have learned something about who they are and why they are good at it. And I have reason now to think that what I have learned about lies about emotions can apply to some lies in a political, criminal, or counter-intelligence context.

I would probably never have learned this if I had not already written *Telling Lies.* A psychology professor who does experimental laboratory research on lying and on emotions does not usually meet people who work in the criminal justice system or the world of the spy and counterspy. These professional lie catchers learned about me not from my scientific publications, which have appeared for the last thirty years, but through the media accounts of my work coincident with the publication of *Telling Lies*. I soon was invited to give workshops to city, state and federal judges, trial attorneys, police, and those who give polygraph examinations for the Federal Bureau of Investigation (FBI), the CIA, the National Security Agency, the Drug Enforcement Agency, the United States Secret Service, and the United States Army, Navy, and Air Force.

Lying is not an academic matter to these people. They take their job and what I have to say with deadly seriousness. They are not students who accept a professor's word because he gives the grade and is the authority who wrote the book. If anything my academic credentials are a disadvantage with these groups. They demand real-life examples, that I confront their experience, meet their challenges, and give them something they can use the next day. I might tell them how hard it is to spot a liar, but they have to make those judgments tomorrow and cannot wait for more research. They want any help I can give, beyond just the warning to be more cautious, but they are very skeptical and critical.

Amazingly, they were also a lot more flexible than I have found the academic world to be. They were more willing to consider changing how they go about their business than most university curriculum committees. One judge asked me during the lunch break whether he should rearrange his courtroom so that he could see the witness's face rather than the back of the head. I had never considered such a simple idea. From there on I always made that suggestion when I talked to judges, and many have rearranged their courtrooms.

A Secret Service agent told me how hard it is to tell whether a person who has made a threat against the president is lying when he or she says the threat was not serious, it was just said to impress a friend. There was a terrible look on this agent's face when he recounted how they had decided that Sarah Jane Moore was a "wacko," not a real assassin, mistakenly releasing her just a few hours before she fired a shot at President Gerald Ford on September 22, 1975. I told the agent that the workshop I could offer might give them only a very slight additional edge, probably adding no more than 1 percent to their accuracy level. "Great," he said, "let's do it."

My colleague Maureen O'Sullivan[1] and I always started our workshops with a brief test of how well each participant could tell from demeanor if someone was lying. Our lie-catching test shows ten different people, the student nurses, who were part of the experiment I described in chapter 2 (pages 52–55). Each person says she is having pleasant feelings as she watches a film showing nature scenes and playful animals. Five of the ten women are telling the truth; the other five are lying. The liars were actually seeing some terrible, gruesome, medical films, but they tried to conceal their upset feelings and convince the interviewer they were seeing the pleasant films.

I had two reasons for giving our lie-catching test. I couldn't miss the opportunity to learn how accurately these people who deal with the most deadly deceits can actually spot when someone is lying. I was also convinced that taking a lie-catching test would be a good opener. It would directly face my audience with how difficult it is to tell when someone is lying. I enticed them by saying, "You are going to have a unique opportunity to learn the truth about your ability to catch lies. You make such judgments all the time, but how often do you find out, for certain, if your judgments are right or wrong? Here is your chance. In just fifteen minutes you will know the answer!" Immediately after taking the test I would give the correct answers. Then I asked them to raise their hands if they got all ten correct, nine correct, and so forth. I tallied the results on a blackboard so they could evaluate their own performance against that of their group. Although it was not my purpose, I knew this procedure also exposed how well each person had done.

I expected that most would not do very well on my test. Having them learn that sad lesson fit with my mission to make such people more cautious about when they can tell whether someone is lying. During the first few workshops I worried that my "students" would object, not wanting to risk being publicly exposed if it turned out they were not able to spot liars. When they found out how badly most of them had done, I expected they would challenge me, questioning the validity of my test, arguing that the lies I showed were not relevant to the lies they dealt with. That never happened. These men and women in the criminal justice and intelligence communities were willing to have their ability to catch lies exposed in public before their peers. They were more courageous than my academic colleagues when I have offered them the same opportunity to learn, in front of their students and colleagues, how well they could do.

Learning how badly they did forced these professional lie catchers to give up the rules-of-thumb many of them had been relying on. They became a lot more cautious about judging deception from demeanor. I further cautioned them about the many stereotypes people have about how to tell whether someone is lying—such as the idea that people who fidget or look away when they talk are always lying.

On the more positive side I showed them how to use the lie-checking list described in chapter 8 (page 241) on some real-life examples. And I gave a lot of emphasis, as I do in earlier chapters, on how emotions can betray a lie, and how to spot the signs of those emotions. I showed them dozens of facial expressions very briefly, at one-hundredth of a second, so they could learn to spot micro facial expressions easily. I used videotaped examples of various lies on which they could practice their newly learned skills.

In September 1991, our findings on these professional lie catchers were published.[2] It turned out that only one occupational group did better than chance—the U.S. Secret Service. A little more than half of them scored at or above 70 percent level accuracy, nearly a third reached 80 percent or more. Although I cannot be certain why the Secret Service did so much better than the other groups, my bet is that it is because many of them had done protection work—watching crowds for any sign of someone who might menace the person they were protecting. That kind of vigilance should be very good preparation for spotting the subtle behavioral clues to deceit.

It is amazing to many people when they learn that all of the other professional groups concerned with lying— judges, trial attorneys, police, polygraphers who work for the CIA, FBI, or NSA (National Security Agency), the military services, and psychiatrists who do forensic work— did no better than chance. Equally astonishing, most of them didn't know they could not detect deceit from demeanor. Their answer to the question we asked before they took our test about how well they thought they would do was unrelated to how well or poorly they actually did, as was their answer to the same question asked immediately after they completed the test.

I was surprised that *any* of these professional lie catchers would be very accurate in spotting lies, since none of them had any prior experience with the particular situation nor with the characteristics of the liars they saw. I had designed the situation shown in the video to approximate the plight of the mental hospital patient who is concealing her plans to take her life, to win freedom from medical supervision so she can carry out her act. She must conceal her anguish and convincingly act as if she is no longer depressed. (See discussion in pages 16–17 and 54–56.) Strong negative emotions felt at the moment were covered with a veneer of positive emotion. Only the psychiatrists and psychologists should have had much experience with that situation, and they as a group were no better than chance. Why should the U.S. Secret Service do so well in spotting this type of deceit?*

It was not obvious to me ahead of time, but thinking about our findings suggested a new idea about when it will be possible to detect deceit from behavioral clues. The lie catcher does not need to know as much about either the suspect or the situation *if* strong emotions are aroused. When someone looks or sounds afraid, guilty, or excited and those expressions don't fit what the words say, it is a good bet the person is lying. When there are many speech disruptions (pauses, "umhh," and so on), and there is no reason why the suspect should not know what to say, and the suspect usually does not talk that way, the suspect is probably lying. Such behavioral clues to deceit will be sparser whenever emotions are not aroused. If the liar is not concealing strong emotions, successful lie detection should require that the lie catcher be better versed in the specifics of the situation and the characteristics of the liar.

Whenever the stakes are high, there is a chance that the fear of being caught or the challenge of beating the lie catcher (what I call duping delight, page 76) will allow accurate lie detection without the need for the lie catcher to have much knowledge about the specifics of either the

*Perhaps the professional groups we tested might have done much better if we had given them a lie to judge which was specific to the situation they usually deal with. We may have only learned who are the good lie catchers regardless of situational familiarity, not who are the good lie catchers when operating in their usual terrain. I think that is not so, but only further research can rule that possibility out.

situation or the suspect. But, and it is an important but, high stakes will not make every liar afraid of being caught. Criminals with experience in getting away with it won't have such fear, nor will the philanderer who has succeeded many times in concealing his past affairs, nor the practiced negotiator. And high-stakes lies may make some innocent suspects who fear being disbelieved appear to be lying, even when they are not. (See the discussion of Othello's error on pages 170–73.)

If the liar shares values with and respects the target of the lie, there is a chance that the liar will feel guilty about lying, and that behavioral signs of that guilt will betray the lie or motivate a confession. But the lie catcher must avoid the temptation of thinking too well of herself, presuming respect to which she is not entitled. The distrustful or hypercritical mother must have the self-knowledge to realize that she has those characteristics and therefore should not presume her daughter will feel guilty about lying to her. The unfair employer must know that he is seen as unfair in the eyes of his employees, and cannot rely upon guilt signs to betray their deceptions.

It is never wise to trust one's judgments about whether someone is lying without *any* knowledge about the suspect or the situation. My lie-catching test did not give the lie catcher any opportunity to become familiar with each person that had to be judged. Decisions about who was lying and who was truthful had to be made based on seeing each person only once, with no other information about that person. Under those circumstances very few people were accurate. It was not impossible, just difficult for most. (I'll explain later how those who were accurate were able to make this judgment with so little information.) We have another version of our test which shows two examples of each person. When lie catchers can compare the person's behavior in two situations, they are more accurate, although even then most do only slightly better than chance.[3]

The lie-checking list in chapter 8 should help in estimating whether in a high stakes lie there will be useful,
misleading, or few behavioral clues. It should help in determining whether there will be detection apprehension,
deception guilt, or duping delight. The lie catcher should
never simply presume that it is always possible to detect
deceit from behavioral clues. The lie catcher must resist the
temptation to resolve uncertainty about truthfulness by
overestimating his own ability to spot a lie.

Although the Secret Service was the only occupational
group which did better than chance, a few people in every
other group also scored highly. I am continuing research to
learn why just some people are very accurate in detecting
deceit. How did they learn it? Why doesn't everyone learn
to spot lying more accurately? Is this really a skill that is
learned, or might it be more of a gift, something you either
have or don't have? That odd idea first came to mind when
I found that my eleven-year-old daughter did nearly as
accurately as the best of the U.S. Secret Service. She has not
read my books or articles. Maybe my daughter isn't so
special; perhaps most children are better than adults in
spotting lies. We are starting research to find out.

A lead on the answer to the question about why some
people are accurate lie detectors comes from what the people who took our test wrote when we asked them what
behavioral clues they used in making their judgments
about whether a person was lying. Comparing those who
were accurate, across all the occupational groups, with
those who were inaccurate, we found that the accurate lie
catchers mentioned using information from the face, voice,
and body while the inaccurate ones only mentioned the
words that were spoken. That finding, of course, fits very
well what I say in the earlier chapters in *Telling Lies,* but
none of the people we tested had read the book before they

took our test. Some people, the ones who were accurate lie catchers, knew that it is much easier to disguise words than expressions, voice, or body movement. Not that words are unimportant—very often contradictions in what is said can be very revealing, and it may well be that sophisticated analyses of speech can reveal lying[4]—but the content of speech should not be the only focus. We still need to find out why everyone does not check the words against the face and voice.

New Findings on Behavioral Clues to Lying

Other research we completed in the last two years further substantiates and adds to what *Telling Lies* says about the importance of the face and voice in detecting deceit. Measuring the facial expressions shown in videotapes of the student nurses when they were lying and telling the truth, we found differences in two kinds of smiles. When they were truly enjoying themselves they showed many more felt smiles (figure 5A in chapter 5), and when they were lying they showed what we call masking smiles. (In a masking smile, in addition to the smiling lips there are signs of sadness [figure 3A], or fear [figure 3B], or anger [figure 3C or figure 4], or disgust.)[5]

The distinctions among types of smiling has been further supported in studies of children and adults, in this country and abroad, in many different circumstances, not just when people lie. We have found differences in what is occurring within the brain and in what people report they are feeling when they show a felt smile as compared to other kinds of smiling. The best clue to whether the smile is truly one in which the person is experiencing enjoyment is the involvement of muscle that surrounds the eye, not just the smiling lips.[6] It is not so simple as just watching for crows-feet wrinkles at the outer corners of the eyes, because that won't always work. Crows-feet are a useful sign of a felt smile only if the smile is slight, the enjoyment experienced not very strong. In a very large or broad smile the smiling lips themselves will create the crows-feet, and so you have to look at the eyebrows. If the eye muscle is involved because it is truly the smile of enjoyment, then the eyebrow will move down, very slightly. It is a subtle clue, but one we have found people can spot without any special training.[7]

We also found that the voice pitch became higher when the nursing students lied about their feelings. This change in voice pitch marks increased emotional arousal, and is not a sign of lying itself. If someone is supposedly enjoying a relaxing, pleasant scene her voice pitch should not get higher. Not all the liars showed both facial and voice signs of their deceit. By using both sources of information, the best results were obtained—a "hit" rate of 86 percent. But that still means that on 14 percent a mistake was made; on the basis of the facial and voice measures we thought the person was being truthful when they lied, and lying when they were truthful. So even though the measures work on the great majority of people, they don't work on everyone. I don't expect we ever will obtain a set of behavioral measures which will work on everyone. Some people are natural performers and won't be caught, and some people are just so idiosyncratic that what reveals lies for others won't for them.

In work in progress Dr. Mark Frank and I have found the first evidence supporting my idea that there are some very good liars, who are natural performers, and some people who are terrible liars and can never succeed in deceiving others. Dr. Frank and I had people lie or tell the truth in two deception scenarios. In one scenario they could have committed a mock crime, taking $50 from a briefcase, which they could keep if they could convince the interrogator they were telling the truth when they claimed not to have taken the money. In the other scenario they could either be lying or telling the truth about their opinion on a hot issue such as abortion or capital punishment. Frank found that those who were successful liars in one scenario were successful in the other, and those who were easy to detect when lying about their opinions were easy to detect when lying about the crime.[8]

This might seem very obvious, but much of the reasoning in the earlier chapters could suggest it is the specifics of the lie, not the person's ability, that determines whether a particular lie succeeds. Probably both factors matter. Some people are so good or so bad at lying that the situation and the specifics of the lie won't matter much; they will consistently get away with it or fail. Most people are not so extreme and for them what determines how well they can lie is who they are lying to, what they are lying about, and what is at stake.

The Odds Against Spotting Lies in the Courtroom

What I learned in teaching police, judges, and attorneys over the past five years suggested a wisecrack—which I now use in my workshops: The criminal justice system must have been designed by someone who wanted to make it impossible to detect deceit from demeanor. The guilty suspect is given many chances to prepare and rehearse her replies before her truthfulness is evaluated by jury or judge, thus increasing her confidence and decreasing her fear of being detected. Score one against the judge and jury. The direct examination and cross-examination take place months, if not years, after the incident, thereby blunting emotions associated with the criminal event. Score two against the judge and jury. Because of the long time delay before the beginning of the trial, the suspect will have repeated her false account so often that she may start to *believe* her own false story; when that happens she is, in a sense, not lying when she testifies. Score three against the judge and jury. When challenged in cross-examination, the defendant typically has been prepared if not rehearsed by her own attorney, and the questions asked often allow a simple yes or no reply. Score four against the judge and jury. And then there is the *innocent* defendant who comes to trial terrified of being disbelieved. Why should the jury and judge believe her, if the police, prosecutor, and the judge, in pretrial moves for dismissal, did not? The signs of fear of being disbelieved can be misinterpreted as a guilty person's fear of being caught. Score five against the judge and jury.

While the odds are against the finders of fact, as the judge and jury are called, being able to rely much upon demeanor, that is not so for the person who does the initial interview or interrogation. Usually it is the police, or sometimes, in cases of child abuse, a social worker. These are the people who have the best chance of being able to tell from behavioral clues if someone is lying. A liar has usually had no chance to rehearse, and is most likely to be either afraid of being caught or guilty about the wrong action. While the police and social workers may be well-intentioned, most are not well trained in how to ask unbiased and non-leading questions. They have not been taught how to evaluate behavioral clues to truthfulness and lying, and they are biased in their typical presumption.[9] They think that nearly everyone they see is guilty, and everyone is lying, and that may well be so for the great majority of those they interrogate. When I first gave my lie-catching test to police officers I found that many of them had judged every person they saw on the videotape as lying. "No one ever tells the truth," they told me. Fortunately, juries are not continually exposed to criminal suspects, and they are therefore not as likely to presume the suspect must be guilty.

Admiral Poindexter's Exploration Flags

The behavioral clues in face, body, voice, and manner of speaking are not signs of lying per se. They may be signs of emotions that don't fit with what is being said. Or they may be signs that the suspect is thinking about what he is saying before he says it. They are flags marking areas which need to be explored. They tell the lie catcher that something is happening which she needs to find out about by asking more questions, checking other information, and so on. Let's look at one example of how these flags can work.

Recall that in mid-1986 the United States sold arms to Iran in hope of obtaining the release of American hostages held in Lebanon by groups directed by or sympathetic to Iran. The Reagan Administration said it was not simply an arms for hostage swap but was part of an attempt to reestablish better relations with the newly emerging moderate Islamic leadership in Iran following the death of the Ayatollah Khomeini. But a scandal of major proportions arose when it was reported that some of the profits made on the sale of those arms to Iran were secretly used, in direct violation of congressional law (the Boland amendments), to buy arms for the *contras,* the pro-American Nicaraguan rebel group that was fighting the new pro-Soviet, Sandinista leadership in this Central American nation. At a press conference in 1986 President Ronald Reagan and Attorney General Edwin Meese themselves revealed the diversion of funds to the *contras.* At the same time they claimed not to have known anything about it. They did announce that Vice Admiral John Poindexter, the national security affairs adviser, had resigned and that his colleague Marine Lieutenant Colonel Oliver North had been relieved of his duties at the National Security Council. News reporting of the Iran-Contra scandal was extensive, and polls taken at the time showed that the majority of the American people did not believe President Reagan's claim that he did not know about the illegal diversions of profits to the *contras*.

Eight months later Lieutenant Colonel North testified before the congressional committee investigating the Iran-Contra affair. North said that he had discussed the whole matter often with the William Casey, director of the Central Intelligence Agency. Casey, though, had died just three months before North testified. North told the committee that Casey had warned him that he (North) would have to be the "fall guy" and that Poindexter might also have to share that role to protect President Reagan.

Now Poindexter testified telling the congressional committee that he alone gave approval to Colonel North's plan to divert profits from the arms sales to the *contras*. "He claims to have exercised this authority without ever telling the President so as to protect Reagan from the 'politically volatile issue' that subsequently exploded on them. 'I made the decision,' Poindexter declared in an even, matter-of-fact tone."[10]

At one point in this testimony, just when he is asked about a luncheon he had with the late CIA director William Casey, Poindexter says he cannot remember what was said at the lunch, only that they had sandwiches. Senator Sam Nunn pursues Poindexter sharply about his failed memory, and within the next two minutes Poindexter shows two very fast micro facial expressions of anger, raised voice pitch, four swallows, and many speech pauses and speech repetitions. This moment in Poindexter's testimony illustrates four important points.

1. When the behavioral changes are not restricted to a single modality (face, or voice, or such autonomic nervous system changes as indicated by swallowing), it is an important flag that something important is happening which should be explored. While we shouldn't ignore signs which are restricted to only one type of behavior, since that may

Former National Security Adviser Vice Admiral John Poindexter

be all we have, it is likely to be more reliable, and the emotion driving the changes to be stronger, when the signs cut across different aspects of behavior.

2. It is less risky to interpret a *change* in behavior than to interpret some behavioral feature which the person shows repeatedly. Poindexter did not often show speech hesitations, pauses, swallowing, or the like. The lie catcher must always look for changes in behavior, because of what I call the Brokaw Hazard in chapter 4 (page 91). We will not be misled by a person's idiosyncrasies if we focus on changes in behavior.

3. When the behavior changes occur in relation to a specific topic or question, that tells the lie catcher this could be a hot area to explore. Even though Senator Nunn and other Congressmen had pushed Poindexter on many topics, Poindexter did not show these behaviors until Senator Nunn pushed him about the lunch with Director Casey.

Poindexter's suspect behavior pattern disappeared when Nunn stopped asking about the lunch and moved on to another topic. Whenever a group of behavioral changes appears to occur in relation to a specific topic, the lie catcher should try to verify that it is indeed topic related. One way to do so is to drop the topic, moving on as Nunn did to something else, and then unexpectedly return to the topic and see if the group of behaviors reappears.

4. The lie catcher should try to figure out alternative explanations of why the behavioral changes are occurring, considering explanations other than the possibility that they are signs of deceit. If Poindexter was lying in his answers about the luncheon, he probably would be upset about doing so. He was known to be a religious man; his wife is a deacon in their church. It is likely that he would have some conflict about lying even if he thought it was justified for national interest. And he would likely be afraid of being caught as well. But there are other alternatives which need to be considered.

Poindexter was testifying for many days. Let's suppose that during the lunch break he always confers with his attorneys, eating a sandwich prepared by his wife. Suppose this day, when he asks his wife if she has made him a sandwich she becomes irritated and says, "John, I can't make you a sandwich every day, week in and week out, I have other responsibilities too!" And if they have the type of marriage in which anger is rarely expressed, Poindexter might be upset about this episode. Later that morning when Nunn asks him about the lunch and he mentions they had sandwiches, the unresolved emotions about the argument with his wife reappear, and it is those feelings which we see, not guilt about lying about some aspect of the Iran-Contra affair or fear of being caught.

There is no way for me to know whether this line of speculation has any grounds. That is my point. The lie

Former Lieutenant Colonel Oliver North

catcher must always try to consider alternative explanations other than lying and gather information which may help rule them out. What Poindexter has revealed is that something about the lunch with Casey is hot, but we don't know what, and therefore we should not leap to the conclusion he is lying without ruling out other explanations.

Oliver North's Ability to Perform

Lieutenant Colonel North's testimony during the Iran-Contra hearings illustrates another point made in *Telling Lies*. North appears to be a good example of what I call a natural performer.[11] I don't mean to suggest that North was in fact lying (although he was convicted of lying in his earlier testimony before Congress) but only that if he was we could not tell from his demeanor. If he were to lie, he would be very convincing. His performance, as performance, was beautiful to behold.[12]

Public opinion surveys taken at the time showed that North was widely admired by the American people. There are many reasons for his appeal. He might have been seen as a David against the Goliath of the powerful government, *viz.* the congressional committee. And, for some people, his uniform helped. He might also have appeared to be a fall guy, unfairly taking the rap for the president or the CIA director. And part of his appeal was his manner itself, his style of behavior. One of the hallmarks of natural performers is that they are likable to behold; we enjoy their performance. There is no reason to think that such people lie any more than anyone else (although they may be more tempted since they know they can get away with it), but when they do lie their lies are seamless.

North's testimony also raises ethical and political questions about the propriety of lying by a public official. In the next chapter I discuss this and other historical incidents.

TEN

Lies in Public Life

*I*N THE LAST CHAPTER I described findings from recent research and research in progress, and also drew upon my experience teaching professional lie catchers. This chapter is not based on scientific evidence. Instead I draw on my personal evaluations informed by thinking about the nature of lying and attempts to apply my research to understanding the larger context in which I live.

Oliver North's Justification for Lying

At one point in his testimony Lieutenant Colonel North admitted that he had some years earlier lied to Congress about the diversion of Iranian funds to the pro-American Nicaraguan *contras*. "Lying does not come easy to me," he said. "But we had to weigh in the balance the difference between lives and lies." North was citing the classic justification for lying argued in philosophy for centuries. What should you say to a man brandishing a gun who asks, "Where is your brother? I am going to kill him." This scenario provides no dilemma to most of us. We don't reveal where our brother is. We lie, giving a false location. As Oliver North said, if life itself is at stake, then you have to lie. A more prosaic example is seen in the instructions parents give to their latch-key children about what to say if a stranger knocks at the door. They are told not to say that they are home alone, but to lie, claiming their parent is taking a nap.

In his book published four years after the congressional hearings, North described his feelings about Congress and the rightness of his cause. "To me, many Senators, Congressmen, and even their staff members were people of privilege who had shamelessly abandoned the Nicaraguan resistance and left the *contras* vulnerable to a powerful and well-armed enemy. And now they wanted to humiliate me for doing what *they* should have done! (page 50) . . . I never saw myself as being above the law, nor did I ever intend to do anything illegal. I have always believed, and still do, that the Boland amendments did not bar the National Security Council from supporting the *contras*. Even the most stringent of the amendments contained loopholes that we used to ensure that the Nicaraguan resistance would not be abandoned."[1] North acknowledged in his book that he misled members of Congress in 1986 when they tried to find out whether he was directly providing aid to the *contras*.

North's lying to defend lives rationale is not justified because, first, it is not certain that his choice was a clear one. He claimed that the *contras* would die because of the Boland amendments, by which Congress had prohibited, at one point, further "lethal" aid to them. But there was no consensus among experts that withholding such aid would mean the death of the *contras*. It was a political judgment, one on which most Democrats and most Republicans strongly disagreed. This is not akin to the certainty that the avowed murderer who threatens to kill will do so.

A second objection to North's claim he was lying to save lives is a problem with who was the target of his lies. He was not lying to the person proclaiming an intent to commit murder. If killing were to occur it would be the Nicaraguan army who would do it, not the members of

Congress. While those who disagreed with the Boland amendments might claim that this would be the consequence, it was not the declared intent of those who voted for the Boland amendments, nor could it be said to be the deliberately sought, even if not declared, purpose of that legislation.

Wise and presumably equally moral people disagreed about what would be the consequences of withholding "lethal" aid, and whether the Boland amendments totally closed all loopholes. Zealously, North could not see, or if he saw he did not care, that there was no single truth here to which all rational men and women agreed. North's hubris was to give his judgment more weight than that of the majority in Congress, and to believe that was a justification for misleading the Congress.

My third objection to North's rationale that he lied to save lives is that his lie violated a contract he had made which prohibited him from lying to Congress. No one is obligated to answer truthfully an avowed murderer. A murderer's declared actions violate the laws to which we and he subscribe. Our children have no obligation to be truthful to a stranger knocking at the door, although the matter would become murkier if that stranger claimed to be in distress. Everyone, however, is obligated to testify truthfully before a congressional committee and can be prosecuted for lying. North had additional reasons for being truthful, by virtue of his profession. Lieutenant Colonel North, as a military officer, had sworn to uphold the Constitution. By lying to Congress North violated the constitutionally provided division of responsibility between the two branches of government, specifically the control of the budget that the Constitution gives to Congress as check against the executive's power to act.[2] North was not without recourse if he felt he was being forced to carry out policies which he believed were immorally endangering others. He could have resigned and then publicly spoken out against the Boland amendments.

The argument continues today, as CIA officials who allegedly lied to Congress are now being prosecuted. One question recently discussed in the press is whether there are a special set of rules for CIA officials, who because of the secret nature of their work might not be obligated to be truthful to Congress. Since North was taking orders from CIA director Casey, his actions might be justified as following the norm for employees of that agency. David Whipple, who is the director of the association of former CIA officers, said, "To my mind, to disclose as little as necessary to Congress, if they can get away with it, is not a bad thing. I have trouble myself blaming any of those guys."[3] Ray Cline, also a retired CIA officer, said: "In the old tradition of the CIA we felt that the senior staff officers should be protected from exposure."[4] Stansfield Turner, who was President Jimmy Carter's director of the CIA from 1977 to 1981, argues that the CIA should not ever be authorized by a president to lie to Congress, and it should be known to agency employees that they will not be protected if they do lie.[5]

The prosecution of North, Poindexter, and more recently CIA officials Alan Fiers and Clair George, for lying to Congress might convey that message. George is the highest official in the CIA to be prosecuted for lying to the Iran-Contra congressional committee in 1987. Since it is widely believed that CIA director Casey did not follow those rules, one can argue that it is wrong to punish people who were led to believe they were not only doing what the president wanted but would be protected if exposed.

President Richard Nixon and the Watergate Scandal

Former president Nixon is probably the public official who has been most often condemned for lying. He was the first president to resign, but it was not simply because he had lied. Nor was he forced to resign because people working for the White House were caught at the Watergate office and apartment complex in June of 1972 attempting to break in to the Democratic party headquarters. It was the cover-up he directed and the lies he told to maintain it. Audiotapes of conversations in the White House, later made public, revealed Nixon to say at the time, "I don't give a shit what happens, I want you to stonewall it, let them plead the Fifth Amendment, or anything else, if it'll save it—save the plan."

The cover-up did succeed for nearly a year until one of the men convicted for the Watergate break-in, James McCord, told the judge that the burglary was part of a larger conspiracy. Then it came out that Nixon had audiotaped all conversations in the Oval Office. Despite Nixon's attempt to suppress the most damaging information on those tapes, there was enough evidence for the House Judiciary Committee to bring articles of impeachment. When the Supreme Court ordered Nixon to turn over the tapes to the grand jury, Nixon resigned on August 9, 1974.

The problem, as I see it, was not that Nixon lied, for I maintain that national leaders must sometimes do so; it was what Nixon lied about, his motivation for lying, and to whom he lied. There was no attempt to mislead another government—the target of Nixon's lie was the American people. There was no possible claim to justification in terms of a need to achieve foreign policy objectives. Nixon concealed his knowledge of a crime, the attempt to steal documents from the Democratic party offices in the Watergate buildings. His motive was to stay in office, to not risk disapproval by the voters if they were to learn that Nixon had known that those who worked for him had broken the law in order to gain an advantage for him in the upcoming election. The first article of impeachment charged Nixon

with obstructing justice, the second article charged him
with abusing the powers of his office and failing to insure
that the laws are faithfully executed, and the third article
charged Nixon with deliberately disobeying subpoenas for
the tape recordings and other documents from the Judiciary Committee. We should not simply condemn Nixon
because he was a liar, although that was a frequent charge
jubilantly made by Nixon-haters. National leaders could
not do their job if they were prohibited from lying in every
circumstance.

President Jimmy Carter's Justified Lie

A good example of a circumstance in which lying by a
public official was justifiable happened during former president Jimmy Carter's term of office. In 1976, former gover-
nor of Georgia Jimmy Carter was elected president after
defeating Gerald Ford who had become president when
Nixon resigned. In the election campaign Carter promised
to restore morality to the White House, after the trying and
scandalous Watergate years. The hallmark of his campaign
was looking into the television cameras and saying, rather
simplistically, that he would never lie to the American
people. Three years later, though, he lied many times to
conceal his plans to rescue American hostages from Iran.

During the early years of Carter's presidency, the Shah
of Iran was overthrown by a fundamentalist Islamic revolution. The Shah had always received American support, so
when he went into exile Carter allowed him to come to the
United States for medical treatment. Infuriated, Iranian
militants seized the U.S. Embassy in Teheran, taking sixty
hostages. Diplomatic efforts to settle the hostage crisis went
on for months with no results, while newscasters on television each night counted out the number of days, then
months, that Americans were being held as prisoners.

Very soon after the hostages were seized, Carter secretly ordered the military to begin training for a rescue operation. That preparation was not simply concealed, but administration representatives repeatedly made false statements to downplay any suspicions about what they were up to. For many months the Pentagon, the state department, and the White House repeatedly claimed that a mission to free the hostages was logistically impossible. On January 8, 1980, President Carter lied at a press conference, saying that a military rescue "would almost certainly end in failure and almost certainly end in the death of the hostages." As he was saying this the Delta military force was rehearsing the rescue operation hidden in the southwestern desert of the United States.

Carter lied to the American people because he knew the Iranians were listening to what he said, and he wanted to lull the Iranian militants guarding the hostages into a false sense of security. Carter had his press secretary Jody Powell deny that the government was planning to rescue the hostages at the very moment when that rescue mission was in progress. Carter wrote in his memoirs, "Any suspicion by the militants of a rescue attempt would doom the effort to failure . . . Success depended upon total surprise.[6]" Remember that Hitler also lied to gain the advantage of surprise over an adversary. We condemn Hitler not because he lied but because of his goals and actions. Lying by a national leader to gain an advantage over an enemy is not in and of itself wrong.

The primary target of Carter's lies was the Iranians who had violated international law by taking hostage U.S. Embassy staff. There was no way to deceive them without deceiving the American people and Congress. The motive was to protect our own military force. And the lie was to be short-lived. Although some members of Congress raised the question of whether Carter had been entitled to act

without notifying them in advance, as called for by the War
Powers Resolution, Carter claimed that the rescue had
been an act of mercy, not an act of war. Carter was condemned because the rescue mission failed, not because he
had broken his promise not to lie.

Stansfield Turner, CIA director under Carter, writing
about the Iran-Contra affair and the need for CIA officials
to be honest with Congress, raised the question about what
he would have done if Congress had asked him if the CIA
was preparing a rescue operation: "I would have been hard-
pressed as to how to respond. I hope I would have said
something like, 'I believe it is inadvisable to talk about any
plans for solving the hostage problem, lest incorrect infer-
ences be drawn and possibly leaked to the Iranians.' I
would then have consulted with the president about
whether I should return and respond to the question forth-
rightly."[7] Mr. Turner does not say what he would have
done if President Carter had instructed him to return to
Congress and deny that there were any plans to rescue the
hostages.

Lyndon Johnson's Lies about the Viet Nam War

More dangerous was former president Lyndon B. Johnson's concealment from the public of adverse information
about the progress of the war in Viet Nam. Johnson had
succeeded to the presidency after the 1963 assassination of
John F. Kennedy, but he ran for election in 1964. During
the campaign Johnson's Republican opponent Arizona
Senator Barry Goldwater said he might be willing to use
atomic weapons to win the war. Johnson took the opposite
line. "We are not about to send American boys nine or ten
thousand miles away from home to do what Asian boys
ought to be doing for themselves." Once elected, and convinced that the war could be won by sending troops, John-

son sent a half million American boys to Viet Nam over the next few years. America ended up dropping more bombs on Viet Nam than had been used throughout World War II.

Johnson thought he would be in a strong position to negotiate a proper end to the war only if the North Vietnamese believed that he had American public opinion behind him. And so Johnson selected what he revealed to the American people about the war's progress. His military commanders learned that Johnson wanted the best possible picture of American success and North Vietnamese and Viet Cong failures, and after a time that was the only information he received from field commanders in Viet Nam. But the charade came down when in January 1968 a devastating North Vietnamese and Viet Cong offensive during the holiday season of Tet exposed to Americans and the world how far the U.S. was from winning that war. The Tet offensive occurred during the next presidential election campaign. Senator Robert Kennedy, who was running against Johnson for the Democratic nomination, said that the Tet offensive "shattered the mask of official illusion, with which we have concealed our true circumstances, even from ourselves." A few months later Johnson announced his decision not to run for reelection.

In a democracy there is no easy way to mislead another nation without misleading your own people, and that makes deception a very dangerous policy when practiced for long. Johnson's deceit about the progress of the war was not a matter of days, or weeks, or even months. By creating the illusion of imminent victory Johnson deprived the electorate of information they needed to make informed political choices. A democracy cannot survive if one political party can control the information the electorate has about a matter crucial to their vote.

As Senator Kennedy noted, I suspect that another cost

of this deceit was that Johnson and at least some of his advisers almost came to believe in their own lies. It is not just government officials who are susceptible to this trap. I believe that the more often anyone tells a lie, the easier it becomes to do so. Each time a lie is repeated there is less consideration about whether it is right to engage in the deceit. After many repetitions, the liar may become so comfortable with the lie that he no longer takes note of the fact that he is lying. If prodded or challenged, however, the liar will remember that he is fabricating. Although Johnson wanted to believe in his false claims about the war's progress, and may have at times thought they were true, I doubt that he ever succeeded in fully deceiving himself.

The Space Shuttle Challenger *Disaster and Self-Deception*

To say one has deceived oneself is quite a different matter. In self-deceit the person does not realize that he is lying to himself. And the person does not know his own motive for deceiving himself. Self-deception occurs, I believe, much more rarely than it is claimed by a culpable person to excuse, after the fact, his wrong actions. The actions which led up to the *Challenger* space shuttle disaster raise the issue of whether those who made the decision to launch the shuttle despite strong warnings about likely dangers might have been the victims of self-deceit. How else can we explain the decision by those who knew the risks to go ahead with the launch?

The space shuttle launch on January 28, 1986, was seen by millions on television. This launch had been highly publicized because the crew included a schoolteacher, Christa McAuliffe. The television audience included many schoolchildren including Ms. McAuliffe's own class. She was to have given a lesson from outer space. But just seventy-three seconds after launch, the shuttle exploded killing all seven on board.

The night before the launch a group of engineers at Morton Thiokol, the firm that had built the booster rockets, officially recommended that the launch be delayed because the cold weather forecast for overnight might severely reduce the elasticity of the rubber O-ring seals. If that were to happen, leaking fuel might cause the booster rockets to explode. The engineers at Thiokol called the National Aeronautic and Space Administration (NASA), unanimously urging postponement of the launch scheduled for the following morning.

There had already been three postponements in the launch date, violating NASA's promise that the space shuttle would have routine, predictable launch schedules. Lawrence Mulloy, NASA's rocket project manager, argued with the Thiokol engineers, saying there was not enough evidence that cold weather would harm the O-rings. Mulloy talked that night to Thiokol manager Bob Lund, who later testified before the presidential commission appointed to investigate the *Challenger* disaster. Lund testified that Mulloy told him that night to put on his "management hat" instead of his "engineering hat." Apparently doing so, Lund changed his opposition to the launch, overruling his own engineers. Mulloy also contacted Joe Kilminister, one of the vice presidents at Thiokol, asking him to sign a launch go-ahead. He did so at 11:45 PM, faxing a launch recommendation to NASA. Allan McDonald, who was director of Thiokol's rocket project, refused to sign the official approval for the launch. Two months later McDonald was to quit his job at Thiokol.

Later the presidential commission discovered that four of NASA's key senior executives responsible for authorizing each launch never were told of the disagreement between Thiokol engineers and the NASA rocket manage-

Crew of the spaceship *Challenger*

ment team on the night the decision to launch was made. Robert Sieck, shuttle manager at the Kennedy Space Center; Gene Thomas, the launch director for *Challenger* at Kennedy; Arnold Aldrich, manager of space transportation systems at the Johnson Space Center in Houston; and Shuttle director Moore all were to later testify that they were not informed that the Thiokol engineers opposed a decision to launch.

How could Mulloy have sent the shuttle up knowing that it might explode? One explanation is that under pressure he became the victim of self-deceit, actually becoming convinced that the engineers were exaggerating what was really a negligible risk. If Mulloy was truly the victim of self-deceit can we fairly hold him responsible for his wrong decision? Suppose someone else had lied to Mulloy and told him there was no risk. We certainly would not blame him for then making a wrong decision. Is it any different if he has deceived himself? I think probably not, if Mulloy truly has deceived himself. The issue is, was it self-deception or bad judgment, well rationalized?

To find out let me contrast what we know about Mulloy with one of the clear-cut examples of self-deceit discussed by experts who study self-deception.[8] A terminal cancer patient who believes he is going to recover, even though there are many signs of a rapidly progressing, incurable malignant tumor, maintains a false belief. Mulloy also maintained a false belief, believing the shuttle could be safely launched. (The alternative that Mulloy knew for certain that it would blow up I think should be ruled out.) The cancer patient believes he will be cured, despite the contrary strong evidence. The cancer patient knows he is getting weaker, the pain is increasing, but he insists these are only temporary setbacks. Mulloy also maintained his false belief despite the contrary evidence. He knew the engineers thought the cold weather would damage the O-ring seals, and if fuel leaked the rockets might explode, but he dismissed their claims as exaggerations.

What I have described so far does not tell us whether either the cancer patient or Mulloy is a deliberate liar or the victim of self-deceit. The crucial requirement for self-deceit is that the victim is unaware of his motive for maintaining his false belief.* The cancer patient does not con-

---

*It might seem that self-deceit is just another term for Freud's concept of repression. There are at least two differences. In repression the information concealed from the self arises from a deep-seated need within the structure of the personal-

sciously know his deceit is motivated by his inability to confront his fear of his own imminent death. This element—not being conscious of the motivation for the self-deceit—is missing for Mulloy. When Mulloy told Lund to put on his management hat, he showed that he was aware of what he needed to do to maintain the belief that the launch should proceed.

Richard Feynman, the Nobel laureate physicist who was appointed to the presidential commission which investigated the *Challenger* disaster, wrote as follows about the management mentality that influenced Mulloy. "[W]hen the moon project was over, NASA . . . [had] to convince Congress that there exists a project that only NASA can do. In order to do so, it is necessary—at least it was *apparently* necessary in this case—to exaggerate: to exaggerate how economical the shuttle would be, to exaggerate how often it could fly, to exaggerate how safe it would be, to exaggerate the big scientific facts that would be discovered."[9] *Newsweek* magazine said, "In a sense the agency seemed a victim of its own flackery, behaving as if space-flight were really as routine as a bus trip."

Mulloy was just one of many in NASA who maintained those exaggerations. He must have feared congressional reaction if the shuttle had to be delayed a fourth time. Bad publicity which contradicted NASA's exaggerated claims about the shuttle might affect future appropriations. The damaging publicity from another postponed launch date might have seemed a certainty. The risk due to the weather was only a possibility, not a certainty. Even the engineers who opposed the launch were not absolutely certain there

---

ity, which is not typically the case in self-deception. And some maintain that confronting the self-deceiver with the truth can break the deceit, while in repression such a confrontation will not cause the truth to be acknowledged. See discussion of these issues in Lockard and Paulhus, *Self-Deception.*

would be an explosion. Some of them reported afterwards thinking only seconds before the explosion that it might not happen.

We should condemn Mulloy for his bad judgment, his decision to give management's concerns more weight than the engineers' worries. Hank Shuey, a rocket-safety expert who reviewed the evidence at NASA's request, said, "It's not a design defect. There was an error in judgment." We should not explain or excuse wrong judgments by the cover of self-deception. We should also condemn Mulloy for not informing his superiors, who had the ultimate authority for the launch decision, about what he was doing and why he was doing it. Feynman offers a convincing explanation of why Mulloy took the responsibility on himself. "[T]he guys who are trying to get Congress to okay their projects don't want to hear such talk [about problems, risks, etc.]. It's better if they don't hear, so they can be more 'honest'— they don't want to be in the position of lying to Congress! So pretty soon the attitudes begin to change: information from the bottom which is disagreeable—'We're having a problem with the seals; we should fix it before we fly again'—is suppressed by big cheeses and middle managers who say, 'If you tell me about the seals problems, we'll have to ground the shuttle and fix it.' Or, 'No, no, keep on flying, because otherwise, it'll look bad,' or 'Don't tell me; I don't want to hear about it.' Maybe they don't say explicitly 'Don't tell me,' but they discourage communication which amounts to the same thing."[10]

Mulloy's decision not to inform his superiors about the sharp disagreement about the shuttle launch could be considered a lie of omission. Remember my definition of lying (in chapter 2, page 26) is that one person deliberately, by choice, misleads another person without any notification that deception will occur. It does not matter whether the lie is accomplished by saying something false or by omitting crucial information. Those are just differences in technique, for the effect is the same.

Notification is a crucial issue. Actors are not liars but impersonators are, for the actor's audience is notified that a role is to be played. Slightly more ambiguous is a poker game, where the rules authorize certain types of deceit such as bluffing, and real estate sales where no one should expect sellers to reveal truthfully at the outset their real selling price. If Feynman is correct, if the NASA higher-ups had discouraged communication, essentially saying, "Don't tell me," then this might constitute notification. Mulloy and presumably others at NASA knew that bad news or difficult decisions were not to be passed to the top. If that was so then Mulloy should not be considered a liar for not informing his superiors, for they had authorized the deceit, and knew they would not be told. In my judgment the superiors who were not told share some of the responsibility for the disaster with Mulloy who did not tell them. The superiors have the ultimate responsibility not only for a launch decision but for creating the atmosphere in which Mulloy operated. They contributed to the circumstances which led to his bad judgment, and for his decision not to bring them in on the decision.

Feynman notes the similarities between the situation at NASA and how mid-level officials in the Iran-Contra affair, such as Poindexter, felt about telling President Reagan what they were doing. Creating an atmosphere in which subordinates believe that those with ultimate authority should not be told of matters for which they would be blamed, providing plausible deniability to a president, destroys governance. Former president Harry Truman rightly said, "The buck stops here." The president or chief executive officer must monitor, evaluate, decide, and be responsible for decisions. To suggest otherwise may be advantageous in the short run, but it endangers any hierarchal organization, encouraging loose cannons and an environment of sanctioned deceit.

Judge Clarence Thomas and Professor Anita Hill

The widely conflicting testimony by Supreme Court nominee Judge Clarence Thomas and law professor Anita Hill in the fall of 1991 offers a number of sobering lessons about lying. The dramatic televised confrontation began just days before the Senate was expected to confirm Thomas's nomination to the Supreme Court. Professor Hill testified before the Senate Judiciary Committee that between 1981 and 1983, when she was an assistant to Clarence Thomas, first in the Office of Civil Rights in the Department of Education, and then when Thomas became head of the Equal Employment Opportunity Commission, she had been the victim of sexual harassment. "He spoke about acts that he had seen in pornographic films involving such matters as women having sex with animals and films showing group sex or rape scenes. . . . He talked about pornographic materials depicting individuals with large penises or large breasts involved in various sex acts. On several occasions Thomas told me graphically of his own sexual prowess. . . . He said that if I ever told anyone of his behavior, that it would ruin his career." She spoke with absolute calm, she was consistent and to many observers very convincing.

Immediately after her testimony Judge Thomas totally denied all her charges: "I have not said or done the things Anita Hill has alleged." After Hill's testimony Thomas said, "I would like to start by saying unequivocally, uncategorically, that I deny each and every single allegation against me today." Self-righteously angry at the committee for injuring his reputation, Thomas claimed he was the victim of a racially motivated attack. He continued: "I cannot shake off these accusations because they play to the worst stereotypes we have about black men in this country." Complaining about the ordeal the Senate had put him through, Thomas said, "I would have preferred an assassin's bullet to this kind of living hell." The hearing, he said, was "a high-tech lynching for uppity blacks."

Time magazine's banner headline that week read: "As the nation looks on, two credible articulate witnesses present irreconcilable views of what happened nearly a decade ago." Columnist Nancy Gibbs wrote in *Time:* "Even after listening to all the anguished testimony, who could ever feel confident that they knew what really happened? Which one was a liar of epic proportion?"

My focus is more narrowly on only the behavior shown

Clarence Thomas

by Hill and Thomas as each testified, not Thomas's testimony before the committee prior to the Anita Hill matter,
nor either one's past history or the testimony of other witnesses about each of them. Considering just their demeanor, I found no new or special information. I could
only note what was obvious to the press, that each spoke
and behaved quite convincingly. But there are some lessons
to be learned from this confrontation about lying and demeanor.

It would not have been easy for either of them to lie
deliberately in front of the entire nation. The stakes for
both were enormously high. Think what the outcome
would have been if either of them had acted in such a way
that they were judged, rightly or wrongly, as lying by the
media and the American people. That didn't happen; both
looked like they meant it.

Suppose Hill was being truthful and Thomas had decided to lie deliberately. If he had consulted the second
chapter in *Telling Lies* he would have found my advice that
the best way to cover the fear of being caught is with a
veneer of another emotion. Using the example from John
Updike's book *Marry Me,* I described on page 33 how the
unfaithful wife Ruth could fool her suspicious husband by
going on the attack, letting herself become angry and making him defensive for disbelieving her. That is exactly what
Clarence Thomas did. His anger was intense, his target was
not Anita Hill, but the Senate. He had the additional benefit of enlisting the sympathy of everyone who feels angry
at politicians, and of appearing as a David fighting the
mighty Goliath.

Just as Thomas would have lost sympathy if he had
attacked Hill, the Senators would have lost sympathy if
they had then attacked Thomas, a black man who says he
is being lynched for being uppity. If he was going to lie it
would also make sense for him not to watch Anita Hill's

Anita Hill

testimony, so the Senators could not as easily ask him about it.

While this line of reasoning should please those who opposed Thomas before the hearing, it does not prove he was lying. He might well have attacked the Senate committee if he had been telling the truth. If Hill was the liar, Thomas would have every right to be furious at the Senate for listening to her stories, brought up at the very last moment, in public, just when it appeared his political opponents had lost their attempt to block his nomination. If Hill was the liar, Thomas might have been so upset and so angry that he could not have stood watching her testimony on television.

Could Anita Hill have been lying? I think it is unlikely, since if she was, she should have been afraid of being disbelieved, and there was no sign of apprehension. She testified coolly and calmly, with reserve, and little sign of any emotion. But the absence of a behavioral clue to deceit does not mean the person is being truthful. Anita Hill had time to prepare and rehearse her story. It is possible she could do so convincingly, it is just not likely.

Although it is more likely that Thomas is the liar than Anita Hill, there is a third possibility which strikes me as most likely. Neither one told the truth and yet neither one may have been lying. Suppose something did happen, but not as much as Professor Hill said, but more than Judge Thomas admitted. If her exaggeration and his denial were repeated again and again, there would be little chance by the time we saw them testify that either one would any longer remember that what each was saying was not entirely true.

Thomas might have forgotten what he did, or even if he remembers it he remembers a well-sanitized version. His anger about her accusations would then be totally justified. He is not lying, as he sees and remembers it, he is telling the truth. And if there was some reason for Hill to resent Thomas, for some slight or affront, real or imagined, or some other reason, she might over time have come to embroider, elaborate, and exaggerate what actually did happen. She too would be telling the truth as she remembers and believes it to be. This is similar to self-deception, the key difference being that in this case the false belief develops slowly over time, through repetitions which each time slowly are elaborated. Some who write about self-deceit might not think this is a difference which matters much.

There is no way to tell from their demeanor which of these accounts is true—is he the liar, is she the liar, or are they both not telling the entire truth? Yet when people hold strong opinions—about sexual harassment, who should be on the Supreme Court, about Senators, about men, and so forth—it is hard to tolerate not knowing what conclusion to draw. Faced with that ambiguity most people resolve it by becoming quite convinced they can tell from demeanor which one is telling the truth. It is usually the person with whom they were most sympathetic to begin with.

It is not that behavioral clues to deceit are useless, but we should know when they will and won't be useful, and how to accept when we cannot tell whether someone is truthful or lying. There is a statute of limitations on charges of sexual harassment—ninety days. One of the very good reasons for having that limitation is that the issues are fresher, and behavioral clues to deceit perhaps more detectable. If we had been able to see each of them testify within a few weeks of the alleged harassment, there would have been a much better chance to tell from their behavior which was telling the truth, and perhaps what was charged and denied might have been different.

A Country of Lies

A few years ago I thought America had become a country of lies: from L.B.J.'s lies about the Viet Nam war, the Nixon Watergate scandal, Reagan and Iran-Contra, and the continuing mystery about Senator Edward Kennedy's role in the death of a woman friend at Chapaquiddick to Senator Biden's plagiarism and former Senator Gary Hart's lie during the 1984 presidential campaign about his extramarital affair. It is not just politics; lies in business have come to the fore, in Wall Street and savings and loans scandals, and lies in sports, such as baseball Hall of Fame Pete Rose's to conceal his gambling and Olympic athlete Ben Johnson's to conceal his use of drugs. Then I spent five weeks lecturing in Russia in May 1990.

Having been in Russia before, as a Fulbright professor in 1979, I was astonished by how much more frank people now were. They were no longer afraid to talk to an American, or to criticize their own government. "You have come to the right country," I was often told. "This is a country of lies! Seventy years of lies!" Again and again I was told by Russians how they had always known how much their government had lied to them. Yet in my five weeks there I saw how stunned they were to learn about new lies they had not earlier suspected. A poignant example was the revelation of the truth about the suffering of the people of Leningrad during World War II.

Very soon after Nazi Germany's invasion of Russia in 1941, the Nazi troops surrounded Leningrad (now St. Petersburg). Their siege lasted 900 days. One and a half million people reportedly died in Leningrad, many of starvation. Nearly every adult I met told me about family members they had lost during the siege. But while I was there the government announced that the figures for the number of civilians who died in the siege had been inflated. On the day in May when the whole country celebrates the victory over the Nazis the Soviet government announced that casualties in the war had been so high because there were not enough officers to command the Soviet troops. Soviet leader Stalin, the government said, had murdered many of his own officers in a purge before the war began.

It is not just the revelation of past unsuspected lies, but new lies continue. Just a year after Mikhail Gorbachev

came to power there was a disastrous nuclear accident at
Chernobyl. A radiation cloud spread over parts of Western
as well as Eastern Europe, but the Soviet government at
first revealed nothing. Scientists in Scandinavia recorded
high levels of radiation in the atmosphere. Three days later
Soviet officials admitted a large accident had occurred and
said that thirty-two people had died. Only after several
weeks had elapsed did Gorbachev speak publicly, and he
spent most of his time criticizing the Western reaction. The
government has never admitted that people in the area
were not evacuated early enough and many suffered from
radiation sickness. Russian scientists now estimate that as
many as 10,000 may die from the Chernobyl accident.

I learned about this from a Ukrainian physician who
shared my compartment on the overnight train to Kiev.
Communist party officials had evacuated their families, he
said, while everyone else was told it was safe to stay. This
physician was now treating young girls with ovarian cancer, a disease normally not seen in such young people. On
the ward for children suffering from radiation sickness,
their bodies glowed at night. I was not able to be certain,
because of our language difficulty, whether he was speaking literally or metaphorically. "Gorbachev lies to us like
the rest of them," he said. "He knows what has happened
and he knows that we know he is lying."

I met a psychologist who had been assigned to interview those living in the vicinity of Chernobyl, to evaluate
how they were dealing with the stress three years later. He
thought their plight would be partially alleviated if they
did not feel so abandoned by their government. His official
recommendation was for Gorbachev to speak to the nation
and say, "We made a terrible mistake, underestimating the
severity of the radiation. We should have evacuated many
more of you and much more quickly, but we had no place
to put you. And once we learned about our mistake we

should have told you the truth and we didn't. Now we want you to know the truth and to know that the nation suffers for you. We will give you the medical care you need and our hopes for your future." His recommendation went unanswered.

Anger about the lies about Chernobyl is not over. Early in December of 1991, more than five years after the accident, the Ukrainian parliament demanded that Mikhail Gorbachev and seventeen other Soviet and Ukrainian officials be prosecuted. The chairman of the Ukrainian legislative commission which investigated the incident, Volodymyr Yavorivsky, said, "All the leadership, from Gorbachev down to the decipherers of coded telegrams, were aware of the level of active radioactive contamination." The Ukrainian leaders said that President Gorbachev "had personally covered up the extent of radiation leakage."

For decades Soviets learned that to achieve anything they had to bend and evade the rules. It became a country in which lying and cheating were normal, where everyone knew the system was corrupt and the rules unfair, and survival required beating the system. Social institutions cannot work when everyone believes every rule is to be broken or dodged. I am not convinced that any change in government will quickly change such attitudes. No one now believes what anyone in the current government says about anything. Few I met believed Gorbachev, and that was a year before the 1991 failed coup. A nation cannot survive if no one believes what any leader says. This may be what makes a population willing, eager perhaps, to give their allegiance to any strong leader whose claims are bold enough, and actions strong enough, to win back trust.

Americans joke about lying politicians—"How can you tell when a politician is lying? When he moves his lips!" My visit to Russia convinced me that, by contrast, we still expect our leaders to be truthful even though we suspect they will not be. Laws work when most people believe they are fair, when it is a minority not the majority who feel it is right to violate any law. In a democracy, government only works if most people believe that most of the time they are told the truth, and that there is some claim to fairness and justice.

No important relationship survives if trust is totally lost. If you discover your friend has betrayed you, lied to you repeatedly for his own advantage, that friendship cannot continue. Neither can a marriage be more than a shambles if one spouse learns that the other, not once but many times, has again and again been a deceiver. I doubt any form of government can long survive except by using force to oppress its own people, if the people believe its leaders always lie.

I don't think we have come to that. Lying by public officials is still newsworthy, condemned not admired. Lies and corruption are part of our history. They are nothing new, but they are still regarded as the aberration not the norm. We still believe we can throw the rascals out.

While Watergate and the Iran-Contra affair can be viewed as proof that the American system has failed, we can also see them as proof of just the opposite. Nixon had to resign. When Supreme Court Chief Justice Warren Burger administered the oath of office to Gerald Ford to replace Nixon, he said to one of the Senators present, "It [the system] worked, thank God it worked."[11] North, Poindexter, and now others are prosecuted for lying to the Congress. During the Iran-Contra Congressional hearings, Congressman Lee Hamilton chastised Oliver North with a quotation from Thomas Jefferson: "The whole art of government consists in the art of being honest."

Epilogue

WHAT I HAVE WRITTEN should help lie catchers more than liars. I think it is easier to improve one's ability to detect deceit than to perpetrate it. What needs to be understood is more learnable. No special talent is required to understand my ideas about how lies differ. Anyone who is diligent can make use of the lying checklist in the last chapter to estimate whether or not a liar is liable to make mistakes. Becoming better able to spot clues to deceit requires more than simply understanding what I have described; a skill must be developed through practice. But anyone who spends the time, looking and listening carefully, watching for the clues described in chapters 4 and 5, can improve. We and others have trained people in how to look and listen more carefully and accurately, and most people do benefit. Even without such formal training, people can on their own practice spotting clues to deceit.

While there could be a school for lie catchers, a school for liars would not make sense. Natural liars don't need it, and the rest of us don't have the talent to benefit from it. Natural liars already know and use most of what I have written, even though they don't always realize that they know it. Lying well is a special talent, not easily acquired. One must be a natural performer, winning and charming in manner. Such people are able, without thought, to manage their expressions, giving off just the impression they seek to convey. They don't need much help.

Most people need that help, but lacking a natural ability to perform, they will never be able to lie very well. What I have explained about what betrays a lie and what makes a lie appear believable won't help them much. It may even make them worse. Lying can't be improved by knowing what to do and what not to do. And I seriously doubt that practice will have much benefit. A self-conscious liar, who planned each move as he made it, would be like a skier who thought about each stride as he went down the slope.

There are two exceptions, two lessons about lying that can help anyone. Liars should take more care to develop fully and memorize their false story lines. Most liars don't anticipate all of the questions that may be asked, all of the unexpected incidents that may be met. A liar must have prepared, rehearsed answers for more contingencies than he will likely encounter. Inventing an answer on the spot quickly and convincingly, an answer that is consistent with what already was said and what may need to be maintained in the future, requires mental abilities and coolness under pressure, which few people have. The other lesson about lying, which any reader will have learned by now, is how hard it is to lie without making any mistakes. Most people escape detection only because the targets of their deceits don't care enough to work at catching them. It is very hard to prevent any leakage or deception clues.

I have never actually tried to teach anyone to lie better. My judgment that I couldn't help much is based on reasoning, not evidence. I hope I am correct, for I prefer for my research to help the lie catcher more than the liar. It is not that I believe lying to be inherently evil. Many philosophers have argued convincingly that at least some lies can be morally justified, and honesty can sometimes be brutal and cruel.[1] Yet my sympathy is more with the lie catcher than the liar. Perhaps it is because my scientific work is a search for the clues to how people truly feel. The disguise interests me, but the challenge is to uncover the real, felt emotion beneath it. Discovering how felt and false expressions differ, to find that concealment is not perfect, that the false only resembles but differs from real expressions of emotion is satisfying. The study of deceit, in these terms, is about much more than deceit. It provides an opportunity to witness an extraordinary internal struggle between voluntary and involuntary parts of our life, to learn how well we can deliberately control the outward signs of our inner life.

Despite my sympathy for lie catching as compared to lying, I realize that lie catching is not always more virtuous. The friend who kindly conceals boredom would be properly offended if unmasked. The husband who pretends amusement when his wife badly tells a joke, the wife who feigns interest in the husband's account of how he fixed a gadget, may feel abused if the pretense is challenged. And, in military deception, of course, one's national interests properly may be with the liar, not the lie catcher. In World War II, for example, who in an Allied country did not want Hitler to be misled about which French beach—Normandy or Calais—was the one on which Allied troops would land?

While Hitler obviously had the perfect right to try to uncover the Allied lie, lie catching is not always warranted. Sometimes intent is to be honored, regardless of what is truly thought or felt. Sometimes one has the right to be taken at one's word. Lie catching violates privacy, the right to keep some thoughts or feelings private. While there are situations in which it is warranted—criminal investigations, buying a car, negotiating a contract, and so on—there are arenas in which people assume the right to keep to themselves, if they choose, their personal feelings and thoughts, and to expect that what they choose to put forth will be accepted.

It is not just altruism or respect for privacy that should give pause to the relentless lie catcher. Sometimes one is better off misled. The host may be better off thinking the guest enjoyed himself; the wife happier believing that she can tell a joke well. The liar's false message may not only be more palatable, it may also be more useful than the truth. The carpenter's false claim "I'm fine" to his boss's "How are you today?" may provide information more relevant than would his true reply, "I am still feel terrible from the fight I had at home last night." His lie truthfully tells his intention to perform his job despite personal upset. There is, of course, a cost for being misled even in these benevolent instances. The boss might better regulate his work assignments if he recognized the carpenter's true distress. The wife might learn to tell jokes better or resolve not to tell them at all if she saw through her husband's deceit. Yet I believe it worth noting that *sometimes* lie catching violates a relationship, betrays trust, steals information that was not, for good reason, given. The lie catcher should realize at least that detecting clues to deceit is a presumption—it takes without permission, despite the other person's wishes.

There was no way to know when I started out to study deceit just what I would find. Claims were contradictory. Freud claimed: "He that has eyes to see and ears to hear may convince himself that no mortal can keep a secret. If his lips are silent, he chatters with his finger-tips; betrayal oozes out of him at every pore".[2] Yet I knew of many instances of quite successful lying, and my first studies found people did no better than chance in detecting deceit. Psychiatrists and psychologists were no better than anyone else. I am pleased with the answer that I have found. We are neither perfect nor imperfect as liars, detecting deceit is neither as easy as Freud claimed nor impossible. It makes matters more complex, and therefore more interesting. Our imperfect ability to lie is fundamental to, perhaps necessary for, our existence.

Consider what life would be like if everyone could lie perfectly or if no one could lie at all. I have thought about this most in regard to lies about emotions, since those are the hardest lies, and it is emotions that interest me. If we could never know how someone really felt, and if we knew that we couldn't know, life would be more tenuous. Certain in the knowledge that every show of emotion might be a mere display put on to please, manipulate, or mislead, individuals would be more adrift, attachments less firm. Consider for a moment the dilemma for the parent if the one-month-old infant could disguise his emotions and falsify as well as can most adults. Any cry could be the cry of "wolf." We lead our lives believing that there is a core of emotional truth, that most people can't or won't mislead us about how they feel. If treachery was as easy with emotions as with ideas, if expressions and gestures could be disguised and falsified as readily as words, our emotional lives would be impoverished and more guarded than they are.

And if we could never lie, if a smile was reliable, never absent when pleasure was felt, and never present without pleasure, life would be rougher than it is, many relationships harder to maintain. Politeness, attempts to smooth matters over, to conceal feelings one wished one didn't feel—all that would be gone. There would be no way not to be known, no opportunity to sulk or lick one's wounds except alone. Consider having as a friend, co-worker, or lover a person who in terms of emotional control and disguise was like a three-month-old infant, yet in all other respects—intelligence, skills, and so on—was fully able as any adult. It is a painful prospect.

We are neither transparent as the infant nor perfectly disguised. We can lie or be truthful, spot deceit or miss it, be misled or know the truth. We have a choice; that is our nature.

Appendix

Tables 1 and 2 summarize the information for all the clues to deceit described in chapters 4 and 5. Table 1 is organized by the behavioral clue, table 2 by the information conveyed. To learn what information on a particular behavior can reveal, the reader should consult table 1, and to learn what behavior can provide a particular type of information, we look at table 2.

Recall that there are two principal ways to lie: concealment and falsification. Tables 1 and 2 both deal with concealment. Table 3 describes the behavioral clues to falsification. Table 4 provides the complete checklist of lies.

TABLE 1

THE BETRAYAL OF CONCEALED INFORMATION, ORGANIZED BY BEHAVIORAL CLUES

Clue to Deceit	*Information Revealed*
Slips of the tongue	May be emotion-specific; may leak information unrelated to emotion
Tirades	May be emotion-specific; may leak information unrelated to emotion
Indirect speech	Verbal line not prepared; or, negative emotions, most likely fear
Pauses and speech errors	Verbal line not prepared; or, negative emotions, most likely fear
Voice pitch raised	Negative emotion, probably anger and/or fear
Voice pitch lowered	Negative emotion, probably sadness
Louder, faster speech	Probably anger, fear, and/or excitement
Slower, softer speech	Probably sadness and/or boredom
Emblems	May be emotion-specific; may leak information unrelated to emotion
Illustrators decrease	Boredom; line not prepared; or, weighing each word
Manipulators increase	Negative emotion
Fast or shallow breathing	Emotion, not specific
Sweating	Emotion, not specific
Frequent swallowing	Emotion, not specific
Micro expressions	Any of the specific emotions
Squelched expressions	Specific emotion; or, may only show that some emotion was interrupted but not which one
Reliable facial muscles	Fear or sadness
Increased blinking	Emotion, not specific
Pupil dilation	Emotion, not specific
Tears	Sadness, distress, uncontrolled laughter
Facial reddening	Embarrassment, shame, or anger; maybe guilt
Facial blanching	Fear or anger

TABLE 2

THE BETRAYAL OF CONCEALED INFORMATION, ORGANIZED BY TYPE OF INFORMATION

Type of Information	*Behavioral Clue*
Verbal line not prepared	Indirect speech, Pauses, Speech errors, Illustrators decrease
Nonemotional information (e.g., facts, plans, fantasies)	Slip of the tongue, Tirade, Emblem*
Emotions (e.g., happiness, surprise, distress)	Slip of the tongue, Tirade, Micro expression, Squelched expression
Fear	Indirect speech, Pauses, Speech errors, Voice pitch raised, Louder and faster speech, Reliable facial muscles, Facial blanching
Anger	Voice pitch raised, Louder and faster speech, Facial reddening, Facial blanching
Sadness (Maybe guilt & shame)	Voice pitch lowered, Slower and softer speech, Reliable facial muscles, Tears, Gaze down, Blushing
Embarrassment	Blushing, Gaze down or away
Excitement	Increased illustrators, Voice pitch raised, Louder and faster speech
Boredom	Decreased illustrators, Slower and softer speech
Negative emotion	Indirect speech, Pauses, Speech errors, Voice pitch raised, Voice pitch lowered, Manipulators increased
The arousal of any emotion	Changed breathing, Sweating, Swallowing, Squelched expression, Increased blinking, Pupil dilation

*Emblems cannot convey as many different messages as slips of the tongue or tirades. Among Americans there are about sixty messages for which there are emblems.

TABLE 3

CLUES THAT AN EXPRESSION IS FALSE

False Emotion	*Behavioral Clue*
Fear	Absence of reliable forehead expression
Sadness	Absence of reliable forehead expression
Happiness	Eye muscles not involved
Enthusiasm or involvement with what is being said	Illustrators fail to increase, or timing of illustrators is incorrect
Negative emotions	Absence of: sweating, changed respiration, or increased manipulators
Any emotion	Asymmetrical expression, Onset too abrupt, Offset too abrupt or jagged, Location in speech incorrect

TABLE 4

LYING CHECK LIST

	HARD	EASY
	FOR THE LIE CATCHER TO DETECT	

QUESTIONS ABOUT THE LIE

	HARD	EASY
1. *CAN THE LIAR ANTICIPATE EXACTLY WHEN HE OR SHE HAS TO LIE?*	YES: line prepared & rehearsed	NO: line not prepared
2. *DOES THE LIE INVOLVE CONCEALMENT ONLY, WITHOUT ANY NEED TO FALSIFY?*	YES	NO
3. *DOES THE LIE INVOLVE EMOTIONS FELT AT THE MOMENT?*	NO	YES: especially difficult if A. negative emotions such as anger, fear, or distress must be concealed or falsified B. liar must appear emotionless and cannot use another emotion to mask felt emotions that have to be concealed
4. *WOULD THERE BE AMNESTY IF LIAR CONFESSES TO LYING?*	NO: enhances liar's motive to succeed	YES: chance to induce confession
5. *ARE THE STAKES IN TERMS OF EITHER REWARDS OR PUNISHMENTS VERY HIGH?*	Difficult to predict: while high stakes may increase detection apprehension, it should also motivate the liar to try hard	

	HARD	**EASY**
	FOR THE LIE CATCHER TO DETECT	
6. *ARE THERE SEVERE PUNISHMENTS FOR BEING CAUGHT LYING?*	NO: low detection apprehension; but may produce carelessness	YES: enhances detection apprehension, but may also fear being disbelieved, producing false positive errors
7. *ARE THERE SEVERE PUNISHMENTS FOR THE VERY ACT OF HAVING LIED, APART FROM THE LOSSES INCURRED FROM THE DECEIT FAILING?*	NO	YES: enhances detection apprehension; person may be dissuaded from embarking on lie if she or he knows that punishment for attempting to lie will be worse than the loss incurred by not lying
8. *DOES THE TARGET SUFFER NO LOSS, OR EVEN BENEFIT, FROM THE LIE? IS THE LIE ALTRUISTIC NOT BENEFITING THE LIAR?*	YES: less deception guilt if liar believes this to be so	NO: increases deception guilt
9. *IS IT A SITUATION IN WHICH THE TARGET IS LIKELY TO TRUST THE LIAR, NOT SUSPECTING THAT HE OR SHE MAY BE MISLED?*	YES	NO

	HARD	EASY
	FOR THE LIE CATCHER TO DETECT	
10. *HAS LIAR SUCCESSFULLY DECEIVED THE TARGET BEFORE?*	YES: decreases detection apprehension; and if target would be ashamed or otherwise suffer by having to acknowledge having been fooled, she or he may become a willing victim.	NO
11. *DO LIAR AND TARGET SHARE VALUES?*	NO: decreases deception guilt	YES: increases deception guilt
12. *IS THE LIE AUTHORIZED?*	YES: decreases deception guilt	NO: increases deception guilt
13. *IS THE TARGET ANONYMOUS?*	YES: decreases deception guilt	NO
14. *ARE TARGET AND LIAR PERSONALLY ACQUAINTED?*	NO	YES: lie catcher will be more able to avoid errors due to individual differences
15. *MUST LIE CATCHER CONCEAL HIS SUSPICIONS FROM THE LIAR?*	YES: lie catcher may become enmeshed in his own need to conceal and fail to be as alert to liar's behavior	NO
16. *DOES LIE CATCHER HAVE INFORMATION THAT ONLY A GUILTY NOT AN INNOCENT PERSON WOULD ALSO HAVE?*	NO	YES: Can try to use the guilty knowledge test if the suspect can be interrogated
17. *IS THERE AN AUDIENCE WHO KNOWS OR SUSPECTS THAT THE TARGET IS BEING DECEIVED?*	NO	YES: may enhance duping delight, detection apprehension, or deception guilt

	HARD	**EASY**
	FOR THE LIE CATCHER TO DETECT	

18. *DO LIAR AND LIE CATCHER COME FROM SIMILAR LANGUAGE, NATIONAL, CULTURAL BACKROUNDS?*	NO: more errors in judging clues to deceit	YES: better able to interpret clues to deceit

QUESTIONS ABOUT THE LIAR

19. *IS THE LIAR PRACTICED IN LYING?*	YES: especially, if practiced in this type of lie	NO
20. *IS THE LIAR INVENTIVE AND CLEVER IN FABRICATING?*	YES	NO
21. *DOES THE LIAR HAVE A GOOD MEMORY?*	YES	NO
22. *IS THE LIAR A SMOOTH TALKER, WITH A CONVINCING MANNER?*	YES	NO
23. *DOES THE LIAR USE THE RELIABLE FACIAL MUSCLES AS CONVERSATIONAL EMPHASIZERS?*	YES: better able to conceal or falsify facial expressions	NO
24. *IS THE LIAR SKILLED AS AN ACTOR, ABLE TO USE THE THE STANISLAVSKI METHOD?*	YES	NO
25. *IS THE LIAR LIKELY TO CONVINCE HIMSELF OF HIS LIE BELIEVING THAT WHAT HE SAYS IS TRUE?*	YES	NO

	HARD	**EASY**
	FOR THE LIE CATCHER TO DETECT	

	HARD	EASY
26. *IS SHE OR HE A "NATURAL LIAR" OR PSYCHOPATH?*	YES	NO
27. *DOES LIAR'S PERSONALITY MAKE LIAR VULNERABLE EITHER TO FEAR, GUILT, OR DUPING DELIGHT?*	NO	YES
28. *IS LIAR ASHAMED OF WHAT LIAR IS CONCEALING?*	Difficult to predict: while shame works to prevent confession, leakage of that shame may betray the lie	
29. *MIGHT SUSPECTED LIAR FEEL FEAR, GUILT, SHAME, OR DUPING DELIGHT EVEN IF SUSPECT IS INNOCENT AND NOT LYING, OR LYING ABOUT SOMETHING ELSE?*	YES: Can't interpret emotion clues	NO: signs of these emotions are clues to deceit

QUESTIONS ABOUT THE LIE CATCHER

	HARD	EASY
30. *DOES THE LIE CATCHER HAVE A REPUTATION OF BEING TOUGH TO MISLEAD?*	NO: especially if liar has in the past been successful in fooling the lie catcher	YES: increases detection apprehension; may also increase duping delight
31. *DOES THE LIE CATCHER HAVE A REPUTATION OF BEING DISTRUSTFUL?*	Difficult to predict: such a reputation might decrease deception guilt, it may also increase detection apprehension	
32. *DOES THE LIE CATCHER HAVE A REPUTATION OF BEING FAIR-MINDED?*	NO: liar less likely to feel guilty about deceiving the lie catcher	YES: increases deception guilt

| | **HARD** | **EASY** |
| | **FOR THE LIE CATCHER TO DETECT** | |

	HARD	EASY
33. *IS THE LIE CATCHER A DENIER, WHO AVOIDS PROBLEMS, AND TENDS TO ALWAYS THINK THE BEST OF PEOPLE?*	YES: probably will overlook clues to deceit, vulnerable to false negative errors	NO
34. *IS LIE CATCHER UNUSUALLY ABLE TO ACCURATELY INTERPRET EXPRESSIVE BEHAVIORS?*	NO	YES
35. *DOES THE LIE CATCHER HAVE PRECONCEPTIONS WHICH BIAS THE LIE CATCHER AGAINST THE LIAR?*	NO	YES: although lie catcher will be alert to clues to deceit, he will be liable to false positive errors
36. *DOES THE LIE CATCHER OBTAIN ANY BENEFITS FROM NOT DETECTING THE LIE?*	YES: lie catcher will ignore, deliberately or unwittingly, clues to deceit	NO
37. *IS LIE CATCHER UNABLE TO TOLERATE UNCERTAINTY ABOUT WHETHER HE IS BEING DECEIVED?*	Difficult to predict: may cause either false positive or false negative errors	
38. *IS LIE CATCHER SEIZED BY AN EMOTIONAL WILDFIRE?*	NO	YES: liars will be caught, but innocents will be judged to be lying (false positive error)

Reference Notes

ONE • INTRODUCTION

1. I am indebted to Robert Jervis's book *The Logic of Images in International Relations* (Princeton, N.J.: Princeton University Press, 1970) for much of my thinking about international deceit and for bringing to my attention the writings of Alexander Groth. This quote was analyzed in Groth's article "On the Intelligence Aspects of Personal Diplomacy," *Orbis* 7 (1964): 833–49. It is from Keith Feiling, *The Life of Neville Chamberlain* (London: Macmillan, 1947, p. 367).
2. Speech to the House of Commons, September 28, 1938. Neville Chamberlain, *In Search of Peace* (New York: Putnam and Sons, 1939, p. 210, as cited by Groth).
3. This work was reported in a series of articles in the late 1960s and in a book I edited entitled *Darwin and Facial Expression* (New York: Academic Press, 1973).
4. This work is reported in my first article on deception: Paul Ekman and Wallace V. Friesen, "Nonverbal Leakage and Clues to Deception," *Psychiatry* 32 (1969): 88–105.
5. Roberta Wohlstetter, "Slow Pearl Harbors and the Pleasures of Deception," in *Intelligence Policy and National Security*, ed. Robert L. Pfaltzgraff, Jr., Uri Ra'anan, and Warren Milberg, (Hamden, Conn.: Archon Books, 1981), pp. 23–34.

TWO • LYING, LEAKAGE, AND CLUES TO DECEIT

1. *San Francisco Chronicle*, October 28, 1982, p. 12.
2. *The Compact Edition of the Oxford English Dictionary* (New York: Oxford University Press, 1971), p. 1616.
3. See Paul F. Secord, "Facial Features and Inference Processes in Interpersonal Perception," in *Person Perception and Interpersonal Behavior*," ed. R. Taguiri and L. Petrullo (Stanford: Stanford University Press, 1958). Also, Paul Ekman, "Facial Signs: Facts, Fantasies and Possibilities," in *Sight, Sound and Sense*, ed. Thomas A. Sebeok (Bloomington: Indiana University Press, 1978).

4. Argument persists about whether or not animals can deliberately choose to lie. See David Premack and Ann James Premack, *The Mind of an Ape* (New York: W. W. Norton & Co., 1983). Also, Premack and Premack, "Communication as Evidence of Thinking," in *Animal Mind—Human Mind,* ed. D. R. Griffin (New York: Springer-Verlag, 1982).

5. I am grateful to Michael I. Handel for citing this quote in his very stimulating article "Intelligence and Deception," *Journal of Strategic Studies* 5 (March 1982): 122–54. The quote is from Denis Mack Smith, *Mussolini's Roman Empire,* p. 170.

6. This distinction is used by most analysts of deceit. See Handel, "Intelligence," and Barton Whaley, "Toward a General Theory of Deception," *Journal of Strategic Studies* 5 (March 1982): 179–92 for discussions of the utility of this distinction in analyzing military deceits.

7. Sisela Bok reserves the term *lying* for what I call falsification and uses the term *secrecy* for what I call concealment. The distinction she claims to be of moral importance, for she argues that while lying is *"prima facie* wrong, with a negative presumption against it, secrecy need not be" (Bok, *Secrets* [New York: Pantheon, 1982], p. xv.

8. Eve Sweetser, "The Definition of a Lie," in *Cultural Models in Language and Thought* ed. Naomi Quinn and Dorothy Holland, (in press), p. 40.

9. David E. Rosenbaum, *New York Times,* December 17, 1980.

10. John Updike, *Marry Me,* (New York: Fawcett Crest, 1976), p. 90.

11. Ezer Weizman, *The Battle for Peace* (New York: Bantam Books, 1981), p. 182.

12. Alan Bullock, *Hitler* (New York: Harper & Row, 1964, rev. ed.), p. 528. As cited by Robert Jervis, *The Logic of Images in International Relations* (Princeton, N.J.: Princeton University Press, 1970).

13. Robert Daley, *The Prince of the City* (New York: Berkley Books, 1981), p. 101.

14. Weizman, *Battle,* p. 98.

15. Jon Carroll, "Everyday Hypocrisy—A User's Guide," *San Francisco Chronicle,* April 11, 1983, p. 17.

16. Updike, *Marry Me,* p. 90.

THREE • WHY LIES FAIL

1. John J. Sirica, *To Set the Record Straight* (New York: New American Library, 1980), p. 142.

2. James Phelan, *Scandals, Scamps and Scoundrels* (New York: Random House, 1982), p. 22.

3. Terence Rattigan, *The Winslow Boy* (New York: Dramatists Play Service Inc. Acting Edition, 1973), p. 29.

4. This story is contained in David Lykken's book *A Tremor in the Blood: Uses and Abuses of the Lie Detector* (New York: McGraw-Hill, 1981).

5. Phelan, *Scandals,* p. 110.

6. Robert D. Hare, *Psychopathy: Theory and Research* (New York: John Wiley, 1970), p. 5.

7. Michael I. Handel, "Intelligence and Deception," *Journal of Strategic Studies* 5 (1982): 136.

8. *San Francisco Chronicle,* January 9, 1982, p. 1.

9. *San Francisco Chronicle,* January 21, 1982, p. 43.

10. William Hood, *Mole* (New York: W.W. Norton & Co., 1982), p. 11.

11. Bruce Horowitz, "When Should an An Executive Lie?" *Industry Week,* November 16, 1981, p. 81.
12. Ibid, p. 83.
13. This idea was suggested by Robert L. Wolk and Arthur Henley in their book *The Right to Lie* (New York: Peter H. Wyden, Inc., 1970).
14. Alan Dershowitz, *The Best Defense* (New York: Random House, 1982), p. 370.
15. Shakespeare, Sonnet 138.
16. Roberta Wohlstetter, "Slow Pearl Harbours and the Pleasures of Deception," in *Intelligence Policy and National Security,* ed. Robert L. Pfaltzgraff, Jr., Uri Ra'anan, and Warren Milberg (Hamden, Conn.: Archon Press, 1981).

FOUR • DETECTING DECEIT FROM WORDS, VOICE, OR BODY

1. In "Facial Signs: Facts, Fantasies and Possibilities," in *Sight, Sound, and Sense,* ed. Thomas A. Sebeok (Bloomington: Indiana University Press, 1978), I describe eighteen different messages conveyed by the face, one of which is the mark of unique individual identity.
2. See J. Sergent and D. Bindra, "Differential Hemispheric Processing of Faces: Methodological Considerations and Reinterpretation," *Psychological Bulletin* 89 (1981): 554–554.
3. Some of this work was reported by Paul Ekman, Wallace V. Friesen, Maureen O'Sullivan, and Klaus Scherer, "Relative Importance of Face, Body and Speech in Judgments of Personality and Affect," *Journal of Personality and Social Psychology* 38 (1980): 270–77.
4. Bruce Horowitz, "When Should an Executive Lie?" *Industry Week,* November 16, 1981, p. 83.
5. S. Freud, The psychopathology of everyday life (1901), in James Strachey, tr. and ed., *The Complete Psychological Works,* vol. 6 (New York: W. W. Norton, 1976), p. 86.
6. Freud gave many interesting, briefer examples of slips of the tongue, but they are not as convincing as the one I selected, because they had to be translated from the original German. Dr. Brill was an American, and Freud quoted this example in English. Ibid., pp. 89–90.
7. S. Freud, Parapraxes (1916), in James Strachey, tr. and ed., *The Complete Psychological Works,* vol. 15 (New York: W. W. Norton, 1976), p. 66.
8. John Weisman, "The Truth will Out," *TV Guide,* September 3, 1977, p. 13.
9. A number of new techniques developed to measure the voice promise breakthroughs in the next few years. For a review of these methods, see Klaus Scherer, "Methods of Research on Vocal Communication: Paradigms and Parameters," in *Handbook of Methods in Nonverbal Behavior Research,* ed. Klaus Scherer and Paul Ekman (New York: Cambridge University Press, 1982).
10. These results are reported by Paul Ekman, Wallace V. Friesen, and Klaus Scherer, "Body Movement and Voice Pitch in Deceptive Interaction," *Semiotica* 16 (1976): 23–27. The findings have been replicated by Scherer and by other investigators.
11. John J. Sirica, *To Set the Record Straight* (New York: W. W. Norton, 1979), pp. 99–100.
12. Richard Nixon, *The Memoirs of Richard Nixon,* vol. 2 (New York: Warner Books, 1979), p. 440.
13. Sirica, *To Set the Record Straight,* pp. 99–100.

14. Ibid.
15. John Dean, *Blind Ambition* (New York: Simon & Schuster, 1976), p. 304.
16. Ibid., pp. 309–10.
17. For critical reviews of these various voice stress lie detection techniques, see David T. Lykken, *A Tremor in the Blood* by (New York: McGraw-Hill, 1981), chap. 13 and Harry Hollien, "The Case against Stress Evaluators and Voice Lie Detection," (unpub. mimeograph, Institute for Advanced Study of the Communication Processes, University of Florida, Gainesville).
18. A description of our method for surveying emblems and the results for Americans is contained in Harold G. Johnson, Paul Ekman, and Wallace V. Friesen, "Communicative Body Movements: American Emblems," *Semiotica* 15 (1975): 335–53. For comparison of emblems in different cultures, see Ekman, "Movements with Precise Meanings," *Journal of Communication* 26 (1976): 14–26.
19. Efron's book, *Gesture and Environment,* published in 1941, is back in print again under the title *Gesture, Race, and Culture* (The Hague: Mouton Press, 1972).
20. For a discussion of manipulators, see Paul Ekman and Wallace V. Friesen, "Nonverbal Behavior and Psychopathology," in *The Psychology of Depression: Contemporary Theory and Research* ed. R. J. Friedman and M. N. Katz (Washington, D.C.: J. Winston, 1974).
21. For a current exponent of this view, see George Mandler, *Mind and Body: Psychology of Emotion and Stress* (New York: W. W. Norton & Co., 1984).
22. Paul Ekman, Robert W. Levenson, & Wallace V. Friesen, "Autonomic Nervous System Activity Distinguishes between Emotions," *Science 1983,* vol. 221, pp. 1208–10.

FIVE • FACIAL CLUES TO DECEIT

1. The descriptions of the impairment of voluntary and involuntary systems with different lesions is taken from the clinical literature. See, for example, K. Tschiassny, "Eight Syndromes of Facial Paralysis and Their Significance in Locating the Lesion," *Annals of Otology, Rhinology, and Laryngology* 62 (1953): 677–91. The description of how these different patients might have difficulty or success in deception is my extrapolation.
2. For a review of all the scientific evidence, see Paul Ekman, *Darwin and Facial Expression: A Century of Research in Review* (New York: Academic Press, 1973). For a less technical discussion, and photographs illustrating universals in an isolated, preliterate, New Guinea people, see Ekman, *Face of Man: Expressions of Universal Emotions in a New Guinea Village* (New York: Garland STMP Press, 1980).
3. Ekman, *Face of Man*, pp. 133–36.
4. *The Facial Action Coding System,* Paul Ekman and Wallace V. Friesen (Palo Alto: Consulting Psychologists Press, 1978), is a self-instructional package—containing a manual, illustrative photographs and films, and computer programs—that teaches the reader how to describe or measure any expression.
5. See E. A. Haggard and K. S. Isaacs, "Micromomentary Facial Expressions," in *Methods of Research in Psychotherapy,* ed. L. A. Gottschalk and A. H. Auerbach (New York: Appleton Century Crofts, 1966).

6. *Unmasking the Face,* Paul Ekman and Wallace V. Friesen (Palo Alto: Consulting Psychologists Press, 1984), provides the pictures and instructions on how to acquire this skill.
7. Friesen and I developed a Requested Facial Action Test, which explores how well someone can deliberately move each muscle and also pose emotion. See by Paul Ekman, Gowen Roper, and Joseph C. Hager, "Deliberate Facial Movement," *Child Development* 51 (1980): 886–91 for results on children.
8. Column by William Safire, "Undetermined," in the *San Francisco Chronicle,* June 28, 1983.
9. "Anwar Sadat—in his own words," in the *San Francisco Examiner,* October 11, 1981.
10. Ezer Weizman, *The Battle for Peace* (New York: Bantam, 1981), p. 165.
11. Margaret Mead, *Soviet Attitudes toward Authority* (New York: McGraw-Hill, 1951), pp. 65–66. As cited by Erving Goffman, *Strategic Interaction* (Philadelphia: University of Pennsylvania Press, 1969), p. 21.
12. *San Francisco Chronicle,* January 11, 1982.
13. Harold Sackeim, Ruben C. Gur, and Marcel C. Saucy, "Emotions Are Expressed More Intensely on the Left Side of the Face," *Science* 202 (1978): 434.
14. See Paul Ekman, "Asymmetry in Facial Expression," and Sackeim's rebuttal in *Science* 209 (1980): 833–36.
15. Paul Ekman, Joseph C. Hager, and Wallace V. Friesen, "The Symmetry of Emotional and Deliberate Facial Actions," *Psychophysiology* 18/2 (1981): 101–6.
16. Joseph C. Hager and Paul Ekman, "Different Asymmetries of Facial Muscular Actions," *Psychophysiology,* in press.
17. I am grateful to Ronald van Gelder for his help in this unpublished study.
18. *San Francisco Chronicle,* June 14, 1982.
19. See Paul Ekman and Joseph C. Hager, "Long Distance Transmission of Facial Affect Signals," *Ethology and Sociobiology* 1 (1979): 77–82.
20. Paul Ekman, Wallace V. Friesen, and Sonia Ancoli, "Facial Signs of Emotional Experience," by *Journal of Personality and Social Psychology* 39 (1980): 1125–34.

SIX • DANGERS AND PRECAUTIONS

1. David M. Hayano, "Communicative Competence among Poker Players," *Journal of Communication* 30 (1980): 117.
2. Ibid., p. 115.
3. William Shakespeare, *Othello,* act 5, scene 2.
4. Richards J. Heuer, Jr., "Cognitive Factors in Deception and Counterdeception," in *Strategic Military Deception,* ed. Donald C. Daniel and Katherine L. Herbig (New York: Pergamon Press, 1982), p. 59.
5. Ross Mullaney, "The Third Way—The Interroview," unpublished mimeograph, 1979.
6. Schopenhauer, "Our Relation to Others," in *The Works of Schopenhauer,* ed. Will Durant (Garden City, New Jersey: Garden City Publishing Company, 1933).
7. See Lykken's book *Tremor in the Blood* (New York: McGraw-Hill, 1981) for a full description of how to use the Guilty Knowledge Technique with the polygraph in criminal interrogations.

8. *Scientific Validity of Polygraph Testing: A Research Review and Evaluation—A Technical Memorandum* (Washington D.C.: U. S. Congress, Office of Technology Assessment, OTA-TM-H-15, November 1983).

SEVEN • THE POLYGRAPH AS LIE CATCHER

1. Richard O. Arther, "How Many Robbers, Burglars, Sex Criminals Is Your Department Hiring This Year?? (Hopefully, Just 10% of Those Employed!)," *Journal of Polygraph Studies* 6 (May–June 1972), unpaged.
2. David T. Lykken, "Polygraphic Interrogation," *Nature*, February 23, 1984, pp. 681–84.
3. Leonard Saxe, personal communication.
4. Most of my figures on the use of the polygraph come from *Scientific Validity of Polygraph Testing: A Research Review and Evaluation—A Technical Memorandum* (Washington, D.C.: U. S. Congress, Office of Technology Assessment, OTA-TM-H-15, November 1983). Essentially the same report will appear as an article entitled "The Validity of Polygraph Testing," by Leonard Saxe, Denise Dougherty, and Theodore Cross, in *American Psychologist*, January 1984.
5. David C. Raskin, "The Truth about Lie Detectors," *The Wharton Magazine*, Fall 1980, p. 29.
6. Office of Technology Assessment (OTA) report, p. 31.
7. Benjamin Kleinmuntz and Julian J. Szucko, "On the Fallibility of Lie Detection," Law and Society Review 17 (1982): 91.
8. Statement of Richard K. Willard, Deputy Assistant Attorney General, U.S. Department of Justice, before the Legislation and National Security Committee of the Committee on Government Operations, U. S. House of Representatives, October 19, 1983, mimeograph, p. 22.
9. OTA report, p. 29.
10. The OTA was created in 1972 as an analytical arm of Congress. The report on the polygraph is available by writing to the Superintendent of Documents, U.S. Government Printing Office, Washington, D.C. 20402.
11. Marcia Garwood and Norman Ansley, *The Accuracy and Utility of Polygraph Testing*, Department of Defense, 1983, unpaged.
12. David C. Raskin, "The Scientific Basis of Polygraph Techniques and Their Uses in the Judicial Process, in *Reconstructing the Past: The Role of Psychologists in Criminal Trials*, ed. A. Trankell (Stockholm: Norstedt and Soners, 1982), p. 325.
13. David T. Lykken, *A Tremor in the Blood*, (New York: McGraw-Hill, 1981), p. 118.
14. David T. Lykken, personal communication.
15. Lykken, *Tremor in the Blood*, p. 251.
16. Raskin, "Scientific Basis," p. 341.
17. OTA report, p. 50.
18. Raskin, "Scientific Basis," p. 330.
19. Avital Ginton, Netzer Daie, Eitan Elaad, and Gershon Ben-Shakhar, "A Method for Evaluating the Use of the Polygraph in a Real-Life Situation," *Journal of Applied Psychology* 67 (1982): 132.
20. OTA report, p. 132.
21. Ginton et al., "Method for Evaluating," p. 136.

22. Jack Anderson, *San Francisco Chronicle,* May 21, 1984.
23. OTA report, p. 102.
24. Statement by David C. Raskin at hearings on S.1845 held by the Subcommittee on the Constitution, United States Senate, September 19, 1978, p. 14.
25. OTA report, pp. 75–76.
26. Raskin, Statement, p. 17.
27. Lykken, *Tremor in the Blood,* chap. 15.
28. Gordon H. Barland, "A Survey of the Effect of the Polygraph in Screening Utah Job Applicants: Preliminary Results," *Polygraph* 6 (December 1977), p. 321.
29. Ibid.
30. Raskin, Statement, p. 21.
31. Arther, "How Many," unpaged.
32. Ibid.
33. Garwood and Ansley, *Accuracy and Utility,* unpaged.
34. OTA report, p. 100.
35. Daniel Rapoport, "To Tell the Truth," *The Washingtonian,* February 1984, p. 80.
36. Willard, *ibid.,* p. 36.
37. Lykken, "Polygraphic Interrogation," p. ?.
38. OTA report, pp. 109–110.
39. OTA report, p. 99.
40. Willard, Statement, p. 17.
41. Ginton et al., "Method for Evaluating." Also, John A. Podlesny and David C. Raskin, "Effectiveness of Techniques and Physiological Measures in the Detection of Deception," *Psychophysiology* 15 (1978): pp. 344–59 and Frank S. Horvath, "Verbal and Nonverbal Clues to Truth and Deception During Polygraph Examinations," *Journal of Police Science and Administration,* 1 (1973): 138–52.
42. David C. Raskin and John C. Kircher, "Accuracy of Diagnosing Truth and Deception from Behavioral Observation and Polygraph Recordings," ms. in preparation.

EIGHT • LIE CHECKING

1. Randall Rothenberg, "Bagging the Big Shot," *San Francisco Chronicle,* January 3, 1983, pp. 12–15.
2. Ibid.
3. Ibid.
4. Agness Hankiss, "Games Con Men Play: The Semiosis of Deceptive Interaction," *Journal of Communication* 3 (1980): pp. 104–112.
5. Donald C. Daniel and Katherine L. Herbig, "Propositions on Military Deception," in *Strategic Military Deception,* ed. Daniel & Herbig (New York: Pergamon Press, 1982) p. 17.
6. I am indebted for this example to John Phelan's fascinating account in chapter 6 of his book *Scandals, Scamps and Scoundrels* (New York: Random House, 1982), p. 114. I have only reported part of the story. Anyone interested in detecting lies among people suspected of crimes should read this chapter to learn about other pitfalls that may occur in interrogation and lie detection.

7. I am indebted for my knowledge about interrogations to Rossiter C. Mullaney, an FBI agent from 1948 to 1971, and then coordinator of Investigation Programs, North Central Texas Regional Police Academy, until 1981. See his article "Wanted! Performance Standards for Interrogation and Interview," *The Police Chief,* June 1977, pp. 77–80.

8. Mullaney began a very promising series of studies training interrogators in how to use clues to deceit and evaluating the usefulness of that training, but he retired before completing that work.

9. Alexander J. Groth, "On the Intelligence Aspects of Personal Diplomacy," *Orbis* 7 (1964): 848.

10. Robert Jervis, *The Logic of Images in International Relations* (Princeton, N.J.: Princeton University Press, 1970), pp. 67–78.

11. Henry Kissinger, *Years of Upheaval* (Boston: Little, Brown and Company, 1982), pp. 214, 485.

12. As quoted by Jervis, *Logic,* pp. 69–70.

13. Ibid., pp. 67–68.

14. Michael I. Handel, "Intelligence and Deception," *Journal of Strategic Studies* 5 (1982): 123–53.

15. Barton Whaley, "Covert Rearmament in Germany, 1919–1939: Deception and Mismanagement," *Journal of Strategic Studies* 5 (1982): 26–27.

16. Handel, "Intelligence," p. 129.

17. This quote was analyzed by Groth, "Intelligence Aspects."

18. As cited by Groth, "Intelligence Aspects."

19. Telford Taylor, *Munich* (New York: Vintage, 1980), p. 752.

20. Ibid., p. 821.

21. Ibid., p. 552.

22. Ibid., p. 629.

23. Graham T. Allison, *Essence of Decision: Explaining the Cuban Missile Crisis* (Boston: Little, Brown and Company, 1971), p. 193.

24. Arthur M. Schlesinger, Jr., *A Thousand Days: John F. Kennedy in the White House* (New York: Fawcet Premier Books, 1965). p. 734.

25. Theodore C. Sorensen, *Kennedy* (New York: Harper & Row, 1965), p. 673.

26. Robert F. Kennedy, *Thirteen Days: A Memoir of the Cuban Missile Crisis* (New York: W. W. Norton, 1971), p. 5.

27. Roger Hilsman, To Move a Nation (Garden City, N.Y.: Doubleday & Co., 1967), p. 98.

28. David Detzer, *The Brink* (New York: Thomas Crowell, 1979).

29. Sorensen, *Kennedy,* p. 690.

30. Detzer, *Brink,* p. 142.

31. Robert F. Kennedy, *Thirteen Days,* p. 18.

32. Elie Abel, *The Missile Crisis* (New York: Bantam Books, 1966), p. 63.

33. Sorensen, *Kennedy,* p. 690.

34. Abel, *Missile,* p. 63.

35. Detzer, *Brink,* p. 143.

36. Kennedy, *Thirteen Days,* p. 20.

37. Detzer, *Brink,* p. 143.

38. Ibid., p. 144.

39. Allison, *Essence,* p. 135.

40. Abel, *Missile,* p. 64.

41. Allison, *Essence,* p. 134.

42. Daniel and Herbig, "Propositions," p. 13.
43. Herbert Goldhamer, reference 24 cited by Daniel and Herbig, "Propositions."
44. Barton Whaley, reference 2 cited by Daniel and Herbig, "Propositions."
45. Maureen O'Sullivan, "Measuring the Ability to Recognize Facial Expressions of Emotion," in *Emotion in the Human Face*, ed. Paul Ekman (New York: Cambridge University Press, 1982).
46. Groth, "Intelligence Aspects," p. 847.
47. Jervis, *Logic*, p. 33.
48. Winston Churchill, *The Hinge of Fate* (Boston: Houghton Mifflin, 1950), pp. 481, 493, as cited by Groth, ibid., p. 841.
49. Lewis Broad, *The War that Churchill Waged* (London: Hutchison and Company, 1960), p. 356, as cited by Groth, "Intelligence Aspects," p. 846.
50. Broad, *War*, p. 358, as cited by Groth, "Intelligence Aspects," p. 846.
51. Milovan Djilas, *Conversations with Stalin* (New York: Harcourt, Brace, Jovanovich, 1962), p. 73, as cited by Groth, ibid., p. 846.

NINE • LIE CATCHING IN THE 1990s

1. My colleague and friend Maureen O'Sullivan, at the University of San Francisco, has worked with me for many years to develop this test, collaborated in the research on professional lie catchers, and also gave some of the workshops.
2. "Who Can Catch a Liar" by Paul Ekman and Maureen O'Sullivan appeared in the September 1991 issue of the journal *American Psychologist*.
3. Those findings were reported in "The Effect of Comparisons on Detecting Deceit" by M. O'Sullivan, P. Ekman, and W. V. Friesen. *Journal of Nonverbal Behavior* 12 (1988): 203–15.
4. Udo Undeutsch from Germany developed a procedure called statement analysis, and a number of American researchers are testing its validity in evaluating children's testimony.
5. These findings are reported in "Face, Voice, and Body in Detecting Deceit" by Paul Ekman, Maureen O'Sullivan, Wallace V. Friesen, and Klaus C. Scherer in the *Journal of Nonverbal Behavior*, vol. 15 (1991): 203–15.
6. "The Duchenne Smile: Emotional Expression and Brain Physiology II" by P. Ekman, R. J. Davidson, and W. V. Friesen. *Journal of Personality and Social Psychology* 58 (1990).
7. These findings are reported in M. Frank, P. Ekman, and W. V. Friesen, "Behavioral markers of recognizability of the enjoyment smile." Paper under review.
8. A paper entitled "The ability to lie across situations" currently being written by Mark Frank reports these findings.
9. Professor John Yuille at the University of British Columbia has been directing a program to train social workers in better techniques for interviewing children.
10. *Time* magazine, July 27, 1987, p. 10.
11. In earlier chapters I used the phrase *natural liar*, but that I have found implies that these people may lie more often than others, when I have no evidence that is so. The phrase *natural performer* better describes what I mean, which is that if they lie they ⌐o so flawlessly.

12. Not having met North nor had the opportunity to question him directly I cannot be certain my judgment is correct. His performance on television, however, certainly fits my description.

TEN • LIES IN PUBLIC LIFE

1. Oliver L. North, *Under Fire* (New York: HarperCollins, 1991), p. 66.
2. For a recent discussion of the constitutional issues in this case see an article by Edwin M. Yoder, Jr., entitled "A Poor Substitute for an Impeachment Proceeding," *International Herald Tribune,* July 23, 1991.
3. Stansfield Turner, "Purge the CIA of KGB Types," *New York Times,* October 2, 1991, p. 21.
4. Ibid.
5. Ibid.
6. Jimmy Carter, *Keeping Faith: Memoirs of a President* (New York: Bantam Books, 1982), p. 511.
7. See reference 3.
8. For a recent discussion of the various views on this topic see *Self-Deception: An Adaptive Mechanism?* edited by Joan S. Lockard and Delroy L. Paulhus (Englewood Cliffs, N.J.: Prentice-Hall, 1988).
9. Richard Feynman, *What Do You Care What Other People Think? Further Adventures of a Curious Character* (New York: W.W. Norton, 1988).
10. Ibid., p. 214.
11. *Time,* August 19, 1974, p. 9.

EPILOGUE

1. For the arguments against falsification, see Sisela Bok, *Lying: Moral Choice in Public and Private Life* (New York: Pantheon, 1978). For an argument in favor of concealment in private, not public, life, see Bok, *Secrets* (New York: Pantheon, 1982). For the opposite view, advocating the virtues of lying, see Robert L. Walk and Arthur Henley, *The Right to Lie: A Psychological Guide to the Uses of Deceit in Everyday Life* (New York: Peter H. Wyden, 1970).
2. Sigmund Freud, Fragment of an analysis of a case of hysteria (1905), *Collected Papers,* vol. 3.; (New York: Basic Books, 1959), p. 94.

Index[*]